TRY

PEDIA

RHODA

# PALMISTRY ENCYCLOPEDIA

Rhoda Hamilton

# WELCOME TO PALMISTRY

This is not just a book but the best guide on Palmistry. It is written for the novice as well as the
expert Palmist.

## " OUR HANDS TELL ALL "

Palmistry today is a marvelous tool. Please never
belittle the psychology of Palmistry. Remember our
hands are the mirror of the mind, our virtues and
our vices. It can reveal the stories of our
character, our aims and ambitions and even more
important the possibliity of our achieving them.
Palmistry,Chiromancy, Chirosophy, call it what you
may, it is a science and an art.

# THE AUTHOR

My interest in Palmistry began almost before birth. My mother's interest in Palmistry and E.S.P. were always a strong force in her life. She and along with the association of her friends were my teachers.

I began reading palms at a very young age, and about the year 1960 I began reading for clients. My interest in and the study of Palmistry has increased over the years.

The writing of this Palmistry Reference Book, "The Modern Gypsy" has been one of my life ambitions.

The practice of Palmistry is based upon scientific study, and is not mere guess work; it can indicate potential events that can happen in your life. This information is revealed in the careful study of the hands. Hand Analysis is a science.

I know nothing that offers a better study of human nature than Palmistry. Even the layman can find Palmistry logical, clear and interesting as well as instructional.

The hand reveals the patterns of every life. It is my belief that our hands can be used as a guide. Our fate and character are written and visible in the lines, markings and shapes of our fingers and hands.
Furthermore, I believe that they are there to be read when we are born.

There are doctors, scientists, law enforcement agencies and business executives who use the science of Palmistry as a tool in their professions. It is a wonderful way to understand your children and other loved ones.

## Many Choices

When reading palms, it must be remembered that your clients may have many choices in their life. Some believe that one soul can be inhabited by many other personalities or entities and be influenced greatly by our inherited family tree and our ancestral genetics. Our mind acts as a memory bank, a computer that has stored all the knowledge and experience our ancestors have passed on to us.

The belief is that the same soul can be inhabited in succession by an indefinite number of mortal bodies; that during this one lifetime, our bodies are perpetually changing. These changes are so gradual that we do not realize it is occurring. It's believed that in every body there can be a succession of many personalities. Even during one short lifetime, making us a composite of all that has been and aware of all that will be.

# CONTENTS

# INTRODUCTION

This book has been written with the wish that it may be enjoyed. It is a serious textbook and reference for those interested in the scientific study of Palmistry.

This reference book contains the workable method of reading the hand from beginning to end correctly. The hand reveals the pattern of every life. It is my belief that our hands can be used as a guide to a person's fate and character.

The practice of Palmistry should be based upon your scientific study, and not regarded as mere guesswork. It can tell us the potential of our client's life, events in their life that have happened or will happen. This information can only be the result of the careful study of the hand. Hand analysis is a science; it is also an art. I know of nothing that offers a better study of human nature than Palmistry. Even the layman can find Palmistry logical, informative and interesting, as well as instructive. Futhermore, I believe that our palms are there to be read when we are first born. You can read your children's hands, those of your loved ones and have a better understanding of them.

There are scientific laws in the reading of the hands that must be understood.

There are doctors, scientists, personnel directors, law enforcement agents, head of institutions and business executives who use the reading of the hand as a tool. This is all visible in the lines, markings and shape of your fingers and hands. Every ridge, zone, tone of the skin, color and texture of hair, shape of the hands, mounts, the fingers - their shape and size, the inside tips and length, fingernail size, shape and ridges, the thumb and the flexibility and movement of the hand are all the important tools that we use in the study of Palmistry.

Many Palmists read the left hand as what we are born with, and the right hand as what we make or do with our life. In my book you will be instructed to read both hands together, comparing each as they indicate strengths and weaknesses. Only then can your client understand their choices and be prepared for them. Palmistry, like medicine, is also a matter of intuitive judgement. Each hand has its own meaning; the difference will be in the individual interpretation.

# Palmistry - Cheiromancy

The study of Palmistry is the map of the future. Certain lines and the direction in which they move and crisscross provide important clues about the length of life, your health and happiness, your business, success and your romantic experiences and the study of the shape of the hand and fingers, your nails and skin. The way hands are used when gesturing all help us to understand the character of the people we come in contact with.

One great advantage to hand reading is that you don't have to be clairvoyant or a scientist to learn the valuable lesson it has to teach; a true understanding of human nature.

Palmistry or Cheiromancy is an ancient study. The practice of Palmistry is worldwide today. It has been modernized. Time has been extended with our longevity.

The word Palmistry is derived from two Middle English roots. Paume, which means "the palm of the hand" and estrie, which is of obscure origin and meaning, but which carries with it the idea of "study". It was probably used in England before the end of the 14th century.

Palmistry is defined in the Oxford dictionary as "the act or art of knowing or foretelling the unknown by inspection of the palm of the hand, the art or practice of telling a person's character and fortune by examination of the lines and configurations of the palm".

The more enthusiastic students of hand symbology and hand analysis coined the word Cheirosophy also spelled *Chiro* (The Greek spelling of Xiero meaning hand, and sophia meaning wisdom).

One of our most famous palmists was Count Louis Hamon, known as Cheiro. He gave the Greek classical and scientific names of analyzing palmistry their present names:

**Cheiro-sophy** - Derived from two Greek words meaning "hand" and "wisdom". To the scientific or classical name for palmistry.

**Cheiro-gnomy** - from the two Greek words meaning "hand" and "divination" or "prophecy" - the study of the lines.

**Dermato-glyphics** - from the two Greek words. Derma, meaning "skin", glyphic meaning "carving" - the study of skin patterns.

The three distinct approaches to hand interpretation should be studied separately, then woven into a pattern of cause and effect to obtain a true map to the personality, when reading a hand.

**Cheirognomy** - The study of the shape, size, length, color and formation of the fingers joints and the tips of the fingers, the size and tint of the nails, and even by the hair on the hands. The thumb alone reveals the principal motor forces of life. The first or top, phalanx indicates will power, the second or middle phalanx - Reason and logic the third, or base phalanx The Passions.

**Cheiromancy** - The study of the palms, the lines and marks. The mounts surrounding the palm. You can learn about the condition of the past, present and future. It can tell us about our health, vitality and intelligence. The events of life.

**Chiromancer-**One who interprets the character, the future and the past from markings and signs on the palm of the person's hand.

**Dermataglyphics** - The study of ridge and furrow patterns on our palms. These skin patterns are the basis of police identification the world over.

In India and China, they have used the thumb print as a signature in addition to the signature to prevent forgery of important documents.

Skin patterns here in the United States are being used in biological and genetic research.

Dermatoglyphics is so entirely scientific that it expresses hand patterns in mathematical formulas and in computers.

# The Origin and History
# of Palmistry or Cheirosophy

In my studies the best explanation and research was done by Count Louis Hamon in his book Cheiros Language of the Hand, starting on page 20, let me share it with you.

To consider the origin of this science, we must take our thoughts back to the earliest days of the world's history, and furthermore to the consideration of a people the oldest of all, yet one that has survived the fall of empires, nations, and dynasties, and who are today as characteristic and as full of individuality as they were when thousands of years ago the first records of history were written. I allude to those children of the East, the Hindus, a people whose philosophy and wisdom are every day being more and more revived. Looking back to the earliest days of the history of the known world, we find that the first linguistic records belong to the prople under consideration, and date back to the far-distant cycle of time known as the Aryan civilization. Beyond history we cannot go. The monuments and cave temples of India, according to the testimony of archaeologists, all point to a time so far beyond the scant history at our disposal, that in the examination of such matters our greatest knowledge is dwarfed into infantile nothingness; our age and era are but the swaddling clothes of the child; our manhood that of the infant in the arms of the eternity of time.

In endeavouring to trace the origin of palmistry, we are carried back to the confines of a prehistoric age. History tells us that in the remotest period of the Aryan civilization it had even a literature of its own. Beyond this we cannot go; but as fragments of this literature are even now extant, we must therefore conclude that it had a still more remote infancy; but into that night of antiquity we dare not venture. There are no stars to guide, no faded moons to show us light; and so, standing on the borders of the known, we gaze into the darkness of the unknown, from the vastness of which we occasionally draw the bones of a mammoth or the fragments of a shrine; they are helps to knowledge; they are weeds upon the sands of time; they tell us of days before our days, of races before our race, of verdant islands, of civilization sunk forever in the ocean of antiquity.

Regarding the people who first understood and practiced this study of the hand, we find undisputed proofs of their learning and knowledge. Long before Rome or Greece or Israel was even heard of, the monuments of India point back to the age of learning beyond, and still beyond. From the astronomical calculations that the figures in their temples represent, it has been estimated that the Hindus understood the precession of the equinoxes centuries before the Christian era. In some of the ancient cave temples, the mystic figures of the Sphinx silently tell that such knowledge has been possessed and used in advance of all those nations afterward so celebrated for their learning. It has been demonstrated that to make a change from one sign to another in the zodiacal course of the sun must have occupied at the least 2,140 years, and how many centuries elapsed before such changes came to be observed and noticed it is impossible even to estimate.

The intellectual power which was necessary to make such observations speaks for itself; and yet it to such a people that we trace the origin of the study under consideration. Regarding the spread of the knowledge of palmistry, the Hindu Vedas are the oldest scriptures that have been found, and according to some authorities they have been the foundation of even the Greek schools of learning.

When we consider that palmistry is the offspring of such a race, we should for such a reason alone at least treat it with respect, and be more inclined to examine its claims for justice than we are at present. In the examination of these points we therefore find that this study of the hand is one of the most ancient in the world. History again comes to our assistance, and tells that in the north-west province of India, palmistry was practiced and followed by the Joshi caste from time immemorial to the present day.

It may be interesting to describe here, in as few words as possible, an extremely ancient and curious book on the markings of hands, which I was allowed to use and examine during my sojourn in India. This book was one of the greatest treasures of the few Brahmans who possessed and understood it, and was jealously guarded in one of those old cave temples that belong to the ruins of ancient Hindustan.

This strange book was made of human skin, pieced and put together in the most ingenious manner. It was of enormous size, and contained hundreds of well-drawn illustrations, with records of how, when, and where this or the mark was proved correct.

One of the strangest features in connection with it was that it was written in some red liquid which age had failed to spoil or fade. The effect of those vivid red letters on the pages of dull yellow skin was most remarkable. By some compound, probably made of herbs, each page was glazed, as it were, by varnish; but whatever this compound may have been, it seemed to defy time, as the outer covers alone showed the signs of wear and decay. As regards the antiquity of this book there could be no question. It was apparently written in three sections or divisions: the first part belonged to the earliest language of the country, and dated so far back that very few of the Brahmans even could read or decipher it. There are many such treasures in Hindustan; but all are so jealously guarded by the Brahmans that neither money, art, nor power will ever release such pledges of the past.

As the wisdom of this strange race spread far and wide across the earth, so the doctrines and ideas of palmistry spread and were practiced in other countries. Just as religion suits itself to the conditions of the race in which it is propagated, so has palmistry been divided into systems. The most ancient records, however, are those found among the Hindus. It is difficult to trace its path from country to country. In far-distant ages it has been practiced in China, Tibet, Persia, and Egypt; but it is to the days of the Grecian civilization that we owe the present clear and lucid form of the study. The Greek civilization has in many ways been considered the highest and most intellectual in the world, and here it was that palmistry, or cheiromancy - from the Greek cheir, the hand - grew, flourished, and found favour in the sight of those whose names are as stars of honour in the firmament of knowledge. We find that Anaxagoras taught and practiced it in 423 B.C. We find that Hispanus discovered, on an altar dedicated to Hermes, a book on cheiromancy written in gold letters, which he sent as a present to Alexander the Great, as "a study worthy the attention of an elevated and inquiring mind." We find it also sanctioned by such men of learning as Aristotle, Pliny, Paracelsus, Cardamis, Albertus Magnus, the Emperor Augustus, and many others of note.

Now whether these ancient people were more enlightened than we are, has long been a question of dispute. The point, however, which has been admitted, and the one which concerns this study most, is, that as in those days the greatest study of mankind was man, it therefore follows that in a study like this their conclusions are far more likely to be right than are those of an age famous for its implements of destruction, its steam-engines, and its commerce. Again, if an age like the present will admit, and has admitted that those Greek philosophers were men of extraordinary depth of thought and learning, and that their works, thoughts, and ideas are worthy of the deepest respect, why should we then lightly consider their authority on this subject, and throw aside a study that so deeply occupied their attention? And again, if we go back, as we do, to these men for their learning in other matters, why, in the name of all that is reasonable, should we reject their knowledge in this?

Now, as in the study of mankind there came to be recognized a natural position for the line of head, the line of life, and so on. The time and study devoted to the subject enabled these students to give names to these marks;

6

as the line of head, meaning mentality; the line of heart, affection; the line of life, longevity; and so on, with every mark or mount that the hand possesses. This brings us down to the period when the power of the church was beginning to be felt outside the domain and jurisdiction of religion. It is said that the early Fathers were jealous of the power of this old-world science. Such may or may not have been the case; but even in the present day we find that the church constitutes itself in all matters, both spiritual and temporal, the chosen oracle of God. Without wishing to seem intolerant, one cannot help but remark that the history of any dominant religion is the history of the opposition, knowledge, unless that knowledge proceeds from its teachings.

# Bible References

Verses from the Bible and their exact application to Palmistry have been long and hotly argued about and disputed by commentators who analyzed the verses. Moreover, the translators and commentators seem to have taken special pains to turn and twist about the words and their meanings of the earlier writings of the Bible, to suit the opinion and prejudices of the times when the translations and revisions were made.

Many people who believe in the divine origin and inspiration of the Bible sneer at Palmistry and other occult sciences. Until the pontificate of Sextus V in 1585 the Christian Church found no harm in Palmistry, and several of its priests were highly skilled experts of the ancient science of Palmistry. The only explanation for the church to rise against chiromancy may be traced solely to the Gypsies who made the art of chiromancy to some extent their own, giving Palmistry the worst reputation, and causing the church to use its power against Palmistry and occult sciences.

One example of the turning and twisting of the verses from the Bible, which are the favorite quotations among Palmist writers are:

Book of Job, chap. XXVII, verse 7. The English version runs: "He sealeth up the hand of every man, that all men may know His work."

Whereas the Latin version reads: "In manu omnium hominum Deus signa posuit, ut noverint singuli opera sua," which, in a fair straightforward translation, means: "God has placed a sign in the hand of all men, that each one may know his own works."

All students of Latin and other people would easily recognize the difference. It could be possible that if the scriptures had not been distorted, other religions would still be more favorable to Palmistry.

Verses from the Bible:

Exodus XIII. 9 And it shall be for a sign unto thee upon thine hand.

Exodus XIII. 16 And it shall be for a token upon thine hand.

Numbers XXII. 7 Departed with the rewards of divination in their hands.

Deuteronomy VI. 8 Thou shalt bind them for a sign upon thine hand.

Deuteronomy XI. 18 Bind them for a sign upon your hand.

8

I Samuel IX. 19 And will tell thee all that is in thine heart.

I Samuel XXXVI. 18 Or what evil is in mine hand.

Judges IX. 16 According to the deserving of His hands.

Ezra VII. 14 According to the law of thy God which is in thine hand.

Ezra VII. 25 After the Wisdom of thy God which is in thine hand.

Job XXI. 16 Their good is not in their hand.

Job XXIII. 9 On the left hand, where he doth work, but I cannot behold him; he hideth himself on the right hand, that I cannot see him.

Job XXIV. 20 The mighty shall be taken away without hand.

Job XXXVII. 7 He sealeth up the hand of every man; that all men may know his work.

Psalm VII. 3 If there be iniquity in my hands.

Psalm LXXVII. 10 I will remember the years of the right hand of the Most High.

Psalm CXIX. 109 My soul is continually in my hand.

Proverbs III. 16 Length of days is in her right hand; and in her left hand riches and honour.

Proverbs VII. 3 Bind them upon thy fingers.

Ecclesiastes IV. 6 Both the hands full with travail and vexation of spirit.

Ecclesiastes X. 2 A wise man's heart is at his right hand, but a fool's heart at his left.

Isaiah XLIV. 20 That he cannot say, Is there not a lie in my right hand?

Isaiah XLIX. 16 Behold, I have engraven thee on the palms of my hands.

Ezekiel XXI. 12,22 He looked in the liver; at his right hand was the divination for Jerusalem.

Habakkuk III. 4 He had horns coming out of his hand; and there was the hiding of his power.

Jonah IV. 11 Persons that cannot discern between their right hand and their left hand.

I Corinthians XII. 21 The eye cannot say unto the hand, I have no need of thee.

2 Corinthians VI. 7 By the armour of righteousness on the right hand and on the left.

Revelation I. 16 And he had in his right hand seven stars.

Revelation XIII. 16 To receive a mark in their right hand.

Revelation XIV. 9 Receive his mark in his forehead, or in his hand.

Revelation XX. 4 Neither had received his mark upon their foreheads, or in their hands.

# Making Prints of your Hands

When giving a reading, I always make black ink prints of my client's hands. I have a photocopying machine and prefer to use it when I see an unusual hand and want to keep a copy of it for my records. However, the black ink copies are much more dramatic. They are very nice framed and my clients seem to prefer them. When making these prints, two copies should be made, one for your client and one for your files.

There are several ways to make prints of the palms. A plaster cast is one of the best methods because it shows the form of the hand and the lines of the palm, however they are complicated to make and difficult to store.

Photographs of the hands and palms are simple to make, easy to store, but can be expensive. I have had good results with my camera and my Polaroid, which I carry when I am lecturing.

One of the best methods to make a palm print is the photocopying machine. Today's machines surpass any other method, but they are expensive and most palmists do not own one. I am lucky to have one because of the need in my office and in writing this book. If your client works in an office, I'm sure that they would be allowed to use one. Be sure to recommend this method to them. Suggest that they have an opaque piece of material to cover the top of the machine to block out any light. Also, any printing shop would allow you to use their copy machine for a small fee.

An easy and inexpensive method, and one that is most commonly used, is one using water-soluble black printing ink for the palm prints. Although the prints do not always reveal the exact shape of the hand, lines or ridges, the prints can turn out well with practice and lots of patience. You should always make and extra copy for your record file; in addition to providing a permanent record, the subsequent follow-up prints will reveal any changes in the hand over the years. The prints should be dated, then signed with your name in addition to the client's notes such as the color of skin, texture, nails and flexibility and any unusual markings, etc.

# Equipment needed to Make Palm Prints

1. Black water-soluable printing ink.

The ink comes in a four-inch tube. The brand that I have found is called Speedball. This type of water-based ink is also used by the police department and can be bought at most art supply stores.

2. A rubber roller.

The Speedball Company also makes this type of roller. The roller generally has a metal frame with a wood or plastic handle and is about 7" wide.

3. A supply of good quality unlined paper.

The ink company recommends Printmaster paper, however, a common typewriter paper can work just as well.

4. A soft rubber or styrofoam pad.

This provides a cushion for the paper to help mold and make the impressions of the delicate lines of the palm. I also use the palm of the hand and fingers to gently press the center of the client's palm to reach the hardest area in order to get a good impression.

5. A fairly thick glass.

The back of a baking dish works well, also a piece of marble or marble-like plastic works well; the new plastic cutting boards or a piece of linoleum

To clean up afterwards, liquid dish soap will work best on both the equipment and the hands of your client.

None of the items needed to make the prints are expensive and can be stored in a desk drawer.

## How to Make a Palm Print

Assemble equipment to make palm prints: black water-soluble printing ink, a rubber roller, a supply of good quality paper, a soft rubber or styrofoam pad and a marble slab.

Put about an inch of the water-soluble black ink on the marble slab.

Spread the water-soluble black ink with the rubber roller in a large enough area to cover a hand.

Have your client place their hand on the ink and spread it on the palm over as much area as possible. Then use the rubber roller to cover the balance of the hand.

Place a piece of paper on the rubber pad and gently press, keeping the hand and fingers from moving.

While keeping the hand from moving on the paper, gently press the fingers and palm to the paper.

Lift the hand up carefully off the rubber pad, without moving the fingers or hand. Then press your palm to the center of your client's palm because this area is the hardest to print.

Have your client turn their palm up as you press with your fingers to the center of the palm.

Have the client turn the palm down and, keeping the hand and fingers straight, ease the paper off the hand.

A clear print.

# The Technique of Reading Palms

People who become interested in reading palms will find themselves observing hands when meeting someone for the first time. They will find themselves looking at hands when watching people on television or the movies. When talking with a group they will catch themselves doing a quick reading and it's great fun. I think that I love thumbs the best. The hands for me have always the insight of a person, like eyes will show expression in their movement.

By the reading of the hands we can understand the character of a person. If someone asks me the meaning of the hand, I've always said that it was the character sketch of the subject, as though I was drawing a picture of them.

The best way to become a palmist - a good palmist - is to read hands, lots of them. Start with family, friends or anyone who will allow you to look at their hands. Remember, you cannot memorize all the information available; even I must look to my references when I have an unusual hand. The best doctors and lawyers always use their reference libraries. Today, of course, they have their computers. You must do the same by keeping your reference books on hand and referring to them. It is the best way to continue learning.

Reading the hand of another person is a serious matter which involves a tremendous responsibility, and, as a palmist, you must bear the responsibility for what is said and how you express yourself during the consultation. You should be completely objective and base your information upon what you read in their hands. As a hand analyst you must never use the reading to impress or gain power or control of another life. You must be truthful, kind and non-judgemental. The reading should be as positive as possible and should help your clients to become aware of their talents and abilities.

You should also state any health problems or conflicts in their lives, but avoid giving any advice, for that must be worked out by your clients. You must never discuss a reading with others. There is no one method or technique to giving a reading, it will develop by practice.

After you have made the copies of their hands, you can now get ready for the reading. I always have my recording machine and extra tapes available for my clients. Some like to bring their own machines.

The reading should be done where there is a good light; by a window during the daytime is excellent. If a window is not available, I use a lamp with a flexible neck so that it can be adjusted to the area of the palm I am

15

reading. I keep a copy of my Palmistry Chart on the table so that I can refer to the features and diagrams of the hand or palm as I am discussing them, so my client can have a visible view of the map of the hand. I find it a good tool. You can use any drawing of the hand and palm.

I seat the client across from me in a comfortable chair so that we are as close to the same level as possible. It is very importanmt for them to be at ease. The reading should be enjoyable, even fun.

It must be mentioned here that you are always reading both hands and explaining the differences, if any , to your client.

I start the reading by taking both hands in mine. I explain what I am observing as I read their hands. With both hands in mine, I can feel the strength and thickness of the hand, the color and texture of the skin and the hand's flexibility. I look at the back of the hand - its size and shape, the fingers, color and texture of the fingernails, the hair and the knuckles. At this point I am looking at the size and shape of the palms, the fingers and the fingertips. I always start reading the palms from the tips of the fingers working down to the mounts, taking time to explain the quality of them and continuing until I have covered all the areas and lines. I read the thumb separately and leave the Lines of Affection and Marriage for last; it makes for an anti-climax. I always leave time at the end of the reading for any questions that the client might have.

Note: A good palmist cannot predict the end of life, the correct number of marriages, the number of children nor the amount of travel.

# The Hand - Cheirognomy

Cheirognomy - the Study of the Hands and Fingers. In the study of the hand we must compare its shape and formation, the size, color, the skin texture, the shape , length and condition of the fingers, the fingertips and the shape and condition of the fingernails. You must learn to recognize if the hand is large or small, its color and type, such as square, psychic or spatulate and if the hands are different from each other; if the hand is thick, thin, soft or hard and if the hand is stiff or flexible. The average hand is usually a combination of types. Before 1950 the average hand ratio from the base of the hand to the fingertips was about 50%. After 1950 these proportions started gradually to change. We now find that the fingers as well as thumbs are becoming longer, especially in newborn babies. The average fingers are now slightly longer from the palm to the fingertips, than the length of the palm; the ratio is now about 45% to 55%. Thumbs seem to be longer in the Caucasian countries. Black people's hands have longer fingers more frequently than those of whites. Brown skinned people have hands much the same as the Caucasian people. As the hand is changing with our evolution, so do the hands of individuals evolve with the passing years. We can change the lines in our palms, and if you watch closely, you can see the changes occur. Our hands suggest or indicate our potential, but we have the mental or physical facility to exercise our control over the choices we make.

Scientific research has revealed that the left side of the brain is more highly developed than the right, and each side of the body is controlled by the opposite side of the brain. The right hand is controlled by the left hemisphere of the brain and will therefore reflect more activity, have more changes and interests than the left hand which is controlled by the less active right hemisphere of the brain, which will remain less active showing fewer changes from birth. With left-handed people the rules are reversed; the right hand will show the less active traits, while the left hand will be more active and more changeable.

Everything that has been given as fact in palmistry has been the result of careful observation that has been checked and rechecked thousands of times over the course of centuries; therefore, palmists today can state with a high degree of probability that certain signs or groups of signs will correspond to certain aspects in the character of the client or an event in their future, much to the same degree of success as a doctor might have when comparing data deduced from their patients' symptoms.

The study of fingerprints known as Dermaglyphics, has been recognized by doctors as well as criminologists. These patterns or ridges are different for each person and remain totally unchanged over the years, unlike the lines in the palms of the hands. As physicians use the fingerprints, so do criminologists, who are now using the uniqueness of the fingerprints not only to identify, but to determine the character of the person.

By now it is accepted universally that there exists a fairly precise and constant relationship between an individual's physical characteristics, tendencies and personality. With the study of the hand (Cheirognomy), we study the dimensions and other aspects of the hand and we establish important facts indispensible for a complete palmistry reading.

We seem to take for granted how wonderful our hands are, the many things they are capable of doing. For many years the study of the hand has had the stigma of fortune-telling. Because of this, uninformed people would not accept the investigation and study of palmistry even though it is the most logical, lucid and accessible way to understand and explain the character and health of man.

When learning to read and understand the hand , it is advisable to examine both hands to see if there is any difference between them; usually it will be very minimal. It is very importnat to realize that the hand is a unit; the fingers, the thumb, the back and the palm of the hand from the wrist to the fingertips are the whole hand. When starting a reading we first look at both hands and compare them. You will find that the hand that is used most will be larger, that the texture is firmer, sometimes even course. The hand that does not enjoy physical work will be soft and delicate.

As you examine the hand you should note the size, color, texture of skin, consistancy, the fingers their length, and the fingernails, their shape and condition, then decide what type of hand your client has, square, conic, psychic, etc.

The hand can be thick feel full, fim and stiff. This will indicate an earthy person. They can be stubborn and not easily changed.

Due to the type of work or exercise they do, the hand may broaden, however, the type of hand does not change and can still be identified. Hands that could have been used for delicate work can be changed due to circumstances beyond their control, such as a lack of education, and working at manual labor; they will still reveal very useful hands.

When the base of the palm is thin, it indicates muscular weakness. The thin hand that is healthy usually indicates versatility. These people are open-minded and will most likely have changes in the lines of their palms.

If the hands are very soft, these people tend to be dreamers rather than doers.

A very dry hand indicates a fearful and shy nature.

If the hand is thin and damp, these people are of a nervous type and are often deceitful.

When you feel the bones on the back of the hand, but not on the palm, it is considered normal. Small hands will attempt to do big things and large hands are excellent when they are working hands.

We must learn by experience to understand the size and condition of the hand.

The science of palmistry is founded upon the shape of the hand, the formation of the Mounts, the manner in which the hand is naturally carried and held when walking and gestures when talking. The hand can be divided into three zones and quadrant sections, "The Three Worlds of Palmistry".

The study of the shapes of the hands also gives us information as to the kinds of occupations that would be of interest to the person. The hands determine their capabilities for the types of work and also their ability of their mind and mental aptitude.

Our hands are very unique in their construction; along with our brains, they are the termination point of the countless number of impulses which travel from our hands to our brain as a result of our activity. Our hands are designed to carry out our physical activities through the constant interplay with our muscles and nerve endings. The direct relationship between our brain and hands is one of the main reasons why Palmistry works; our hands reflect our character and personality.

Physicians make use of our hands for certain types of information about our health.

Our fingernail condition and the color and condition of our skin on our hands all help the doctor; they have a bearing on the condition of our health. Medical science is discovering the skin ridges or patterns on the hands can be clues to birth defects.

By the time we are 12 to 14 months old, psychologists say that our hand gestures have begun to communicate feelings of joy, sorrow, anger, surprise, caring and our needs. Our hands serve as a vital part of our everyday speech and they enable us to relate to people we love, as well as those around us.

The hands are highly specialized parts of the body. As our silent partners throughout life, they help us investigate things around us. But not only do they permit us to grasp and move objects, they also detect warmth and texture. The hand is unsurpassed in its sensitivity, mobility and strength.

The hand is one of the most intricate and flexible structures of the body. The hand and wrist are composed of bones, joints and "soft tissues" such as muscles, ligaments, tendons, nerves, and blood vessels.

As infants we touch everything that we can because it provides us with the information, feelings and texture of our surroundings. Hands are one of the most sensitive parts of our body; they inform our brain of impressions, textures, temperature, size or dimensions, changes and movement. Without the information we acquire through our hands and the infant's conception of objects, even the examination of our own bodies would be impossible. We are always touching and exploring and receiving a constant flood of impressions and information which not only helps us to determine our place in our world, but helps us reveal whether the object or person is a threat to us or beneficial.

Our sense of touch is essential to establishing relationships. As infants, our hands reach and grasp and hold onto our mothers for sustenance, warmth and security. As adults, we still need this sense of security in our relationships.

A simple handshake can reveal volumes of information about another person. Without our hands, human relationships would be very limited for our hands show our capacity for feeling.

For the deaf, fingers and hands play a very important part in their lives. The sign language which uses the fingers and hands in finger spelling the alphabet to converse is one of the best ways for them to communicate with others. The sign language is invaluable to them.

# Hand Gestures

You can learn a great deal about a person by watching the way they use or hold their hands, the way a person will shake your hand. The firm handshake means an outgoing, sincere person; the limp "cold fish" handshake, a person that has difficulty dealing with life; or the hand that clings, this is usually a salesman who wants to sell you something.

Watch the way a person holds their hands when walking. If the hands are fully open, they will have nothing to hide; they can be overly frank, a sort of "bull in a china shop" type. The average person walks with their hands slightly cupped.

One of the greatest tools that actors and dancers have are their hands. They not only show emotion, but the hand gestures indicate the nature of the character they are portraying to the audience before a single word is spoken.

If a person seems anxious to keep their hands closed, even when you are trying to give them a reading, they may have things that they do not want to disclose or expose to you. They could have a dark side to their character; they could be deceitful, hypocritical, or even devious. However, at the same time, you must be careful before making any judgement, they may be very shy or very careful. If they are careful, they may not want to hear all that you can see in their hand. This is a person who can keep a confidence or business secret.

Psychiatrists and psychologists watch the gestures of their patients' hands. Medical doctors also use the gestures of their patients, and the appearance and condition of their hands as a tool in diagnostic studies. Judges are aware of the gestures of accused persons as well as witnesses, and use them as a guide. Palmists, of course, feel that you do not really know a person until you have studied their hands.

When hands are crossed in front of a person's chest, it can indicate that this person is set in their ideas, closing out others and making them appear older. If you are trying to sell them something with their hands in this position, you can be sure that they will not be interested.

Beware of a person rubbing their hands together when making a business deal; they are out to fleece you. No matter how attractive the deal may look. you will probably wind up the loser.

A firm handshake indicates a person who is energetic, with a positive outgoing personality. If the hand has an elastic quality, you will know that they also have a flexible outlook on life.

A limp handshake means that you can count on this person to disappear when the going gets tough. Their motto in life is "Let George Do It."

A hard handshake indicates a no nonsense type of person; the only right way is their way. These people can be found in the military; they need physical endurance in their work.

A moist and clinging handshake indicates a weak type of person.

A fingertip handshake is a person who does not want to get involved and may consider that you are beneath them. A politition who is campaigning may also use this type of handshake.

People who keep one or both hands in their pockets when they meet you tend to be secretive or self-conscious. You really don't know what they are thinking.

There are many more gestures too numerous to mention here and there are already many books written on the subject.

# The Consistency of the Hand

Is the hand Flabby, Soft, Elastic, Firm or Hard? One of the many things we must recognize when starting a reading is to know and understand the client's energy. For no matter how brilliant they may be, if they have no energy to carry out their desires, it will be wasted. To determine the consistency of the hand you must take your client's hand in yours as though you were to shake their hand, then firmly close your fingers and gently squeeze to see how much resistance their hand gives to your pressure. Then press your fingers firmly into their palm. This will tell you the degree of hardness, softness, or flabbiness, as well as the resisting power of the muscles of the palm. It also reveals their sexual energy and how it is expressed.

A Flabby hand is the softest hand you will find. When you squeeze the hand the flesh and bones seem to crush together. This hand indicates a person with absolutely deficient physical energy. People with thin, flabby hands generally are not interested in either physical or emotional exertion. They are hands of dreamers, not doers; someone who loves, but expresses their love in words, not in deeds. These people desire ease in their life, both mental and physical. They desire luxury and to be surrounded by beautiful things, but will not work to have them. They would prefer to live in squalor rather than to exert themselves. These people can be highly gifted, but the energy is lacking.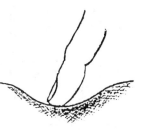

If the hand is Thick and Flabby and the thumb bends back very easily, it indicates a person with little or no will power. They are prone to overindulgence, not only of food, but drugs and alcohol.

The Soft hand will have a boneless, flabby feeling when you take the hand in yours and squeeze it gently, and the palm will be soft to the touch. The Soft hand, though, does not indicate laziness as the Flabby hand does, but it still indicates a deficient energy level. The important difference between the two hands is that the Flabby-handed person will always be lazy, while the Soft-handed person's energy can be developed. These people can build up their energy and develop their talents. However, if the soft hand is thick and chubby, it could indicate overindulgence.

The Elastic hand, when held in yours and squeezed, cannot be crushed, but has the feeling of springiness, gives resistence to your hand and is full of life. When you press your fingertips into their palms, the flesh will spring back like rubber would under the same pressure. There is not a better descriptive word for the consistency of the hand under pressure than elasticity. This type of hand is found on people who are active, energetic and have sexual vitality. They have the capacity to.respond to new ideas and unusual situations. They are full of life, but do not exert themselves. They enjoy a happy medium. They are trustworthy and honest, and make excellent professional business people.

The Firm hand is slightly elastic when held in yours. This consistency indicates a person that is physically active, has a good mind and sexual energy. They are stable, do not like unexpected changes in their lives and would rather have things their way, but will consider anothers' point of view.

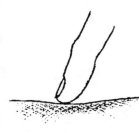

The Hard hands are not seen as often as the soft or elastic hands. The Hard hand will not yield under the pressure of your hand and will have no elasticity. The palm will not spring back to your touch and the texture of the skin will be course. As a rule, these people are less intelligent and it is not easy for them to take on new ideas. Manual labor is what they expect of life. They have physical strength and an abundance of physical energy, but are rigid and set in their ways. Because of their rigid disposition, they lack the openness and adaptability for a successful relationship.

You will find many degrees of consistency between the Hard and the Flabby hand. In the beginning it will be hard to distinguish all the different degrees. It just takes time and many hands. You may also find that a person will have two different degrees of consistency; for example, if the left hand is soft and the right hand is elastic, you will know that their energy has increased. If the left hand is hard and the right hand is softer, you know that this person has become lazy.

# The Back of the Hand

When you become familiar with the principles of Cheirognomy and start your readings, the back of the hand will be observed first.

It is difficult to lay down the order that you observe the hand because, as you study and become familiar with the different types of hands, you will have learned to notice all the various parts, until the recognition is instinctive and you can take in the hand as a whole. All of these details reveal a picture of the person even before they have noticed that they are being inspected.

# Hair on the Hands

In the examination of most hands you will find little or no hair, especially on the backs of hands of women.When, however, excessive hair is seen on the women's hand, it will indicate a tendency toward masculinity. The texture and color of the hair will make a great deal of difference too. You will notice the hair on the back of men's hands most often. The more hair on the back of the hand, depending upon its color and texture, the more physical strength he has. The absence of hair on a man's hand in no way indicates femininity.

Let me mention here that the color of the hair is important. It is impossible to draw any distinction because of the co-mingling of races and nations of the world where we find the very blond hair and the very black hair intermingled. We have so intermarried that all shades of hair are a result.

A profusely hairy hand with course hair will most likely be found on a man indicating an excess of animal instincts. These men have vitality, a strong sexual drive and eat excessively. They tend to have a rough exterior, loving quantity rather than quality and can be aggressive, tending toward an explosive nature. They enjoy a robust constitution and are naturely suited to hard, rough types of work. they are capable of a great deal of physical exertion. This type of person is not capable of too much mental strain, and in times of crisis will usually act with animal instincts. Their health is usually affected by their indulgences.

25

A hairy hand indicates virility and manly qualities. They have vigor and can discipline themselves. They appreciate the better things in life, both in personal relationships and in their appetites. They are firm and responsible, capable of hard work, have a good mind and when necessary, can call on their physical resources to accomplish their duties. The texture of the hair and its color will determine your analysis of the hand.

When the hair on the back of the hand is very sparse, thin and fine it is not a good sign. These people can lack vigor and virility. They can be cunning and evasive. They even suffer from psychological weakness or nervousness.

People that have more hair seem to be more physically aggressive. People with less hair tend to be diplomatic when dealing with others. But again, the intermarriage of our races makes it difficult to be accurate.

# Texture of Skin

One of the first things a palmist notices on the back of the hand is the texture of the skin, its courseness or firmness. The texture of the skin is the key to the person's natural refinement as well as their natural tendency in the choice of an occupation. If the texture is fine, soft or delicate, it indicates a refined, sensitive person who loves to absorb knowledge. Their hands will influence everything they do. If the skin is transparent looking, they are the hands of our saints and prophets, but seen on a weak hand, these people tend to have an abnormal imagination. Those with thin skin are usually overly sensitive and perhaps psychic. People with thick skin are stubborn and insensitive. Course skin is found on the earthy people. The different textures of the skin, however, can be tempered by the other qualities of the palm and fingers.

A question most often asked when discussing skin textures is how does the texture of the skin really lead to a person's choice of occupation and can the texture of the skin change? Of course, hands can change. The hand can change due to circumstances, but in most cases, we tend to choose work or a profession that is most suited to us and the tools we were born with. I have read hands of people who are doing hard labor, not out of choice, but of necessity, and their hands have become rough and course, and in men, course and stiff.

## Smooth or Satiny Texture of Skin

Hands with smooth or satiny type of skin are very pleasant to touch. These people usually have perception and have a love of beauty in art and nature. They have creative talent and are very aware of textures they touch. These people are sensitive and also have a sensitivity to extreme heat or cold.

## Extra Smooth Texture of Skin

This type of skin texture has a fine silky feeling to the touch. These people have a highly developed sense of touch and love to feel fine things. They are often smooth talkers, love self-adornment and try to impress others with their ability to inspire confidence. They are apt to be lazy, but have an alert mind. They love to live high and have excellent taste, but if they go to extremes and do not control themselves, it may cause problems in their life.

## Medium Texture of Skin

The medium texture of skin is the most common type. The skin will feel elastic, not soft; firm, not hard to the touch. These people are practical, well-balanced, have sensitivity and are objective. This type of skin texture is usually found on professional people.

## Course Texture of Skin

Course texture of skin is not often seen. The course texture indicates a lack of refinement. This type of texture can modify all things in the hand by adding courseness, such as stinginess, superstition, vulgarity and aggressiveness. People with this rough textured skin may have difficulty expressing themselves. They enjoy physical labor and need the outdoors in order to release their physical energies. We can use the word "earthy", as this is their type.

# The Color of the Skin of the Hands

The health or disease of a person is indicated by the color of the hands. It is very important that you understand the colors of the hands. The lack of this knowledge will cause a palmist to give a poor reading. Each color of the hand indicates the condition of a person's health. Dead-white hands indicates lack of circulation and a deficiency in the blood. Pink hands indicate a normal healthy person. Red hands indicate an excessive blood supply which can cause high blood pressure. Yellow hands indicate poisoned blood. Blue hands indicate a sluggish condition of the circulation of the blood supply.

When examining the hands for color, notice the palm of the hand, the back of the hand and fingernails, for when combined give a very accurate estimate of the normal color of the hand. The normal color of the palm is rosy and pinkish, regardless of race or color of skin.

The time of the year must also enter into your evaluation. In the winter hands tend to be lighter in color than in the summer when they are exposed to the sun, therefore, the palms must also be examined because they have less exposure to the elements than the back of the hand.

The dead-white skin color gives the impression of pallor and lack of blood supply, while the term "white skin" implies fairnes of the skin. A very course, heavy hand can have pallor, which would indicate a lack of red corpuscles in the blood, but the skin would never have the whiteness of a fine-textured hand that has a natural whiteness. Therefore, you must be able to recognize the watery pallor of a hand from a natural whiteness.

While the white type of hands have written our most beautiful literature, it has a bit of coldness in it. White handed people are dreamy, mystical, unemotional and selfish; they are not enthusiastic, but have a good imagination. These people are not sensual and quite cold in their affections. They can be clever, but would rather be by themselves. They make good poets. They have an active mind. Because they lack warmth they make few friends. When you shake hands with this person, you feel the lack of life, heat energy. generosity, sympathey and enthusiasm. When you have a client with dead white pallor, you must gently ask questions, for they must seek medical help, not only because this is a sign of poor circulation of the blood, but it also indicates a deficiency in the blood which can cause serious health problems.

As whiteness of the hand indicates a deficiency in the blood, the person who has pink colored hands has a healthy blood circulation and a sense of well being with a quality of strength. They have a healthy pink glow not only in their hands but in their faces and eyes. They are full of life, energy and vitality. These people are cheerful, vivacious and full of sparkle. They have a tender loving disposition. They have sympathy for the less fortunate. They enjoy the company of others, are optomistic and show enthusiasm, love and tenderness. They have magnetism and warmth for others. Pink colored hands are a benefit to all who come in contact with them.

Pale pink hands indicate that these people have a delicate constitution. Their circulation is slow and they should be advised to check with a doctor concerning the condition. It it not a dangerous condition and can usually be corrected.

The red or 'ruddy' colored hand indicates a tendency to excess in everything they do, which may be this person's fatal deficiency. There are different degrees of red. The full deep red hand is the hand of a fighter. They can easily lose their tempers which is often violent. They are prime candidates for high blood pressure because of an increased flow of blood. They have an intense, passionate nature and are driven by their passions. They become impatient easily and cannot stand laziness in others. Their increased blood supply enhances their passion for life, however, they must beware that this zeal for life can lead them to excesses in food and drink, which can affect their outlook on life.

The degree of redness in the hand can temper the degree of force in the person. The red color indicates a physically strong, zealous and passionate nature. They cannot do anything in halves. They are intense in everything they do, in love, war, business, art and religion. They have a wonderful vitality and energy. When expressing themselves they do not mince words and tend to overwhelm others. They can be rather slow thinkers; their minds can become dense or coarse and lack keenness. They eat, love and fight with extreme passion.

A yellowish color of the hands is relatively rare; it is a probable indicator of liver disease, which also includes hepatitis and jaundice. Before making any decision, ask your client about their diet. Yellowish hands can be caused by drinking large amounts of carrot juice. If the yellow hands are being caused by a poisoned blood supply, this condition can cause an irritation to the nerves and brain; it weakens the heart muscle and the person will not be able to function well. They will become moody, morose, silent and want to avoid people; they really cannot see the bright side of anything and because of the bilious condition they can be cross, irritable and nervous. They become unhappy people and are not at all pleasant to be around. When you see this problem in the hands and fingernails, always look to the lines for confirmation. If this person has an aggravated

30

problem and the hands are not a pronounced yellow, just slightly, it is wise to give this person warning so they may seek professional medical help and encourage them to do so at once.

Blue or purple color of the hands is caused by poor circulation of the blood, but not necessarily the quality of the blood. This condition can cause physical weakness and affect the heart beats, making them weak and insufficient to move the blood normally. The blood, moving slowly causes the blood to clog in the veins causing the blueness of the hands and fingernails. If the skin is already bluish, the heart has been weakened dangerously. When you see this condition on a client's hand and fingernails, and you have examined the lines on the palm, you must inform them, but be careful to first ask them, "Do you have a heart problem?" If they are unaware of this condition, you must handle this situation very carefully and gently; do not excite them; you must ask with great tact and refinement. You then inform them that their blood circulation is not very good and advise them to seek professional medical help for they are a candidate for heart failure or other illnesses associated with poor circulation and sluggish blood.

Although I have never seen black or gray tints in the hand, my references indicate that they can be brought on by grief, sorrow or even guilt. These black or gray tints can also be caused by colic, bad lungs, heart trouble, liver disorders or dyspepsia. If a client shows these signs, you must suggest that they seek professional medical help.

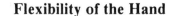

# Flexibility of the Hand

The degree of flexibility and elasticity in the hand indicates one's emotional and mental health. The flexibility also suggests both physical agility and how agile or intuitive the mind is; a flexible hand, a flexible mind, a stiff hand, a stiff mind. The flexibility of the hand also indicates how we adjust to the demands of our environment. Emotionally, those with limber hands adapt well to pressures, in contrast, a very stiff hand indicates a very tense person who has a stiff and rigid outlook on life.

To determine the degree of flexibility in a hand, have your client lay their hand with the palm upwards in the palm of your left hand, and with your right hand press gently downward until you have bent the hand as far backwards as it will go, then test their other hand. At the same time, you must notice whether the whole hand is flexible or if the hand is only bent at the knuckle joints. If the hand is flexible, you will find that the whole hand bends, as well as the fingers. If it is bending at the knuckle joints, it indicates that just the fingers are flexible.

At this point you must decide upon the degree of flexibility of the hand, for there are many variations in degrees of flexibility.

The flexible hand that bends backwards in a graceful arch indicates an elastic mind. Their brain understands and responds very quickly. These people adapt to new surroundings very easily; they are versatile, intuitive and impressionable. Because of this versatility, it is easy for them to think, act and feel all at once. This can cause them to become involved in too many activities without completing any of them. They are open in their feelings in relationships with the opposite sex. Because these people are flexible, it also causes them to have interest in more than one relationship and they lack the ability to make a permanent commitment and have a tendency to be unfaithful.

A moderately flexible hand is seen more often. When the hand is pressed backwards, it bends easily and opens until the fingers straighten themselves naturally and the hand opens to its full extent. The hand is generally elastic in consistency and has energetic force. This is the medium or average flexible hand. People with this type hand are balanced and in control of themsleves. They have good minds, never extravagant or wasteful, and they stay within their bounds both financially and emotionally. They are self-contained, good listeners, and put to good use what they hear. They are open for new ideas. These people take life seriously and understand the difficulties of life. They are thoughtful, broad-minded, earnest and sympathetic people.

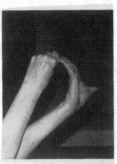

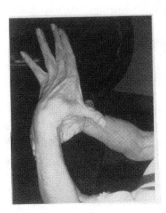  

A very flexible hand can bend backwards to nearly a ninety-degree angle with a minimum of pressure. This type of hand indicates a highly impressionable person, who is easily led by others and has difficulty being committed to one activity or one thing at a time. They are extravagant and unpredictable. If their thumb bends backwards to an extreme they will be generous to others, too generous. They are easily taken advantage of. They will always have difficulty making a commitment to one person and are unpredictable in their attitudes and actions.

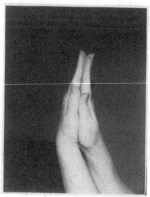

A firm hand hardly bends backwards at all under pressure and the fingers remain straight, indicating a strong type of person. These people are not impulsive. They have trouble if there are too many changes in their life, and have a hard time dealing with new situations and unfamiliar surroundings. They are conservative with their money as well as their feelings, and often keep to themselves.

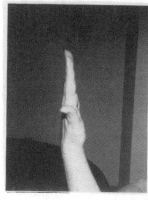

A stiff hand can be extremely rigid and usually hard to the feel. In some cases the fingers will actually turn inward in its natural state. This type of person is very cautious, immobile, close-mouthed (you could safely trust him with your secrets), inclined to be narrow-minded and stingy. They take things very seriously, are responsible people who are dedicated to hard work. The stiffness of the hand also indicates a secretive personality, and they have difficulty sharing their problems or their feelings with others. In their relationships they are inflexible and tend to want things their way, and will find it difficult to compromise with their partners. Although they feel deep affection and love, they seem to have problems sharing their feelings with others. They are afraid of new ideas and new ventures.

# The Hand Shapes

Few hands actually conform to one specific shape, although one shape of hand may be seen more often than any other shape of hand. The classifying of the hand shapes provides us with a general frame work to work with in order to do a thorough hand analysis. The shape and overall appearance of the hand is the primary indicator of the personality and character of a person. Now, with the blending of people that has spread through intermarriage, the different shapes and their combinations are even more important so that we can better understand the temperments and personalities of people from all over the world, which I find very exciting!

## The Elementary Hand

The Elementary hand has short fat fingers; the skin is course with thick flesh and has a heavy palm which is often hard. The hand seems inflexable and stiff. The palm bones make up almost the whole hand so that it has more palm than fingers. The thumb is short, thick and usually square at the end. These people lead a basically physical existence. They have little capacity for education and are slow in their development and ability. They must learn skills of a physical nature. These people work very hard, as this shape of hand is usually accompanied by a powerful physique. They make good professional fighters because of their insensitivity to pain. They are also insensitive to the pain of others and they can become violent. They will use their physical strength to get what they desire. People with Elementary hands have little or no control over their passion. They can be brutes. Like brutes, though, they too may have an amiable side, although they are never appreciative of others, they can be extremely loyal to those who show them tenderness and tolerance.

## The Square Hand

The Square hand can be recognized by its apparent square shaped palm and fingertips that are usually square. These people are the organizers, the planners. They love order, constancy and stability. Common sense and reason will be predominant over their emotions. They are competent and very careful with money, especially when the hand has a rigid thumb. Their minds and hands work well together and have good coordination. They would prefer a steady systematic approach to love and relationships. They

tend to concentrate on the practical aspects of a relationship, but once they have made a commitment, they are loving and warm. They can be critical, suspicious and impatient with detailed work. They are very punctual and reliable in their habits. They love physical action, love to work outdoors. These are practical, earthy people.

## The Spatulate Hand

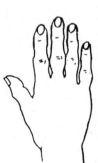

The Spatulate hand is usually wider at the base of the fingers than at the wrist. A spatulate hand with all spatulate fingers is very rare. The spatulate fingertips are wide, resembling a druggist's spatula, and narrowing just below the top of the finger, forming a waist-type shape. The base of the finger tends to be wide. The spatulate hand is known as the energetic hand; people who love action, are innovative, self-confident, and very sensual. These people love to create order and organziation where none has existed. They have a vast amount of energy and enthusiasm. They love adventure and have a wonderful imagination. They can be impulsive, charming and exciting. They are often flirty, and love to taste. They have difficulty making a commitment and enjoy being involved with more than one person at a time. They are sensual people and if their hands are flexible, they tend to pursue their physical pleasures to an extreme.

People with spatulate hands are original, independent, and make excellent leaders; however they often take advantage of a situation and use it to their advantage. They are excellent in commerce, banking, construction, as investment brokers and entrepreneurs.

## The Philosophic Hand

The Philosophic hand, or Knotty hand, can be divided into two classes or sections, one, the materialists and the other, the idealists. One of the most distinguishing characteristics of this hand are the knotted joints of the fingers. The palm is quite square, but longer and more angular than the square hand, with pronounced joints and long fingers. This shape hand indicates a person that is a deep thinker who may be hard to understand and who is sensitive and dignified, the college professor or scientist. People with philosophic hands gather wisdom but seldom gold. They are the students rather than the workers. They have good reasoning powers, are logical, diplomatic, very quick-witted, discriminating and kind-hearted. They tend to be perfectionists. They make good professors, judges, ministers, historians, statesmen and inventors. May I add that this type of hand is found in the Orient, especially in India. I'd like to end with a quote by "Cheiro" of the philosophic hand, "In character they are silent and

36

secretive; they are the deep thinkers, careful over little matters, even in the use of little words they are proud with the pride of being different from others; they rarely forget an injury, but they are patient with the patience of power."

## The Conic Hand

The Conic or Artistic shaped hand is full and well-shaped, with fingers tapering from the lower joint to the fingertips where they end in a rounded thimble-like cone. The texture of the skin is usually fine. This indicates their sensitivity and love of beauty. They appreciate all art and artistic things, but they are not creators of art. They are very romantic, sentimental and impulsive in their relationships. However, they can be intensely devoted to a partner one day and move on to someone else the next. This inconsistency and instability are their major problems. They do things impulsively, they can be rash, moody and have trouble completing what they have started. But you can't help liking them, for they are also very warm and sociable. They love all music and the performing arts, but have a constant need for excitement and activity. They make good actors and dancers.

## The Psychic Hand

The Psychic or Intuitive hand is quite rare, but distinctive. It is beautifully formed, with long, graceful fingers, with the fingertips pointed. The possessor of these hands is sensitive, romantic, impressionable and emotional. Because of this they tend to be nervous and high-strung. They can be overly sensitive, neurotic, even hermits. They can be easily influenced; people tend to impose on them. It would be to their advantage to choose friends or a partner that can add strength and stability in their lives, and advisors in their business. They are suited to being poets, artists and mystics.

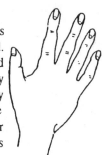

## The Mixed Shaped Hand

The Mixed-shaped hand combines the qualities and characteristics of any of our different hands and finger types. The basic shape of the hand should serve as the foundation of your analysis. The shape of the hand can be of one type, while the fingers are from two or more different shaped hands. You must then look at the mounts, lines and skin texture and, very importantly, the flexibility of the hand. You will find the possessor of this type of hand versatile, energetic, very adaptable when working with people

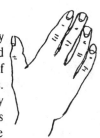

37

and new circumstances. They are original thinkers, combining their ideas in very innovative ways. They love to bring ideas of others, as well as their own, to life. They are tactful, diplomatic and friendly. They love action and adventure. They believe deeply in luck. Because of their versatility, they can be restless, fickle and changeable, and at times easily influenced in their dealing with people. They make good actors and are quite capable of showing different sides of themselves to different people.

# The Hand Size

The hand has been used as a standard of measure for centuries; it measures about four inches. Today it is still used to specify the height of a horse.

Our hands, however, are of different lengths and widths. They sometimes do not match our bodies in their size and proportions. For this reason, Palmists believe that the size of the hand is very significant and can be used as a measure of character and personality.

To determine the size of your hand in comparison to your body, there is a simple test that you can try. Lift your hand up with your palm toward your face, place your chin on your palm where your wrist begins, reach upward to see how far your fingers reach. If your fingertips touch your hair line you have a very large hand; if they touch your forehead, you have a medium sized hand, and if the fingertips just touch the eyebrows, you have small hands for your body structure.

## Small Hands

People with small hands have a great desire to achieve, to reach the top, and they usually set long-range goals for themselves. People with small hands have a bundle of energy; they are achievers and always aim high. Small hands do not have to match or be in proportion to one's body; small hands can be found on large and small bodies. People with small hands can be unscrupulous when seeking their goals, they tend to think big and are known to waste time daydreaming about their future glories. Small-handed people have a large ego; they can be intense and use reasoning rather than their intuition. They have trouble relaxing and seem unfriendly because of their tenseness.

## Medium Hands

When the fingertips reach the forehead, it indicates an even, cool temperment and an ability to deal well with others. The medium hand-type people are usually balanced and have good judgement; they often act as mediators to others. They enjoy good common sense and are practical, with a healthy imagination. The medium sized hand shares the tendencies of the large and small hand and can use all of their capabilities.

## Large Hands

A person with a large type of hand indicates an aptitude for various occupations. They are versatile and have many capabilities. They have a tendency to spread their energies in many directions. They are capable of having different goals, all at the same time. These people are known to have more than one job at one time and are able to be successful in each one of them. They are versatile and enjoy their varied talents. They have the energy and ability to use their talents and skills all at the same time, and because of this they may spread themselves too thin.

Large-handed people are friendly and sociable and like their versatility in their occupations, they enjoy many different types of people. They love to talk and joke.

The size or length of the hand is only one type of measurement used as an indicator of character and personality. In reading palms the use of all the information when put together gives us the knowledge to underestand our clients.

To measure the fingers and the hand, hold the hand so that you have a view of the side of the hand, now measure from the wristbone or base of the hand to the top of the knuckles of the middle (Saturn) finger, then measure from knuckle top to the tip of the middle finger. These measurements can be taken easily with a ruler.

If the fingers measure shorter than the back of the hand, this, of course, is a short fingered type. When you find the measurements are almost the same, this person will share the characteristics and personality of both types of hands.

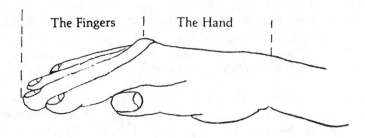

The Fingers    The Hand

# The Palm Size

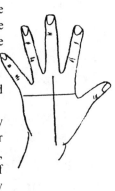

To determine the size of the palm, you start by measuring the width of the palm starting between the thumb and the Mercury finger. You measure the length of the hand from the knuckles to the wrist. If the width of the palm exceeds the length of the hand, it is a wide palm. If the width of the palm is less than the length of the hand, it is a narrow palm.

**In general, men's palms are wider than women's and the wide palm is** associated with masculine qualities. A narrow palm is usually associated with femininity.

People with wide palms are rarely seen, but when identified, they indicate a person who is concerned only with satisfyng their basic or physical needs. People with wide palms are direct, definite, abrupt, vigorous, confident and secure. They can perform tasks with a minimum of effort. People with wide palms usually have well-developed Mounts; they enjoy good health and balanced temperment. If the palms are wide on thick hands, it indicates an excessive imagination. This person will have an aggressive personality and a tendency to be deceptive. A wide hand with a flat palm indicates a person who is very intellectual but not physical.

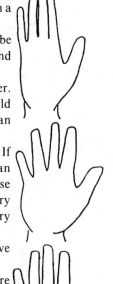

People with wide palms love action; those with narrow palms tend to be easily manipulated, they act more indirectly. They are planners and organizers, but feel insecure where aggressive action is required.

Those with a narrow palm may be very lively with a quick wit and clever. They may be inclined to be gloomy and cynical. They think that the world and life can be evil. When faced with conflict they would rather retreat than be brave.

The narrow or oblong palm indicates an emotionally sensitive person. If a person has a palm that is wider at the base than at the top, they have an introverted personality. If the palm is wider at the knuckles than the base area of the palm, this person will have an extroverted personality, very firey and expressive. They are active and excitable and can be very intuitive.

If a narrow palm is found on a very small hand, it indicates a sensitive person and an introverted personality.

People with a square palm love action; they prefer mobility and are attracted to physical activity.

Square palms with short fingers indicate a person who is practical, dependable and reliable. People with square palms are usually cheerful, extroverted and ambitious.

# The Tree of Life

Through the combined cooperation of the twenty-seven bones of our hand, dozens of muscles and millions of nerves, the human hand is a marvel of design and function. Our hands express our love, our needs and our desire to communicate; they have created our civilization and culture. Our hands are our tools for creative expression and the mirror of our inner selves.

Think of your hand as a tree with the fingers as branches. Any deviation in the straightness of the tree trunk or branches due to outside influences, pressures and other circumstances, so it is with our hands and fingers. "As the tree is bent, so the tree will grow."

By their nature hands grow straight from the wrist and the fingers extend directly from the palm of the hand. Any curving or bending of the skeletal part is usually caused by outside pressures of life; parents, family, society and our experiences.

Just as we examine a tree to find out how it has been affected by its surroundings, so we can examine our hands.

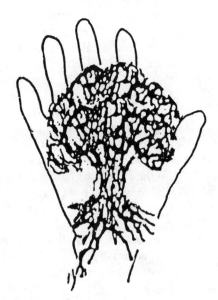

When we look at the skeleton of the hand, we see joints between the bones that become knuckles when the flesh is added. The palmar area of the hand also includes four metacarpal bones which extend from each finger. The phalanx of the thumb has a different skeletal structure from the fingers; it has its own significance. In this book there is a special chapter dedicated to the thumb, because of its significance.

Any deviation from the skeletal structure of a normal hand should be noted as a unique characteristic that has been developed by one's own lifetime experiences. You must understand what the effects of the differences in the structure would signify.

PHALANX

Phalanx of the Thumb

Metacarpal Bones
or Metacarpus

## The Divisions of the Palm

There are three main divisions of the palm. The illustration that I like to use is a tree. From the base or roots of the tree we draw life and from the center one-third section or Mars area, conscious energy, physical courage and fortitude. The use of the tree as a symbol is especially suited here. With the tree's energy flowing upwards from the trunk to the upper third of the palm where the leaves, flowers and fruit represent man"s highest expression of brain power, thought and will.

The fingers of the hand have the same three divisions and the symbols are repeated on the palm.

43

# The Divisions and Quadrant Sections

The knowledge of the Divisions and the Quadrant Sections of the hand is very important for a good understanding of your client. It is necessary to be able to view each section of the hand and their interplay with each other.

## The Divisions

There are three zones of the hand or three worlds of Palmistry that have been based on the superstition that a person is guided either by the mind, the affairs of everyday life, or the base qualities of animal instincts. As far back as we can recall, there have been three divisions of the body, the soul and spirit, the mental abstract and the material: air, fire and water. Going back even further, an old notion, heaven, earth and hell. In psychological terms, superego, ego and unconscious part of the psyche. These three divisions can be applied to the hand, and in Palmistry they are also known as instinctual energy, social energy and mental energy. Even though we use different terms, the idea behind each of these terms remains the same.

## The Mental Energy Division.

The fingers of the hand make up the mental section of the hand. It indicates the mind in a broad sense and includes the spiritual nature, conscience and the power of rationalization. If the fingers are long, the Mental Division is emphasized and increases the person's desire to control their lives and usually it indicates an idealistic mind. If the fingers are short, it would indicate that the person is not idealistic but will have another form of energy that will predominate. If the fingers are unusually long, it indicates that this person is often preoccupied with their ideas. They are very sensitive and aware of other people's feelings. They are very loyal. You must always observe the fingertips for further information that is important.

## The Social Energy Divisions

The Social Energy Section of the hand includes and affects all the resources available for carryng out all aspects relating to the family and society. The more prominent this section is the more aware and involved this person will be with humanitarian interests and the promotion and

44

welfare of mankind by trying to eliminate the pain and suffering of others. If this area of the palm is prominent, it also indicates a capacity for dealing with groups of people and is known as a people-oriented type of hand. These people are adaptable and can recognize the needs of others. This section of the palm refers directly to a person's ego. If there appears to be prominent mounts in this section of the palm, it indicates that this person's ego is not built on idle energy, they need activity to be happy. Certain high mounts in this area indicate powers of projection for these people, which adds ambition and the ability to reach goals. However, the primary indication of such prominent mounts gives these people an awareness of the world around them.

A prominent social energy area will indicate a person who is very involved with other people. They love to share and communicate their ideas with others. These people are ambitious and are always involved with others and the the activities going on around them.

## The Instinctual Energy Division

The Instinctual Energy Section of the hand represents all the biological drives of a person, their instinctive functions and routines. This source of energy must be generated and maintained to carry out all the tasks which are represented by the Mental Energy Division and the Social Division in addition to its own function. In a sense, the instinctual energy division can be compared to the roots of a tree.

ZONE OF INSTINCTUAL ENERGY

If the instinctual area of the palm is prominent, it indicates that whatever this person does, they will do it with a great deal of personal strength and resource for they will have the vitality and an extraordinary amount of energy.

45

# THE QUADRANT SECTIONS

## The Active and Passive

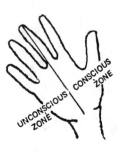

If you draw a horizontal line to divide the palm of the hand in two at the point where the thumb is joined to the base of the hand and across the palm to the percussion side of the hand, the two sections will form the Active and Passive Zones. The reason for this division will become clear when you realize that the fingers do all the active tasks; the demands of the brain. The base of the hand is known as the Passive Section. It indicates a person's expression and their way of acting out their inner desires.

## The Conscious and the Unconscious

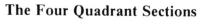

If you draw a vertical line down the middle section of the hand from the center of the middle finger (Saturn) to the center of the base of the palm, it divides the hand into two sections which are known as the Conscious and the Unconscious Zones. The thumb and index finger (Jupiter) are clearly the Conscious Section of the hand. The Unconscious side of the palm, which includes the ring finger (Apollo) and the little finger (Mercury) is the Active Unconscious one quarter section. This section of the palm indicates memories and dreams which they express symbolically and creatively through the arts or writing rather than directly as part of their early life. The base of the thumb to the center of the palm is known as the Passive Conscious Section and the base of the outer percussion side of the hand is known as the Passive Unconscious Section.

## The Four Quadrant Sections

The Four Quadrant Sections of the hand are very useful as a further dimension of information. These four sections are the functions of the mind and nervous system. They are the Conscious, the Unconscious, the Active and the Passive and their combined meanings.

The thumb and index finger (Jupiter) along with one half of the middle finger (Saturn) in the upper section of the hand is known as the Active Conscious Quadraant. Half of the middle finger (Saturn), the ring finger

46

(Apollo) and the little finger (Mercury) is the Active Unconscious of the upper section.

The base of the thumb to the center of the palm then down to the base of the palm is known as the Passive Conscious Section. The base of the outer percussion side of the hand is the Passive Unconscious Section.

ACTIVE
UNCONSCIOUS

ACTIVE
CONSCIOUS

PASSIVE
UNCONSCIOUS

PASSIVE
CONSCIOUS

## The Three Latitudinal Zones

Another concept on the division of the hand is called the Three Latitudinal Zones which are formed by drawing two horizontal lines, one from the tip of the thumb across the palm below the base of the fingers, and the second line starting from just above the ball of the thumb across the palm to the percussion side of the hand.

The top section is known as the Emotional Conscious and Zone. This represents our link with the world around us; like a tree spreading out its branches. Depending upon the prominence of these mounts in this section of the hand; the zone of our emotional expression, it determines how we use our power, our inspiration, our ambition, our artistic creativeness and business intellect. This area of the palm enjoys the sense of touch and holds the strongest power of connection with people and objects.

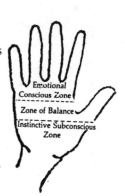

Emotional
Conscious Zone

Zone of Balance

Instinctive Subconscious
Zone

The middle section is known as the Balance Zone. It is the zone of logic, practical or common sense, good reason and represents the blending of our thoughts and feelings. It is the area of our palm that filters and absorbs our unconscious drives and helps to guide them. It helps to bring together our aspirations, desires, high ambitions and goals, and our intellectual abilities with our physical and instinctive drives.

The lower section is known as the Instinctive Subconscious Zone. It is the unconscious part of our psyche, our morality and our motivating forces. Depending on the prominence of the mounts in this section of the palm, this zone relates to our intution, imagination and libido, including our deepest and hidden desires.

# The Tree As A Symbol

I believe that the symbol of the tree is the best illustration of a hand that I have found. A tree is the symbol of life; the hand shows the capacity for life. There are three divisions to the hand as there are three divisions to the tree. The base of the hand symbolizes the roots of the tree, the palm symbolizes the trunk of the tree and the fingers symbolize the branches, leaves, flowers and fruit.

To locate the base or lower third of the hand, draw an imaginary horizontal line across the wrist and another just above the ball of the thumb across the palm of the hand; this area signifies intuition and emotion.

The palm or middle section is located between the imaginary line just above the ball of the thumb and the Heart Line. The middle division takes its energy from the God of Energy, Mars the Warrior. It has its darker side, such as being quarrelsome, yet may not necessarily have much force. It also relates to courage, our social contacts and our ability to make a living.

The upper third located between the Heart Line and the Fingertips signifies the conscious and emotional zone. It is closely united with physical courage. The outside or percussion side of the palm indicates the degree of development of the instinctive courage or fortitude of the person. As the tree reaches its highest point, so man's highest expression is the power of thought. This upper third is the area of mental interest and the foudation of the repetition of a renewed tree pattern in the fingers; renewed life.

The tree is the symbol of life, and the hand shows the capacity for life.

# The Longitudinal Zones

The Three Longitudinal Zones of the palm of the hand are formed by an imaginary vertical line between the index (Jupiter) finger and the middle (Saturn) finger downward to the wrist. The second line is between the middle (Saturn) finger and the ring (Apollo) finger downward to the base of the hand.

The first section is known as the Active Conscious Zone, which represents the energy we consciously use in our dealings with the material world. This section of our palm relates to our attitude and the assertion of our ego in our daily life as an intellectual and individual and physical levels. It is the area of practical knowledge, outward movement and the application of our principles in our work, study and how we deal with our relationships.

The Zone of Balance located in the center of the middle of the palm, serves as a meeting place where our different energies can blend. The Fate Line, when seen in a palm, occupies this middle section which indicates a career, advancement in life and the degree to which we will achieve our goals in life.

The Passive Subconscious, which occupies the outer, or Percussion side of our hand, represents our hidden energy reserve. It relates to our inborn or inherited nature and creativities. It is part of our emotional awareness and natural instinctive abilities.

The Three Longitudinal Zones

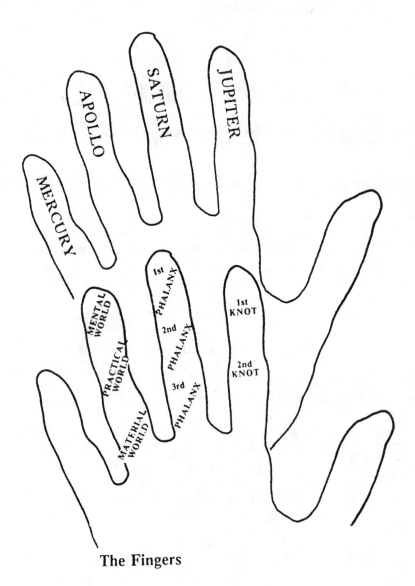

**The Fingers**

# The Fingers

*Conic*
*Spatulate*
*Square*
*Pointed*

## Classification of the Fingers

The average person thinks of the hand as having five fingers, but in palmistry, we give the thumb a separate classification and because of its importance, it is given special attention. So, when a palmist refers to the fingers, they are only including four. The four fingers can be long or short, knotty or smooth, straight or crooked, or bent and leaning towards another finger.

The fingertips are classified as square, spatulate, conic or pointed. Each finger is named for the mount at its base and takes on the qualities of the mount. The first finger is the index, the Jupiter finger; the second, middle finger, or Saturn finger; the third or ring finger is the Apollo or Sun finger; the fourth, the little finger is the Mercury finger.

The most developed finger of the hand usually indicates the important area of the person's life. To determine the length of the finger is to compare them to each other. The length and shape of the palm is considered as well. Long fingers on a long palm is natural, as are short fingers on a short hand.

Next, examine the joints of the fingers. Are they smooth or knotty? If the fingers are knotty, are both the joints knotty, and to what degree?

Now the flexibility. Take each finger by itself. If one finger is more flexible than the others, then the qualities of the mount it is named for will be more pronounced. Have your client put their palms together and reach backwards with their fingers as far as they can. This can also indicate the degree of their flexibility.

The Phalanxes of the fingers are the three spaces between the knuckles of the finger. The first phalanx is the area from the fingertips to the first crease of the finger. The second phalanx is the middle area between the first and second creases of the finger, and the third phalanx is located between the second crease of the finger and the crease at the base of the finger, which joins its mount. The phalanxes provide information about the growth and personality of a person. The first phalanx at the fingertips indicates our capacity for thought, both abstract and pictured. The middle phalanx indicates common sense; the third phalanx nearest the palm indicates our interest in physical things.

The shape of the finger is very important, whether it is straight, crooked or curved; if the finger is bending laterally from one side or the other, or if the finger seems to be twisted. When a finger is bent, it increases the shrewdness of the qualities of its mount. A finger that is twisted indicates a liability and obligation to the moral or physical defects of the mount's qualities. By comparing the fingers they will indicate crookedness, their natural angle of opening, the way they are set on the palm.

The fingertips of each finger must be recognized and classified. Notice if any one finger is longer or more erect than the others, or if one or more of their fingers lean toward each other. If a finger is leaning toward another, it gives up some of its qualities to the finger it leans toward.

The fingernails, the mounts, the lines, the shape of the hand and their condition all must be taken into consideration.

## The Length of the Fingers

The first thing I must impress on you when determining the growth, development and classification of the fingers of the hand is that the fingers on both hands must be compared, for the fingers may differ from each other. Your client may have more than one personality and characteristics. Only by reading both hands and discussing them with your client can you know which path in life they have chosen.

## The Jupiter Finger

The first finger, named Jupiter, is also referred to as the index finger. When it is normal or of average length, it is slightly shorter than the Apollo finger, which indicates how well a person gets along with others, their relationship with people and their attitude towards their community. People with an average length Jupiter finger will have no desire to be a boss; they would rather work in the background with a partner. However, if the Head Line is poor and they have a weak thumb, it would cause them to have a lack of self-confidence.

A person with a short Jupiter finger also shows a lack of self-confidence. They do not enjoy social activities and always feel conspicuous.

A very short Jupiter finger indicates a person with an inferiority complex. They do not feel worthy of love or worthy of any attention. They feel unattractive. If the Head Line is poor and the thumb is weak, it indicates a timid and very cautious person. They are followers and not leaders. Any kind of responsibility or authority frightens them as their temperament makes them unable to cope with the responsibility. Routine, undemanding work would best suit them.

A long Jupiter finger is usually as long or longer than the Apollo finger. These people have a good self-image and are attractive to others. They deal well with the world and have self-confidence. They are ambitious, take pride in their work and like to be in charge, which makes them excellent executives. With a good Head Line and strong thumbs, their ability for leadership and responsibility is increased. They are good at making quick decisions and have a gift for getting things done. In the field of education they maintain discipline and respect from their students.

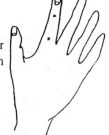

But if you find a Jupiter finger that is long and the Head Line is poor and a weak thumb, it indicates a person with a bossy and selfish disposition. These people always want to be the center of attention.

A very long Jupiter finger, that is, the finger is as long or longer than the Saturn finger, can have a negative or a positive aspect. At this point in your reading, you must be very sure to examine the hand as a whole, not just the fingers.

The extra-long Jupiter finger can indicate a conceited, overconfident, overbearing and tyrannical personality. This is known to be the sign of dictators.

The positive hand with a very long Jupiter finger indicates a very confident person that can exert a tremendous amount of influence over others. They are born leaders and rulers.

# The Saturn Finger

The Saturn finger is the second, or middle, finger of the hand, which represents the finger of solitude, wisdom, service, duty, and restrictions. It deals with the spiritual or philosophical side of our nature. Next to our thumbs, it is one of the most important parts of the hand.

The average or normal length of the Saturn finger is about one-half tip longer than the Jupiter or Apollo fingers. When the Saturn finger is straight and in proportion to the other fingers, it indicates a prudent and sensible outlook on life. With an intelligent hand, a normally developed Saturn finger indicates excellent powers of study and concentration. These people will have the ability to think clearly and calmly. They can set their goals in life with competence and intelligence. At times, though, they must have their privacy.

If the Saturn finger is longer than normal, not only longer, but stronger and bony-looking and appears to dominate the hand, this type of Saturn finger is seen in the hands of people who know loneliness. They would rather live in the country than the crowded city. They hate to endure delays, restrictions of various kinds. They have to learn self-discipline and gain knowledge and experience in the "school of hard knocks." They will eventually manage to win success and happiness.

A very long Saturn finger is a burden. These people have a strong sense of duty and responsibility, and take life too seriously, which can cause them to become melancholy and morose.

When the Saturn finger is short, these people have an easy-going nature. They just coast along, having a good time, really not interested in any problems that exist in the world around them.

# The Apollo Finger

The Apollo finger is the third finger of the hand and also is referred to as the Sun finger and the Ring finger. This finger rules both the emotional and the mental aspects of a person's personality, and how they will express their feelings to others.

The average or normal length of the Apollo finger is about one-half of a tip shorter than the Saturn finger, and a little longer than the Jupiter finger. These people are warm, social, sympathetic and enjoy the finer things in life, with a love and appreciation of the arts.

A long Apollo finger indicates a person with a great deal of patience. They are artistic and have the ability to be successful in their choice of career. They are willing to take a chance and gamble on their hunches. They can be very charming and are usually well-liked. They are not the type of people to make quick judgments or to criticize others. They are good listeners. They are well-balanced and quietly self-confident.

If the Apollo finger is extra long, it indicates a love of gambling and speculation. They are known to take chances in their careers, as well as the gaming tables. They love notoriety and, because they are very artistic and have the ability to express themselves in drama, art, music or poetry, you will often see the extra long Apollo finger on actors, actresses, and other people who enjoy the spotlight.

If the Apollo finger is short, it indicates there has been very little growth in this person's personality and in their lives. They are impatient in everything they do, and with the people around them. They have a tendency to bring out the negative side of others. They are apt to make snap judgments and quick decisions. They dislike detail work and rush to get things done quickly. They don't like social activities.

# The Mercury Finger

The Mercury finger is the fourth finger of the hand, also known as the Pinkie, or little finger.

The average or normal length of the Mercury finger is when the tip of the finger reaches the top crease or knuckle of the Apollo finger. It is one of my favorite fingers. This little finger has a lot of power. It represents our one-to-one relationships. It also deals with communications at all levels, sexually, with the writer or in the spoken word, all forms of communication. Especially as a speaker, for although they may be speaking before a large audience, they must reach each person individually. This one-on-one communication applies between our loved ones, as well as with the public. People with a normal Mercury finger are also good listeners. They are always aware of their environment.

A long Mercury finger gives the ability to perceive, become aware through their senses, of the unseen. These people may have spontaneous flashes and hunches, and their hunches are usually reliable. When the Mercury finger is long, philosophical discussions and conversations about the abstract and unknown fascinate these people. They are versatile, born actors, story-tellers and mimics. They make excellent business people and, because they are in tune with their environment, they know instinctively what the public needs are. They always have the desire to improve themselves as well as others.

When the Mercury finger is short, it indicates a person who will not find it easy to carry out their aims and ideas in their life. They have a lack of stability and concentration. If the Head Line and thumb are strong, they may eventually have success, but have to work very hard for everything, and it will be a struggle for them. These people always feel the world is treating them badly. They can become withdrawn into themselves and because of this will lose a great deal of their psychic ability and they will not be able to depend on their hunches. They seem to have lost touch with their environment and will ignore what others say and feel.

# The Growth and Development of the Fingers

In the skeleton of the hand we can see the joints between the bones that become the knuckles of our hands when our flesh covers them. The palm area includes the four melocarpal bones between the wrist and the phalanx, or bones of the fingers, which extends from each finger and the third phalanx of the thumb. The different skeletal structure of the thumb as opposed to the fingers, carries its own significance.

Let us imagine our hands as two trees with our fingers the branches. Any bending or deviation of the shape of the branches due to outside influences, pressures, circumstances, including those inherited or genetic, will affect the tree growth. This principle also illustrates the principle of our finger growth. Any deviation from the skeletal structure should be investigated.

## The Average Growth

When looking at the hand and its fingers, you will find when the hand is lying on a flat surface with the fingers and thumb close together, the average thumb should reach to the middle of the bottom phalanx of the Jupiter finger.

When the top of the Jupiter finger reaches the middle of the top phalanx of the Saturn finger, this person realizes their own potential and feels secure in their own abilities to lead and teach others. They have security within themselves.

The second finger, Saturn, is one-half of a tip longer than Apollo or Jupiter fingers. This indicates a sense of balance and an understanding of themselves, and not to become too serious in dealing with others.

The third finger, Apollo, is about the same length as the index finger (Jupiter). These people are usually social, warm and sympathetic, and appreciate all the finer things in life.

The fourth finger, Mercury, or the little finger. The top of the little finger should reach the crease line of the third phalanx of the Apollo finger. This type finger indicates a person who communicates well and has a good relationship with their family and lovers.

## The Phalanxes of the Fingers

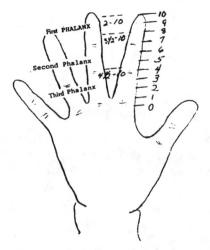

Each of our fingers and our thumb is divided into three sections, and each section is a phalanx of the finger. The phalanx provides us with information about the growth of our fingers, which provides us with reliable clues to our vocational aptitudes, our personality and the outstanding aspects of our character and make-up.

Normally, each of the sections or phalanxes is equal in measurement when compared. If we were to divide the length of the finger into ten equal parts, the first phalanx, or the tip of the finger, should be two parts of the whole finger. The middle, or center phalanx of the finger, should be three and one-half parts of the whole finger, and the third phalanx, or base of the finger should be four and one-half parts of the whole finger.

The first phalanx is located at the fingertip, or fingernail portion of the finger. It indicates our spiritual responses.

If the first phalanx of the finger is thick, it indicates a pursuit of religious inspiration and pleasure. These people receive sensual enjoyment from religion and art.

If the second phalanx of the finger is thick, these people have ambition, possess material things, and are always in pursuit of their own personal pleasures.

If the second phalanx of the finger is thick and long, the money-making side of this person becomes uppermost in importance to them.

The second phalanx is located in the middle or center of the finger between the two creases or knuckles of the finger. It indicates our mental responses.

The third phalanx is located at the base of the finger nearest the palm of the hand. It indicates our physical responses.

If the third phalanx of the finger is very long and very thick it indicates this person's sensuality and their gratification of their appetite for sex and luxury will be the most important part of their lives.

The extreme thickness of the third phalanx of the finger indicates a great love for eating and drinking.

If the third phalanx is extremely thick and the first phalanx is short and the second phalanx normal, this person will not care for mental pursuits at all, but will only care to make money and to have plenty to eat and drink. This type of finger is not sensual, as just having the third phalanx thick, but these people want their gratification in food, luxury and comfort.

The thickness of the phalanxes will always indicate a coarseness and desire and need for excess.

The thumb's first phalanx is located at the top, or fingernail portion and indicates willpower, determination and temper one has.

The second phalanx of the thumb is located between the first and second crease of the thumb. It indicates our logic and reason.

The third phalanx of the thumb is considered part of the Mount of Venus. It indicates our love of music, sympathy, passion, enjoyment, our desire to be liked.

# The Jupiter Finger

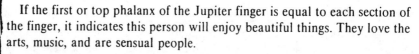

If the first or top phalanx of the Jupiter finger is equal to each section of the finger, it indicates this person will enjoy beautiful things. They love the arts, music, and are sensual people.

If the first phalanx of the Jupiter finger is longer than the other two phalanxes, it indicates these people will be over-indulgent sexually and are attracted to glitter and gaudy things.

If the first phalanx of the Jupiter finger is shorter than the other two phalanxes, these people do not know how to enjoy life and will have problems with their self image.

If the second or middle phalanx of the Jupiter finger is equal to the other phalanxes of the finger, this person will have ambition, self-esteem, a good ego and the drive to succeed in life.

If the center or middle phalanx of the Jupiter finger is longer than the two other phalanxes, this person will be self-centered, selfish and have a dictatorial personality.

If the second phalanx of the Jupiter finger is shorter than the other two phalanxes, these people are self-destructive. They try to remain inconspicuous and usually lead an insignificant life, depending on the other aspects of their hands.

The third phalanx, located at the base of the Jupiter finger, when equal to the other two phalanxes, indicates a spiritual person. They have faith in their destiny and have healing powers. They always attempt to live up to their ideals.

If the third phalanx of the Jupiter finger is longer than the other two phalanxes of the finger, these people can become religious fanatics, dreamers, alcoholics or drug addicts.

If the third phalanx of the Jupiter is shorter than the other two phalanxes, these people lack faith, have no insight to their personality, and often play the martyr rather than stand up for themselves.

# The Saturn Finger

When the first or top phalanx of the Saturn finger is equal to the other two phalanxes of the finger, these people enjoy teaching, have an expansive personality, love to travel and meet people from all over the world, both young and old. They are writers and enjoy philosophy.

If the first phalanx of the Saturn finger is longer than the other two phalanxes of the finger, these people always are looking for perfection; they are restless and impulsive.

If the first phalanx of the Saturn finger is shorter than the other two phalanxes, these people have a lack of faith in themselves and will give up too easily.

When the second or middle phalanx of the Saturn finger is equal to the other phalanxes, these people are the workers; they are stable, give a sense of security, are the father or mother figures. Tradition is very important to them.

If the second or middle phalanx of the Saturn finger is longer than the two other phalanxes of the finger, these people are worriers, fuss over petty things and trivial details. They find fault in everything. They have strict religious morals and are very judgmental.

If the second or middle phalanx of the Saturn finger is shorter than the other two phalanxes of the finger, these people lack purpose in life. They tend to be closed-minded and have problems with authority.

When the third phalanx, or base of the Saturn finger, is equal to the two other phalanxes of the finger, these people tend to be eccentric, enjoy new ideas, changes, and new methods in their life and work. They are our humanitarians.

If the third phalanx or base of the Saturn finger is longer than the two other phalanxes, these people will fight for any cause and are superficial and uneffective.

If the third phalanx, or base of the Saturn finger, is shorter than the two other phalanxes of the finger, these people do not want to become involved. They tend to be anti-social and feel that others are persecuting them.

60

# The Apollo Finger

When the first phalanx or top of the Apollo finger is equal to the other two phalanxes, this person will do well as a teacher, writer and communications worker.

If the first phalanx of the Apollo finger is longer than the other two phalanxes of the finger, it indicates this person may have problems in communication, such as dysphasia, a difficulty in speaking. They may also have difficulty in reading.

If the first phalanx of the Apollo finger is shorter than the two other phalanxes of the finger, it indicates this person will have negative feelings. They will anger easily and feel resentment toward others.

The second or middle phalanx of the Apollo finger, when equal to the two others, indicates this person is intuitive, protective, home-oriented and imaginative.

If the second or middle phalanx of the Apollo finger is longer than the other two phalanxes, it indicates this person can be over-emotional, tending toward fantasies.

If the second or middle phalanx of the Apollo finger is shorter than the other two phalanxes of the finger, these people are afraid of life. They tend to detach or isolate themselves.

When the third phalanx or base of the Apollo finger is equal to the two other phalanxes, these people have a good self-image, are creative, productive and emotionally balanced.

If the third phalanx of the Apollo finger is longer than the other two phalanxes, these people tend to have compulsive behavior; they are selfish, boastful and have excessive ego.

If the third phalanx of the Apollo finger is shorter than the other two phalanxes of the finger, this person will have a poor self-image and low self-esteem.

# The Mercury Finger

When the first or top phalanx of the Mercury finger is equal to the two other phalanxes, it indicates a person who is very sexual. They have an investigative mind, always studying, searching, and inquiring.

If the first or top phalanx of the Mercury finger is longer than the other two phalanxes, it indicates these people are sexually permissive; they never seem to appreciate anyone, never have long relationships and cannot find happiness.

If the first or top phalanx of the Mercury finger is shorter than the two other phalanxes, these people will suffer from impotency, have sexual and social problems. They can be cold and have little insight.

When the second or middle phalanx of the Mercury finger is equal to the other two phalanxes of the finger, these people are loving, caring and trusting. They have good relationships. They are receptive and can compromise when necessary in a good relationship.

If the second or middle phalanx of the Mercury finger is longer than the other phalanxes, it indicates these people will have difficulty making up their minds. They tend to be taken advantage of because they are very open and receptive.

If the second or middle phalanx of the Mercury finger is shorter than the other two phalanxes, this person has a fear of being taken advantage of or used. They are not trustworthy.

The third phalanx or base of the Mercury finger, when equal to the two other phalanxes, it indicates these people have investigative minds. They speak and communicate well. They are responsible people who work in healing and medicine.

If the third phalanx of the Mercury finger is longer than the two other phalanxes, these people are always finding fault. They are always seeking perfection and have a frigid nature.

If the third phalanx of the Mercury finger is shorter than the other two phalanxes, it indicates that these people are irresponsible, have problems finding and keeping their jobs and have no compunction about letting others support or take care of them.

# The Crooked or Curved Finger

## The Apollo Finger

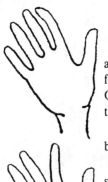

If the Apollo finger is crooked, it indicates this person will have many drawbacks in life. Their achievements will be hard to come by, if they can ever be reached at all. Money tends to be the idol of the crooked fingers, but does not necessarily make them happy.

When the Apollo finger is crooked or twisted, it is always a bad sign. It indicates a twist or flaw in the personality and characteristics of this person. These people will use any means to achieve their goals. They are unscrupulous, devious, secretive and crooked.

An Apollo finger curving toward the Saturn finger is rare, but if seen, this person has a serious conflict between duty and the pursuit of their pleasures. Because of their conflict, try to make this person understand that everyone needs recreation and pleasure, and they will still be able to do their work well, probably even better.

## Jupiter Finger

When the Jupiter finger curves in toward the Saturn finger, this indicates a person with enduring persistence and self-will. Once they have set a goal for themselves, they will keep on stubbornly until they have achieved it. Once they have set their mind that they want something, or even someone, they will be very persistent.

When the Jupiter finger curves toward the thumb, these people want to be independent, and have a tendency to be possessive and jealous.

When the Jupiter finger curves toward the Saturn finger, it indicates a serious and dutiful outlook on life.

If the curve is exaggerated, then this person's true motives will be hard to know. They find it hard to disclose what they are thinking, especially if it means revealing their emotions.

# The Knotty Fingers

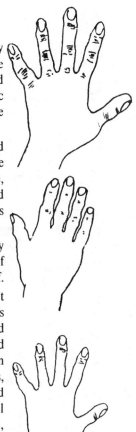

When looking at the fingers of a client's hand you will automatically classify them as smooth or knotty and then to what degree the fingers are knotty. If the fingers are knotty, the back of the hand will show ridges and have a bony structure. Knotty fingers tend to have pointed or conic fingertips. Doing hard manual work, even for years, will not produce knotty fingers.

Fingers can change, especially fingers of small children. If they have had smooth fingers when young, in later life knotty fingers can develop. If the knuckles are developed at an early age, these people will have patience, great power of concentration and perseverance. They will have a vivid imagination, a highly original mind and will be logical mathematicians as well.

All the fingers of the hand may not have knotty fingers and in every case, each finger must be considered separately, because the meaning of each knot depends on its location on the finger, as well as the finger itself.

There are three types of knotty fingers; the Philosophical knot located at the joint between the first and second phalanxes of the finger, which is referred to as the knot of mental order and indicates the harmonious and well-balanced mind. The second knot is referred to as the Orderly knot and is located at the joint between the second and third phalanxes. It is known as the knot of material order and indicates the love of order and neatness, both at home and in business. The third knot is less frequently found, and is located towards the tip of the finger, above the first joint. This knot will emphasize whatever the fingertip shape may be. It will add a more logical, practical or efficient approach to the person's life and enable them to invent new techniques and methods to improve their chances for achievement.

When the fingers of the hand are knotty, in most cases they are an excellent type of fingers to have. These fingers belong to the great thinkers of the world. They have a philosophical outlook on life. Contentment and peace of mind is more important to them than fame and fortune. They can be alone, but are not lonely, for they enjoy their own company and have lots of inner resources. They are dignified, rather than detached. They do not like small talk and often appear rude with their standoffish lack of interest. People with those knotty fingers are often absent-minded professor types and, because of their brilliant minds, are often accused of being

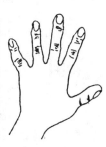

cranks. But they delight in discussions of higher mathematics or the metaphysical.

People with knotty fingers will act slowly and thoughtfully and will analyze and reason things out. They are philosophical people, always seeking the truth and striving to get to the bottom of a situation. With their analytical tendencies, before they can make a decision they must investigate and confirm any decision. They must examine all aspects from all standpoints. They simply cannot do anything impulsively or emotionally and they are not easily swayed by sentiment. Because of their analytical minds, many of them are more likely to be atheists.

These people are investigators, reasoners, searchers of the truth, honest, energetic, hard to change, thinkers, doubters, slow to arrive at conclusions, patient and systematic. They love detail in their work and are great organizers. They are thoughtful, slow at arriving at conclusions and they cannot be rushed into anything. They are fearless, advocates for human rights. They have a sense of justice and love of freedom. They are very loyal, but a little on the cold side as lovers. If the Head and Heart lines are close together, they will not have much of a sense of humor. They tend to become over-absorbed in their work, and are worriers.

Knotty fingers can develop from arthritis or an injury. Be sure to ask your client if either has occurred. Usually you can recognize these problems, but it is always best to ask.

Square fingertips with the first knuckle pronounced indicates these people will excel in reasoning. It will bring out an extreme personality and they will become methodical. They will always enjoy a good debate. They like to work and are often scholars in science and research. They also make good lawyers and professional people.

Square fingertips with the first and second knuckles pronounced indicates the love of the natural sciences. These people like to dig and excavate ruins. They are our archeologists and historians. They have lots of energy and are ruled by their minds, not by their emotions. Square fingertips on knotty fingers bring out the extreme personality of these people and they become very methodical.

Spatulate fingertips with the first knuckle knotty indicates a very realistic and obstinate person who can be very irritable. They like the exact sciences, and only believe in what they see, feel, or can touch. These people are not sentimental, even though they are humanitarians and will work for the welfare of the human race.

Spatulate fingertips with the second knuckle knotty indicate these people want order and harmony in their lives. Because of their love of order they can be forceful and demand things around them are regimented.

65

Spatulate fingertips with the first and second knuckles knotty indicate that these people do not like to take advice from others. They, themselves can become a nuisance with their continued desire to give advice. They always think their help is the best for other people.

Conic fingertips with the first knuckle knotty decreases the intensity of the knotty fingers and adds the best of combinations. This is the ideal type of knotty fingers. These people can be slightly aloof in their manner, but they are also very ambitious and work toward making a success of their lives. These knotty fingers add idealism, allowing this person to be more open and flexible.

Conic fingertips with the second knuckle knotty adds sensuality to this person.

Conic fingers with knotty knuckles are not as noticeabale as other shapes of fingers, because the conic hand and fingers tend to be fleshy.

Conic fingertips with the first and second knuckles knotty is a very nice sign. These people can be investors, musicians and imaginative writers. They have lots of energy and are achievers.

Pointed fingertips with knotty knuckles are rarely seen. These people have trouble distinguishing between their ideals and realism. They tend to be tearful people because they believe the world is not the way they think it should be.

Pointed fingertips with the first knuckle knotty adds stability to this personality.

Pointed fingertips with the second knuckle knotty makes these people more productive and adds a little more practical sense to their personality. It gives them the desire to succeed, especially in money matters.

The consistency and flexibility of a knotty-fingered hand is very important, for if the hand is soft or flabby, it will add laziness. If the hand is firm and strong, it adds energy.

# The Smooth Fingers

Smooth fingers do not have any pronounced knuckles and are smooth not only at the back of the fingers, but also along the sides. People with smooth fingers have a quick mind and can instantly grasp the real nature of a situation and provide a key to the problem. They are not easily taken off guard, for their mind is very elastic and they are able in a flash to see any opportunity and turn even a mishap into an advantage. They do not care to get to the bottom of every subject, but rely on their impressions which come to them without their having to stop and reason out all the problems they may encounter. They are guided by their first impressions and are seldom wrong in their intuitive deductions.

They are the lovers of beauty, but not the creators. These smooth-fingered people see the beauty of life; they love the artistic side of life and are graceful and attractive.

In business smooth-fingered people are more often successful because of their ablity to react and think fast. They usually can go by their first impressions, especially if their emotions are not involved. They are impulsive people and can do things without thinking them out.

They can communicate well, but talk off the top of their heads. They tend to be easy-going and enjoy being around other people. Because they are impulsive and impressionable, they sometimes act hastily, without thinking about the possible reactions of others.

In religion they vary from the very profound believers to the agnostics. They do not reason out their religious beliefs, but are willing to take the word of others.

Smooth fingered people are usually very agreeable and pleasant partners. Their love of beauty is very important in their surroundings, even when eating or sleeping as well as in their dress and the decoration of their home and place of business.

Quickness of thought, inspiration, not reasoning, calculation or premeditation, but impulsiveness and spontaneity are the guilding forces of the smooth fingered people.

They love and appreciate the arts and many people believe that the smooth conic type hand and fingers are our greatest artists. It is not so; the ideal hand of an artist is one that has large knotty fingers and square or spatulate fingertips. The other factor of the true artist is their thumbs.

Conic hands usually have small thumbs. Most successful artists have large square thumbs.

You will find smooth fingers in all walks of life, but the degree of the smoothness must be taken into consideration.

The smooth fingered Latins love ritual and decorations in their churches as well as in their homes, rather than the simple surroundings of the knotty-fingered, square tipped Puritans.

If the smooth-fingered person has square fingertips, their usual quickness and inspiration will become more practical and they will be less idealistic.

If the smooth-fingered person has spatulate fingertips, the force of the spatulate fingertips will intensify and add originality, activity and independence to their personality.

If the smooth-fingered person has pointed fingertips, these people are the most artistic of all the smooth-fingered people.

# The Knuckles

Knuckles form at the third row of the joints, at the back of the hand, at the material end of the fingers. This signifies order of material things and the standards of tidiness and cleanliness of a person.

When the knuckles form an even line at the back of the hand, it indicates that this person will take very good care of their personal health and be very neat. They tend to be meticulous about cleanlines and fastidious about their health.

If the knuckles form an uneven line at the back of the hand, this will indicate that this person will not take good care of themselves; they will be untidy and will not be careful about their personal health or cleanliness. They lack discipline and are not punctual.

If the Jupiter knuckle is pronounced, it indicates this person will always want neatness in their personal clothing and their personal belongings.

If the Saturn knuckle is pronounced, it indicates this person has a gift for making everything look nice when finished. They always add the perfect touch.

If the Mercury knuckle is pronounced, it indicates the instinctive love or gift of tidiness.

In young children the instinct toward tidiness may be submerged or hidden for awhile, but will reappear when needed and as they grow older, will be more prevalent.

## Spaces Between the Fingers

The degree of widths between the fingers and the hands gives us very useful and accurate information. For the fingers to be well-balanced they should be evenly set and normally spaced on the palm of the hand. To determine the width or narrowness of their separation, there are various methods that can be used. It is very important that the fingers are held in a natural position, as any strain would defeat the purpose.

One way to determine the width of the spaces between the fingers is to have your client place their hands in a natural position on unlined white paper and draw an outline of their hand and fingers. Because the position of the fingers can change and reflect their current state of mind, have them lift their hands and put them down more than one time. You will find in most cases that the spaces between the fingers are rarely the same, even in each of their hands.

In my readings, unless the client requests an outline of their hands, I prefer to ask them to hold their hand up and extend their palm toward me. When the hands are held this way in a natural position, I find reading and interpreting the spaces between the fingers easier for both of us.

The degree of width between the fingers indicates the amount of security or insecurity a person has. The wider the spaces are between the fingers, the more need for freedom this person will have. They also possess a sympathetic nature. They love action and are spontaneous. The more space between the fingers, the more financially secure the person will be.

The closer together the fingers are spaced, the more restricted these people's behavior will be. They are courteous and will always think before they act. They are always careful and thorough. The narrower the spaces between the fingers, the more restricted their financial resources will be.

If the fingers of the hand touch each other, this type of person will need someone to lean on.

When the spaces of the hand are divided equally, it indicates a good sense of security and diplomacy.

# Narrow Spaces Between the Fingers

When the spaces between the fingers are narrow and almost touching, it indicates a person who will need security and lives in a conventional world. They are very content to leave things as they are. Their attitude is, if everything is going along fine, "please don't rock the boat." They tend to put up a defense mechanism, whether consciously or unconsciously, to protect themselves. They have a cautious, formal attitude. Because of their self-imposed restrictions, they don't enjoy new ideas or the unexpected, however they have the desire and ability to finish whatever they start.

They have the reputation for being stingy, but this does not bother them. They want to hold on to what they have. Their motto is, "neither a borrower nor a lender be." If they are married they will want to set aside money that would be theirs alone. Because of their tightness with money, they miss many good opportunities, for it would mean they would have to take some risks. If only the Jupiter and Saturn fingers are closely spaced, these people will take a small risk and be able to spend money a little more freely, but they will always have money put aside for a rainy day. They still have a need for the sense of security.

If the spaces between the Jupiter (index) finger and the Saturn (middle) finger are narrow, it indicates a person that does not have freedom of thought or action. These people are cautious and have an inhibited frame of mind; they are not open to new ideas.

The Saturn (middle) finger and Apollo (ring) finger usually are very close together and difficult to separate. However, in some hands these two fingers will separate and open very easily. This is quite rare and has been used as a sign in some religious and cults. When these fingers do fall well apart, it indicates a person who has an inborn capacity for action and freedom of thought. They are unconventional, Bohemian type, non-conformist in their thinking and their mode of dress. They are flexible and love informality. Some become reformers. They are successful and usually have financial security.

If the Saturn and Apollo fingers are narrowly separated, it indicates a person who is restricted of freedom of action, one who cares about the future but they do not seem to be able to avoid or control their restrictions. Their lives are routine. They always seem to worry about their finances, for the narrow spaces between the Apollo and Saturn fingers always seem to indicate worry over money matters. These people save money and desire to have a secure future. They always put money away for a rainy day.

If the Apollo (ring) fingers and the Mercury (little) fingers are spaced closed together, it indicates this person may be dependent on others. They have trouble acting on their own and always seem to be blocked or hampered in their actions.

## Moderate Spaces Between the Fingers

When the spaces between the fingers are equally and moderately divided, it indicates a good sense of security and diplomacy. These people make friends easily. They enjoy new experiences, but have no great desire for adventure. They are logical and secure.

If the Apollo fingers are almost equal in length to the Saturn fingers, it indicates a desire to take risks. Although they need a sense of financial security, they do not worry about it. They have an adventurous spirit and are very enterprising. They enjoy the gambles and chances they take to succeed. These people will never really have any financial worries.

# Wide Spaces Between the Fingers

The degree of width between the fingers indicate the degree of security each person needs. Wide spaces between the fingers indicates this person is secure within themselves. These people with wide spaces are free spirited. They have a sense of adventure and love the unusual and eccentric. They have no fear of experimenting with the unknown or to try a new profession, even if it means moving to a new location. They are not afraid of failure. They look upon each new experience as an adventure. They are secure people. They are unconventional, non-conformist, out of the mainstream in their actions and dress, but will always make a good living. They can never be held down to the rules of etiquette. They are always fun to be with, but they can be reckless and rash and throw caution to the winds and find themselves in trouble. These lovely people would be quite impractical to be married to or to have a serious relationship with.

If the separation of the fingers is very wide, this person will always be easy to approach. They enjoy others and are the "hail fellow well met," type. They are spontaneous and like variety. They are never bound by convention. They have a good personality. They are sympathetic towards others. They will always need their freedom. They have a tendency to take up too many new projects which they may not be able to complete.

If the spaces between the Jupiter (index) finger and the Saturn (middle) finger are widely separated, it indicates an independent thinker. The wider the space, the more inventive they are. They must have their freedom and can never be bound by the views of others, but will always form their own opinions. They make good leaders.

If the Apollo (ring) fingers and the Mercury (little) fingers are widely separated, it indicates an independent person. They have the capacity to do things on their own. They will do what they want without allowing outside influences to hamper their activities or caring what others think of them. They can be unconventional and love the unusual and out-of-the-ordinary things. They have the courage to pursue and achieve their goals.

# Space Between the Hands

To determine the space between the hands, ask your client to stand up using their hands on the tabletop to help them into the standing position.

The wider the space left between their hands, the more alert and ready for quick action they are. They will act on a moment's notice and think about it later.

The closer the hands are together on the table, the more thought this person will put into their actions and projects before they begin.

If the two hands touch each other, it indicates self-imposed restriction on their behavior; these people are inhibited.

If just the two thumbs are touching each other and they are arranged in perfect alignment to each other, with the thumbs extending away from their hands, it indicates that this person will be very tactful and considerate of others.

If the two hands are touching and leaning on each other, this indicates a person who will need support in anything they undertake.

## Arched or Straight Position

When the hands are placed on the table in a natural position, the fingers will either stretch out flat, or they will be arched or curved. The arched or curved position indicates the person is uncertain at this point in their life. The higher the arch, the more uncertain they feel.

If the arch is only on one hand and the fingers of the other hand lie flat on the table, it indicates something is occurring at the present time. Always note which of the hands is lying flat and which has the arch. As you read the whole hand, it may become clear what the problem may be.

If both hands have arched fingers their feelings of uncertainty will be an old experience that they have not been able to solve.

If the arched fingers are on the hand of a person that holds their hands close together, there is a problem they are trying hard to work out.

If the fingers of the hand are lying flat and straight, it indicates a person with a lack of independence in either thought or action. They become a slave to formality and to make their acquaintance one would have to be careful for they are hard to get acquainted with. They tend to be stingy and constantly concerned for their future, especially if the fingers are held tightly together.

# The Flexible Fingers

There are many degrees of flexibility of the fingers and fingertips. The degree of flexibility is determined by how far the fingers can bend back in graceful arc with ease. The degree of flexibility determines the ability the person will have to adapt to new circumstances and new ideas.

There are several ways to judge the flexibility of the fingers and fingertips. I ask my clients to put their two palms together in front of us. Then I ask them to reach backwards as far as they can in an easy manner. The degree of flexibility can be easily seen by both of us. If the fingertips are also flexible, they will bend backwards independently.

Flexible fingers indicate a very alert mind. You do not have to be very close to someone to notice whether their fingers sweep back, for the fingers are very pliable. Because of this, so is the person's whole attitude. They are happy-go-lucky and have an open mind. They are more tolerant than most people and less sorrowful. They are interested in the scientific and occult studies. They are potentially psychic and deeply absorbed in people. They love to gossip and drink up information. They have a fast mind, sometimes too fast for their own good.

These supple-fingered people are attractive and are able to adapt to new and unexpected situations. They are fairly open with their feelings and have the ability to be a good partner in a relationship. However they sometimes desire more than one relationship and will have trouble making a commitment.

The flexible fingers also indicate an unconventional and inquisitive mind. Security and position mean very little to them. Money and opportunities for advancement just slip through their flexible fingers. They are young in spirit and open to new experiences and ideas, and understand the new generation, even if they do not agree with everything they do. Life is a constant adventure for them. They can adapt easily to their surroundings, no matter how different things may become from what they have experienced before.

# The Very Flexible Fingers

Very flexible fingers are capable, if bent toward the back of the hand, of achieving a ninety-degree angle with a minimum of pressure. These people lack the ability to hold onto any material things. They never seem able to save money and are generous to a fault. They can never keep a secret; they simply cannot hold their tongue. They are very impressionable in a relationship and can be easily controlled by others. They have difficulty making a commitment to one person and can be very unpredictable. They are extremely curious, have a tendency to eavesdrop and gossip. They are very entertaining at parties and their friends never have a dull moment when they are with them, for they can be very interesting, lively and jovial company.

# Double Jointed Fingers

When I see extremely flexible fingers I always ask if they are double-jointed. These people have all the aspects of the flexible fingers, and more. They are a great asset to the theatrical world. These people have a dramatic flair and make the greatest gymnasts and acrobats.

# The Stiff Fingers

Stiff fingers that are very straight and rigid, that cannot bend backwards, indicate a rigid-minded person. These people long for the good old days. They are set in their ways, narrow-minded, hostile toward any change or progress, and unbending. This type of person will never change their mind; they always need a secure base of operation, and tend to stay put. They are very cautious and stubborn. Safety comes first because of their fear of change.

In a relationship they want to have things their way and cannot compromise with their partner. While they may be deeply in love they have trouble expressing their feelings. They are more apt to show their anger.

These people are born skeptics and are suspicious of any new ideas. The younger generation leaves them bewildered. Tradition appeals to them.

They tend to stay with one type of profession or work. They stubbornly cling to their own point of view. They are inflexible as leaders and poor politicians; however they are very reliable and responsible people.

## Inward Bent Fingers

When all the fingers are bent inwardly, especially at the fingertips, and the hand seems to have lost its beauty and shape and taken on the appearance of an animal claw, you must first ask your client if their fingers bend inwardly naturally or has this been caused by an accident or illness.

People with inward bent fingers are known to be grasping and greedy with an animal's appetite; self-gratification rules them. They know what they want and do not care how they get it. They have a passion for acquiring and hoarding riches. They love material things and to get them, will not let anything or anyone get in their way. Other people's feelings mean nothing to them. They are selfish and can be extremely mean. They are cowardly and suspicious when prevented from accomplishing their selfish efforts, and they will become very ruthless.

# The Set of the Fingers

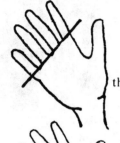

Chances are that you will never see an absolutely straight set or arch of the fingers.

A low set first finger (Jupiter) indicates lack of push and self assertion. These people are shy and feel awkward in the presence of company. They feel superior to others, but they lack the necessary poise and ease of manner to put themselves across successfully.

The second finger (Saturn) is almost always set a little higher than the rest of the fingers.

The low set third finger is an indication that this person's capabilities have been blocked or obstructed in some way. This type of low set Apollo finger can be seen in the hands of frustrated actors, artists and other gifted people. These people may have to do other types of work in order to support themselves. They will have to struggle hard against circumstances or some lack within themselves before they can achieve their aims. Nothing ever seems to come easily for them.

The low set fourth (Mercury) finger also indicates the need for the person to struggle hard against circumstances or the lack within themselves before they can achieve their goals in life. Nothing ever seems to come easily for them.

## The Arch of the Fingers

The line that connects the fingers to the palm of the hand or the way the fingers are mounted on the palm of the hand is important. It indicates how one supports oneself. Look at the palm with the fingers spread out slightly, now move the fingers slightly toward you and draw an imaginary line at the base of the four fingers. This is the set of the fingers, the way the fingers are mounted on the hand.

## The Norman Arch

The Norman Arch is also called the Norm. It is an even line under the base of the four fingers with a slight drop beneath the index (Jupiter) finger and the little (Mercury) finger. This is considered an average line, healthy and normal. Like an architectural arch it is strong and balanced.

## The Tudor Arch

The Tudor Arch is a fairly straight line that runs across the base of the fingers and is a strong, equal base for all fingers. Although it is rarely seen, this set of the fingers indicates that this person will do well in life. They have all the qualities that make for success, self-confidence, assurance, common sense and a good attitude toward life. These people trust their own judgement and have a gift for making the most of their talents and opportunities.

# The Perpendicular Arch

The Perpendicular Arch is made up of right angles, upright or vertical, low set at the index (Jupiter) and the little (Mercury) finger. This tented arch indicates a person lacking in self-confidence; they feel inferior.

# The Uneven Arch

left hand          right hand

The Uneven Arch line tends to droop at the little (Mercury) finger of the right and left hand. This type of line indicates a person whose confidence has been weakened or impared at an early age. Because of this, life is like a battle to them and their distrust of people has cut off any communication that they may have had with those around them.

# The Low Jupiter Finger Arch

left hand          right hand

The low set index or Jupiter finger is an indication that this person lacks self-confidence. This arch shows a very severe inferiority complex, as well as a great dependence on others. They feel helpless and powerless.

# The Fingertips

The fingertips in the study of Palmistry (cheirognomy) are very important. There are four classifications of the fingertips, the Spatulate, the Square, the Conic and the Pointed. Because most of us are individual in our own way, one person's hands can have different or mixed fingertips on their hands. Their hands are given a special name; they are called mixed hands. The shape of the hand and the fingertips can be different also. In reading hands I have found it quite common for people to have their hand shape different from that of their fingertips, except for the Conic hand, which almost always has Conic fingertips, but you will see the Conic fingertips on other shaped hands.

To understand the reasoning in the shape of the fingertips, the easiest rule to remember is, the more pointed the tip of the finger, the more idealistic the person will be. The broader the fingertip, the more practical they are and the more common sense they will have.

## The Square Fingertips

The Square fingertips are clearly and unmistakably square at the ends of the finger, and are generally found on a square hand. The square fingertips indicate order and regularity. People with square fingertips cannot stand disorder. They want everything systematically arranged and according to a rule, "A place for everything, and everything in its place." This type person is always on time and also expects everyone else to be on time. They are creatures of habit and are always polite. They enjoy studying and reading for pleasure things pertaining to history, mathematics and sciences. They love art and tend to paint natural scenery or still life. Because they are so good with their hands, they make wonderful sculptors. Their fingers and minds coordinate so well together, it makes them skillful in everything that takes good coordination. They are usually methodical. These useful fingertips are found in all the practical walks of life.

# The Spatulate Fingertips

The Spatulate fingertip received its name because of its resemblance to a druggist's spatula, used in dispensing drugs. The Spatulate fingertips are the broadest of the fingertip types. These fingertips are quite often seen on a square hand, as well as the spatulate hand. Most spatulate fingers tend to be knotty. A person with spatulate fingertips is very practical. They see the realism in everything and have good common sense. The spatulate fingertips have also been called the fingertips of real life, because these people like action, exercise and management. They are always on the go and have wonderful enthusiasm for life. When relaxing, they enjoy reading or watching television pertaining to tales of action, hunting and sports of all kinds. They are very fond of animals. They are our true lovers. These people are practical, but also original and creative. Their minds and fingertips coordinate well and work skillfully together.

# The Conic Fingertips

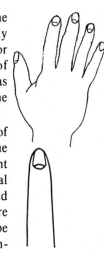

The Conic fingertips are gently tapered or slightly rounded at the fingertips and are distinctly cone-shaped. The conic hand usually has only conic fingertips, but the conic fingertips can be found on the square or spatulate hands. The conic type fingertips have many degrees of development. In some references you will find the conic fintertips typed as a pointed fintertip, which are associated with the psychic hand. I give the pointed fingertips their own classification.

When you see true conic fingertips on a hand, you will always think of art, beauty, quietness, intuition, grace, harmony, and idealism. The true conic fingertips indicate a person of intelligence, with excellent judgment and a good sense of humor. The conic fingertips can be found on professional people and executives. They are artistic, impulsive, quick-witted and intuitive. They have a refined nature and tend to be idealistic. They are non-conformist and need expansion in their work. They love to be surrounded by beautiful and artistic things. Because of their non-conformity, their likes are from one extreme to the other. In food they can be gourmets or love just plain hamburgers. In their reading material they can enjoy the romance novels to the study of history and science. They are very sympathetic, emotional, and are often easily led. As lovers they can be

84

fickle. The conic fingertips indicate people that are poetic, artistic, lovable and very attractive.

## The Pointed Fingertips

The Pointed fingertips are an exaggerated form of the Conic fingertips. Their appearance is so distinctive that, once you see them and recognize their type, you will never mistake them for any other type of fingertips. The more pointed the fingertips are, the more life will be a disappointment to these people. Although the hand is beautiful to look at, they are useless. This type of fingertip indicates a person who is very idealistic and spiritual. They live in a fantasy world. They are very impractical. Though they see beauty in everything and everybody, they have a hard time facing life. Life to them is unreal. They are the dreamers and the poets. They can be meddlesome and inquisitive about everything. They are hypersensitive and unsure of themselves.

The Psychic hand has the pointed fingertips, but pointed fingertips can also be found on the other shaped hands.

## The Mixed Fingertips

It is rare that you will find a hand that has only one type of fingertips. The Conic or Psychic hand may be an exception. This difference is what makes us interesting as individuals, and provides us with the information about our character and personality. This is why we must investigate all the different aspects of our hands and fingers.

When you find a hand with a combination of two or more different types of fingertips, you must be able to recognize the difference and explain to your client their differences and their meaning. For example, the combination of the Square fingertips and the Conic fingertips. The Square fingertips indicate a security minded, practical and realistic person. The Conic fingertips indicate a person who loves freedom, the arts and music, with a sense of humor and intelligence. Even though these two types of fingertips are quite different from each other, the mixture could add creativity to the practical and realistic side of the person.

85

## The Sensitivity Pads

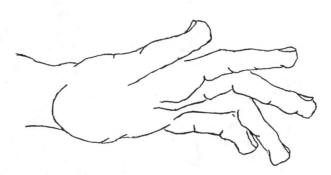

Also known as "Droplets" or "Drops of Water." I refer to them as "Antennas." These are little mounts on the first phalanx of the fingertips. These little pads of flesh can, in some cases, be quite prominent. If you hold the hand horizontally with the palm down at eye level, they can be seen on the tips of the fingers and thumb. These little mounts are seen very infrequently, but are very interesting signs. These little antennas add a great sensitivity. However, the pads can be of different prominence and not always on all the fingertips of a hand. The degree of sensitivity, therefore, can vary.

People with these little antennas are very aware of their surroundings and have a sensitivity to the things they touch. When meeting someone for the first time, they have an immediate reaction, either positive or negative, and for them this will be confirmed. They can feel and understand others' pain. These sensitive people must learn to protect themselves, for they can be affected by their surroundings and other people's emotions. They are found on the hands of physicians, nurses, surgeons, pianists and others whose occupations involve sensitivity. These people are highly sensitive, both intellectually and emotionally.

# THE FINGERNAILS

## The Size, Shape, Condition, Texture and Color

The Study of fingernails is one of the most important parts of Palmistry. Their shape, size, texture, condition and color relates to the character, health, personality, temperament, the nervous system and glands. The fingernails are a remarkably accurate guide to many diseases. Doctors recognize the value of observing and studying the fingernails of their patients. It can inform them of their patients hereditory diseases, especially the diseases of the heart, nerves, lung and spine. We are born with our fingernail shapes and they will remain with us for the rest of our lives, only the condition of the fingernails can change. This information can help us understand ourselves as well as others. When studying the fingernails you will find that the fingers of the hand can have more than one type of fingernail plus the condition and shape of the fingernail also relates to the finger that the nail belongs to.

## The Healthy Fingernail

A fingernail when healthy grows thin and transparent. This condition can change when health is threatened. We know there are more nerve endings in our fingertips than anywhere else in our body. Because our fingertips are so sensitive we must have the fingernails to protect the delicate nerve endings. The very delicate skin under the nail is known as the "quick" the blood circulation and nerve centers in the quick can become impaired by nerve damage or illness which will change the quality of the nails.

The Shape of our nails are determined at the time of our birth. The perfect fingernail can be described as matching their hand type, skin, texture and hand structure. The Fingernail should feel satiny smooth and be pliable, this indicates the nerves are alive and elastic. The fingernail tops should be attached to the skin and moulded at a moderate distance from the fingertips. There should be moons visible at the base of the nail. The cuticle should be soft and barely noticeable. The fingernails when held sideways should appear straight with the exception of the Almond shaped fingernail which has a gentle curve. The healthy fingernail when seen from side to side should have a gentle curve. The color of the fingernail should be a rosy pink color.

87

## Size of the Fingernail

### Small Fingernail

This type of fingernail shows a determined person. They know their own mind right or wrong. They tend to be assertive and overbearing. however they must learn to be tolerant, more open to others views and be more objective.

### Small Square Fingernails

The small Square fingernail is not a good sign. This fingernail often is an indication that the possessor is narrow minded, can be petty and have a limited field of action. These people tend to be fanatic in their beliefs and have trouble discussing things calmly. They freqently have problems of a sexual nature and are capable of explosions of jealousy. They may even become suicidal under extreme stress.

### Medium Fingernail

The person with a medium size fingernail is less active or forceful, than those with a large size fingernail. They have the ability to be discriminating and are accurate critics.

### Medium Square Fingernail

The person with a medium square fingernail is practical, orderly and a hardworker. They have good common sense. At times they can be very critical and short tempered but they are able to control themseves.

### Medium Square Fingernail with an Oval Base

People with this type of fingernail are practical, orderly and hard working. They have good common sense but at times are too discriminating and critical of others. They have short tempers but can keep it under control.

# Large Fingernails

People with Large Fingernails love companionship and are very social and friendly. They are broad-minded, capable, good natured, a dreamer, romantic and very interested in the artistic. They enjoy good health and have great endurance. They are tolerant and usually have sound judgment.

# Large Square Fingernails

These people are careful about their appearance and are very neat. They get along well in the public system because they can take orders well. They have keenness of intellect, quickness of insight, and enjoy material success. Because of the squareness of the nail, they are broad-minded, open and sincere.

# Unusually Wide Square Fingernails

This type of fingernail indicates hormonal (endocrine) disorders.

# Short Fingernails

Short Fingernails are often found on people who are highly critical and impatient toward themselves, as well as others, and impatient with life in general. They are always putting things in order, keeping things tidy and in their place. They never seem to be satisfied, so they are constantly rearranging. As a rule, they are hard workers, love competition, and reliable as bosses. However, they are hard to please. They do well in the legal profession or as critics. Short Fingernails can be an indication toward heart weakness and are mentally inclined towards nerves and depression. Look at the base of the fingernail. If the moons are small, this can add to the weakness.

# Short Fingernails That Are Square Spatulate, Round or Oval

When the Short Fingernail is square or spatulate in shape, the owners tend to be sarcastic and vindictive. If the fingernails are short with an oval shape, these people are judgmental and fault-finding. Round, Short Fingernails give their owners an argumentative disposition. They do not like to lose any arguments. They are skeptical and love to contradict. They have a quick wit. They are suspicious, always impatient, and they have a tendency to be hot-tempered and irritable. Short, Round Nails indicate a tendency towards laryngitis, bronchitis, and nose and throat ailments.

## Long Fingernails

Persons with Long Fingernails are very susceptible to all diseases, especially the upper parts of their bodies, such as the lungs and chest. They are even more susceptible if their fingernails are ribbed or fluted with the ribs running upwards from the base of the fingerrnail to the edge of the nail. Long Fingernails belong to people with vivid and refreshing imaginations. They are emotional, sympathetic and frank. Because of their weakness, they often lack physical strength and are frail. They can and do lead useful lives, but at a slower pace.

## Long, Narrow Fingernails

If the Fingernail is Narrow and Long, then their health problems are already present. Their health may be very delicate. This type of fingernail indicates a spinal weakness. If the fingernail is extremely curved and very thin, it can indicate curvature of the spine and weakness of the body.

## Long, Square, Wide or Rounded

Long, Square Fingernails indicate lack of vitality and poor circulation. Long, Wide Fingernails are a warning of lung weakness. Long Fingernails that are rounded at the cuticle and are grooved or striated indicate bronchial and repiratory problems.

## Talon Shaped Fingernails

These nails are usually very long. They resemble the claws of a predator. This person is strong-willed and determined to get all they can without any thought of the consequences.

# SHAPES OF THE FINGERNAILS

## Oblong Fingernails

The possessors of the Oblong Fingernails have a gentle, agreeable nature. These people are the peacemakers of the world. They dislike arguments or rivalry of any kind. They are not assertive and do not like aggressiveness. They enjoy good health. The Oblong Nail tends to appear blue at its base or cuticle which indicates poor circulation.

If the Oblong Nail tends to be long and narrow, it can be a sign of narrow-mindedness or lack of versatility. These people are nervous and unable to do strenuous work and do not have good vitality.

## Oval Fingernails

There are basically three types of Oval Fingernails: The Long Oval, the Short Oval and Medium Oval which has a Square Fingernail with an Oval base.

The Oval Fingernails are the most common type of nails. They denote a pratical and well-balanced nature. You can recognize the fingernails by their round shape, particularly where the nails separate from the skin at the end of the finger. They should be nicely rounded. The nail that is square at the end of the finger denotes practical common sense and a critical sense of humor.

## Long, Oblong Fingernails

The Long Fingernail that is oblong shaped can indicate poor health. These people have agreeable personalities. They are gentle and they are the peacemakers of our human society. They dislike quarreling, disputes, or any form of assertiveness.

## Horizontal Fingernails

The Horizontal Fingernail can be similar to the Large, Square Fingernail, but lacks the height. This type of nail denotes an asssertive person with a positive attitude.

## Wide, Horizontal Fingernails

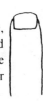

The Wide, Horizontal Fingernail denotes a tendency to look for trouble, even a fight. The possessor of this nail can be quarrelsome and overbearing. They have a sound constitution and are muscular. They are usually healthy and are active. They enjoy taking on jobs that show their stamina.

## Spatulate Fingernails

This fingernail is usually found on spatulate fingers. Their possessors have a sarcastic sense of humor. They are creative, imaginative, and original in thought through art. If the base of the nail is a fairly straight line, it gives an indication of organizational ability.

## Almond-Shaped Fingernails

These nails have the look of the nut of an almond. They are the only nails of their kind. they are unusual, even rare. The nail is square at the base of the nail, then becomes a narrow, oval shape at the end, resembling an almond. People possessing these nails are gentle, cultured, intellectual and deal excellently with others. They are sensitive, emotional and caring. They are easy to understand with great insight and a love for beauty.

There is also an Almond-Shaped Fingernail that is longer, and it is rounded at the base of the nail as well as at the top. It resembles an elongated oval fingernail. It is quite elegant looking and is found most commonly on a woman's hand.

Health-wise, this fingernail indicates a weakness toward the malfunction of the thyroid, pituitary glands and the heart. These people are not strong or energetic. They tend to be hypochondriacs and always imagine symptoms of illness.

These people are easy-going, calm, tend to be shy, modest and reserved. They are not practical. They are self-centered and see beauty in art and in nature. They are interested in the occult, are intuitive, have strong beliefs and tend to be spiritual.

Smaller versions of the Almond Nail with striations on the surface are called Date Stone Nails. These nails can be caused by a glandular deficiency, a sluggish circulatory system, or neurosis.

## Wedge-Shaped Fingernails

This nail is softly rounded at the base of the fingernail and wide at top. These people are extremely sensitive. They enjoy being by themselves and love acquiring knowledge. If their intellect is well developed, they will have quickness of insight and a keen intelligence. If the wedge fingernail lacks depth, these people may push themselves in a stressful situation. They can become quarrelsome and a little quick tempered.

## Clawlike Fingernails

The clawlike fingernail people have strong or even violent personal relationships. Though they tend to be talkative, they can be unmanageable, spiteful or even mean. They can be possessive, self-centered, domineering and arrogant. This Talon Shaped Fingernail indicates grasping people, strong willed and very determined to get all they can without thought of the consequences.

## Filbert or Hazelnut Fingernails

These fingernails tend to look round, like a large circle. They usually are medium sized nails. As a Palmist, I have rarely seen this type of fingernail. The base of the nail is attractively rounded and has a graceful appearance.

These people are usually broad-minded, tolerant, tend to be unrealistic, given more to idealism than reality, easy going, and they are often very creative. They have a strong constitution and good physical stamina. Their thinking is logical and they express themselves in a clear and concise manner.

## The Clubbed Fingernails

This fingernail has an exaggerated upward curve and curls around the fingertips. The Clubbed Fingernail may be inherited. However, this fingernail indicates a tendency toward emphysema, tuberculosis, heart disease, ulcerative colitis, or cirrhosis.

## Hippocractic or Watchglass Fingernails

These fingernails are curved in the shape of a watch crystal, which gives it its nickname, Watchglass Fingernails. These nails indicate a general weakness of the respiratory system, such as tuberculosis and has been found on people who are heavy smokers. The Hippocratic Fingernail can also reveal a predisposition for heart disease, especially if the nails are bluish in color. If the fingernails are yellowish, it indicates cirrhosis of the liver. Whenever you see a person with this type of nail and they are smokers, even when the curvature is mild, you should advise them to stop smoking.

## Spoon-Shaped Fingernails

These fingernails look depressed or concave and appear flat or scooped-like. Spoon-Shaped Fingernails are associated with nutritional deficiency anemia, syphilis, thyroid disorders, rheumatic fever and chronic skin disorders. It also indicates lung problems that could lead to tuberculosis.

## Narrow Fingernails

The Narrow fingernails are not too good to own. They indicate a tendency towards delicate health. People with Narrow Fingernails tend to suffer from nervous fatigue. They do not have vitality or much vigor. They tend to be nervous and apprehensive. They are not able to take on strenuous work due to their general weakness of body and will. They seem to have to preserve their energy just to get through the day. This person also has narrow interests.

Narrow, Curved and Long Fingernails indicate weakness of the back, and if very narrow, then spinal trouble. People with this type nail usually suffer from a weak back in childhood days and in old age.

## Fan-Shaped Fingernails

The Fan-Shaped Fingernails resemble the Triangular Fingernail except that the base of the nail is slightly rounded. These people often suffer from nervous disorders and mental diseases. They have a very low tolerance for frustration.

# Flat Fingernails

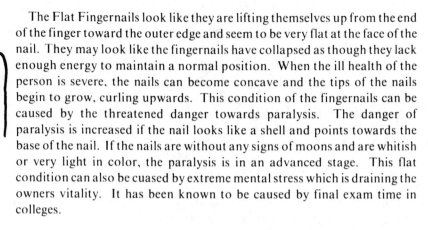

The Flat Fingernails look like they are lifting themselves up from the end of the finger toward the outer edge and seem to be very flat at the face of the nail. They may look like the fingernails have collapsed as though they lack enough energy to maintain a normal position. When the ill health of the person is severe, the nails can become concave and the tips of the nails begin to grow, curling upwards. This condition of the fingernails can be caused by the threatened danger towards paralysis. The danger of paralysis is increased if the nail looks like a shell and points towards the base of the nail. If the nails are without any signs of moons and are whitish or very light in color, the paralysis is in an advanced stage. This flat condition can also be cuased by extreme mental stress which is draining the owners vitality. It has been known to be caused by final exam time in colleges.

## Dished Fingernails

The Dished Fingernails curve inwards, giving the contour of a disk. This nail indicates a tendency towards alcoholism and nervousness. This may also be an indication of a mineral deficiency and poor circulation.

## Shell-Shaped Fingernails

The Shell-Shaped Fingernails are usually either short or a medium size. There are striations on their surface which gives them the look of a shell. This type fingernail indicates tension and illness such as hypertension, nervous disorders, mental disease, or a low tolerance for frustration.

If the Shell-Shaped Fingernail is pointed towards the base or cuticle, there is a danger of paralysis. sometimes a long peiod of rest can eliminate the striations on the nails and the illness becomes less of a threat.

These people enjoy studying by themselves and can become accomplished scholars. They often push themselves too far and cause stress and tension. They love a good debate, but can be quarrlesome. They can be quick-tempered and restless and they have alot of nervous energy.

# Curved Fingernails

This fingernail is very curved both from the top bac < of the nail towards the finger and across the fingernail. It is a very bad sign. This fingernail indicates tuberculosis of the lymphatic glands and consumption.

When the fingernail is thick and hard and very curved, both from the top of the nail back towards the finger and across the fingernail, it indicates an animalistic nature. These people can be cruel.

# Triangular Fingernails

The Triangular-Shaped Fingernail comes to a point at the base of the nail or cuticle. If the nail is short and flat-shaped and inclined to lift up or curve up at the edge, it indicates a weakness and ever paralysis.

These people have a critical personality.

# CONDITIONS OF THE FINGERNAIL

## Mee's Fingernails

The white lines or ridges of the Mee's Fingernails run horizontally across the nail. These ridges are not as deep as those of the Beau's Fingernails. The condition of the fingernails can be caused by high fever, arsenic poisoning, or coronary heart disease. They may also be caused by nervous exhaustion.

## Beau's Lines

These are deep, horizontal ridges or dents which begin at the root of the fingernail and move to the end of the nail. They indicate the person has had some nervous shock, an acute infection, nutritional deficiencies, or other physical and emotional traumas. The fingernail's condition can be caused by any severe illness that temporarily interferes with nail growth, such as measles, mumps, heart attack or conditions such as carpaltunnel syndrome.

## The Fluted, Ribbon, or Longitudinal Ridges Fingernails

These fingernails all have the same common problems. These grooves originate under the cuticle and extend to the end of the nails. This is caused by a trauma associated with chronic diseases such as rheumatism, disorders of the thyroid gland, skin disorders, bronchial or ciculatory problems due to lack of oxygen in the blood.

## Pitted Fingernails

Pitted Fingernails occur in many cases of psoriasis. When the fingernail is pitting in rows, the nail resembles hammered brass. This problem sometimes occurs as a result of a disease called olopecia areata which causes total loss of hair.

Pitted Fingernails with ridges across the nail are a sign of eczema.

Pitted, red-brown spots (oil drop sign), and nail loss occur in many cases of psoriasis.

## Chewed-Up Fingernails

We have all seen Chewed-Up Fingernails and realize the cause. This person is suffering from shyness usually caused from nervousness.

## Chronically Chipped

Chronically Chipped, Sawtooth Fingernails indicate malnutrition vitamin deficiencies, radiation exposure or chemical damage.

# THE TEXTURE OF THE FINGERNAILS

The texture of the nails can describe the person's attitude toward the world. A careful and thorough study of the hand and nails can provide information about the health conditions and actual presence of diseases and deficiencies. The natural state of the nail should be pliable and the nail shoud bend easily without breaking. The nails make us aware of the health of the client and able to recognize any serious problems. Hopefully, this enables us to guide the client so they can avoid these health problems by making a change in their lifestyle and health habits in order to be able to enjoy a healthy, active and happy life.

## Soft Nails

These nails split easily which indicates a nutritional deficiency such as protein or calcium that can cause the person to suffer from arthritis. A person with soft nails may be easily impressed. They are considered a soft touch. If the nails are extremely soft, they lack willpower.

## Hard Nails

People with hard nails lack sensitivity. Hard nails are a sign of vigor, physical and mental strength. They have natural power, vitality and good health.

## Thick Nails

People with thick nails are usually thick and dull. Their nails indicate a lack of sensitivity and a lack of mental and emotional response to nature, beauty or art.

## Thin Nails

Thin nails are usually shiny and smooth. These people are sensitive and discriminating and have fine mental and emotional responses to beauty and nature.

## Brittle Nails

A person with brittle nails is just that - brittle. They cannot handle stress and may be easily broken. They are resistant to change and have fixed opinions. They are rigid and lack the strength to carry out their convictions. If the brittle nails are thick, this person can withstand more stress than if the nail is thin and brittle. They have a thicker exterior and very fixed ideas about life.

## Flexible Nails

When the nail is in its natural state, the nail should be pliable. It should bend easily without breaking. Like their nails, these people are flexible and can bend and not break with the storms and trials of life. They are caring, but cautious.

# COLOR OF THE NAIL

Nails come in a very wide variety of colors, shapes and sizes. To recognize the healthy nail, it should be slightly longer than wide, more elastic than brittle and gently curved with a nice rosy-pink color. The nail should match the hand type, skin texture and hand structure. Thicker nails for the thicker hand and thin nails for thin hands. The nails should feel smooth.

The study of nails of the hand is a remarkably accurate guide to many diseases.

This part of Palmistry is recognized by the medical professionals who as an aid to diagnosing lung disease, circulatory problems, heart disease, anemia, nervous disorders and other health problems.

There are more nerve endings in our fingertips than anywhere else in the body. There are literally thousands of tiny nerve endings on each finger giving it its sensitivity. The fact is, our fingertips are so sensitive that we have to have the fingernails to protect the delicate nerve buds and the fibers underneath.

The usual color variations are white, blue, yellow and shades of red (rosy pink). When studying the nails, their color, shape and texture, the other aspects of the hand have to be taken into careful consideration.

Like the complexion of our exterior skin, the skin behind the nails is the window of the nails and can tell us about the individual's state of health.

## Pink Nails

If the pink nails are smooth, bright and slightly lustrous, it indicates a balanced mental disposition, adequate nutritional intake, good health and an outgoing temperament. The nails will turn white when pinched, but will return to pink when the pressure is removed. If, however, the color returns very slowly, low blood pressure can be indicated.

## White Nails

These pale, white nails, like pale skin, lack the intensity of red nails. This person lacks red corpuscles. The condition is associated with anemia.

Their physical energy is lacking because of poor circulation. They have low vitality, usually poor nutrition, and low blood flow.

A personality trait is coldness to others. Nails that are white in the middle of the nails and pink at the outer edges can indicate this person has short fits of anger and rage.

## White Spots or Dots

These white spots can also be called liver spots. Temporary liver disorders can be caused by emotional conflicts or disappointment. When white spots appear, they should act as a warning to take care of any liver problems. Another sign that white spots indicate is a loss of vitality. These white spots are general signs of anxiety or stress and can be found often on people who suffer from chronic depression. They may also indicate a calcium deficiency, especially if the nails have a tendency to be soft.

White spots that grow together over the nail surface and obscure the clearness and the tranparency of the nail can be a sign of hypersensitivity that can result in a severe liver condition.

White spots on the nails usually come and go as they tell the condition of the system. These spots are seen on timid and nervous people when they have a sudden demand upon their nervous system such as a new important position of responsibility or an appearance before the public.

## Yellow Nails

Yellowish nails may indicate liver trouble or poor circulation that slows the growth of the nail and produces a thicker, rougher, yellow-tinted nail. Other problems that this nail can indicate are diabetes and heart disease. In extreme cases lack of oxygen makes the nail bed appear blue. When nail growth becomes slow and the nails thicken and become very hard and appear yellow or yellow-green, it is known as the yellow-nail syndrome. This condition can be caused by chronic respiratory, thyroid and lymphatic deseases.

## Orange Nails

People with nails that show an orange discoloration should have their liver checked. This condition can also be causing mental confusion.

## Red Nails

Red nails indicate a strong blood circulation with a tendency to anger.

This person usually becomes over-excited and may suffer from hypertension. They can be prone to high blood pressure and heart problems. They should avoid all stimulants. It would be wise for them to relieve their pent-up emotions with outside activities that they would enjoy.

## Blue or Bluish Nails

The blue or bluish nails indicates a probability that the heart is not functioning normally. It also reveals a problem with circulation. If all the nails on both hands are bluish, the trouble is more generalized, while several blue or bluish nails mean local circulatory problems.

When someone is having a coronary heart attack, the base of the nails will become blue, the color will creep upwards and then the nails will become so dark that they will appear to be almost black. When the attack passes and oxygen floods the bloodstream, the darkness disappears.

If there is no indication of disease and and the nails have a tinge of blue, then their personality will be reserved, even cold. Their warmth and passion are hidden. They should start an exercise program which would be very helpful to them by increasing their blood circulation and hopefully, they will be able to express themselves more.

## Dark Tips of the Nails

Dark tips of the fingernails are a sign of kidney failure. There is scientific research at this time at the University of Mississippi Medical Center regarding this. The research has found that half of the dark nails are a highly specific sign of kidney failure.

## Black Spots on the Nails

Black spots not due to a bruise are usually from sorrow or grief, but this is a very rare sign.

## Brown or Black Nails

Brown or black discolorations on the nail, paticularly those that spread from the nail to the surrounding finger tissue, indicate malignant melanoma. There may be a single large patch or collection of small freckle-like discolorations. The thumbs are the most common areas to show this problems.

## Lindsay's Nail

In the Lindsay's nails the half near the nail tip appears pink or brown and the half near the cuticle appears white. This nail is also referred to as the "half and half nail". This condition of the nail is a sign of chronic kidney failure.

## Splinter Nails

These nails are also referred to as the Splinter Hemorrahages. This nail has longitudinal red streaks on the nails that signify bleeding of the capillaries. The multiple lines may be a sign of chronic high blood pressure, psoriasis, a skin disease, or an infection of the lining of the heart which is potentially a life threatening condition.

## Terry's Nail

The Terry's nail grows so that most of the skin under the nail appears white, with the normal pink area reduced to a band near the tip of the nail. Cirrhosis of the liver can be the cause.

# Moons on the Fingernails

Moons are at the bottom of the nails where the nails are embedded in the skin. There are normally moon-shaped white portions visible. These moons tell quite a tale.

Like the moon of the solar system, the moon of the nails represents feelings and perceptions. The moon on the nail is a full circle or full moon. The further back the cuticle is, the more potential there is for feelings and perception. Moons should ideally appear on all the fingernails which would indicate good health and strong constitution. In some people, the moons can be completely hidden. That is because the cuticle has grown to cover it and it means that these people must work harder to increase their degree of perception and feelings. When there is an absence of moons on the fingernails, or no moons, or only small crescent moons, there is a strong tendency towards low blood pressure and poor or irregular circulation.

A large moon can show a strong heart, good circulation and generally fortunate circumstances. This moon is usually on each fingernail or none at all.

When the moons are unusually large, it can mean too much pressure on the heart and rapid heart beat. The valves can become over-strained and there can be a danger of a burst of some blood vessel in the heart or in the brain. There is a tendency toward nervous hypersensitivity and excitable temper. There can be weakness and over-active thyroid glands. Their feelings are submerged in the unconscious mind.

## Small Moons

Small moons can indicate poor circulation, weak action of the heart and anemia that can affect the brain.

## Half Moons

Clear half moons are the best ones you can have. They indicate a balanced blood pressure, good circulation and a fairly cool and stable temper.

## Blue Moons

A blue tint to the moon at the base of the nail indicates impaired circulation, heart disease, and Raynaud's Syndrome which are spasms of the arteries of the fingers and toes that are the result of exposure to extreme cold. Sometimes this is caused by rheumatoid arthritis or the auto-immune disease, lupus erythemalosus.

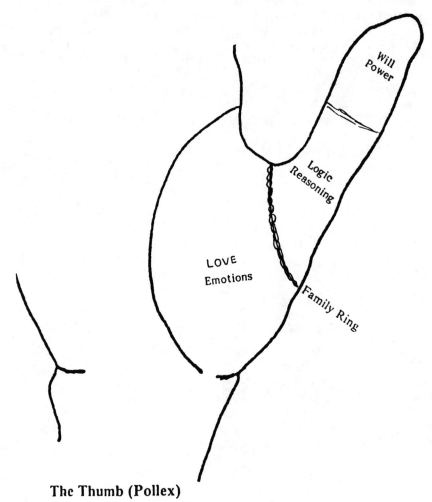

Will
Power

Logic
Reasoning

LOVE
Emotions

Family Ring

**The Thumb (Pollex)**

107 A

# The Thumb (Pollex)

The Thumb is one of the most important and distinctive features on the hand. The Thumb is considered the "WILL" of the personality and one of the most important features of the hand. I consider the thumb very important when analyzing the hand and most interesting when studying Palmistry. It is the key to character and personality. Its length, shape and inclination all give valuable clues to its owners make-up and individuality. Just at a glance you can judge the amount of will power and reasoning ability that can control and guide the life of the individual. The thumb can show whether you deliberately make the best of all your talents and abilities or whether your success will depend upon chance.

If we were to learn only the meanings given to the thumb in palmistry, we would have the ability to understand the character and strength of anyone with whom we come in contact.

The thumb as in the fingers are divided into two phalanxes. One is at the base of the thumb or root on the Mount of Venus. That is why the thumb can be classified both as being the study of *Chierognomy* (the shape of the hands and fingers) and *Chieromancy* (the lines and mounts).

The first phalanx, which has the thumb nail denotes the amount of will power, determination and temper one has. The second phalanx denotes logic and reason.

The Mount of Venus (also called the third phalanx) denotes love, sympathy, passion, enjoyment, love of music, love of dancing and a desire to be liked, in other words sensuous.

# The Phalanx of the Thumb

The thumb is divided into three parts. The fingernail or top phalanx is the phalanx of will and temperament. The second is the phalanx of logic. The third is part of the Mount of Venus, love, emotion, passion, and enjoyment.

## Long Second Phalanx

The Long Second phalanx is the phalanx of logic. If this phalanx is long and prominent it shows a very logical mind. These people are usually brilliant and intelligent but sometimes go into detail too much and want to argue. They have trouble in taking decisive action that could lose them chances of making headway in life. They have a habit of talking too much. Although they do it brilliantly, they have wonderful ideas but become unhappy when their colleagues use their ideas as their own. They will just have to learn to keep their ideas to themselves. They really never learn to practice this self discipline. These people should find careers in an area where their wonderful ideas and abilities will allow them to succeed. Being very perceptive makes them intelligent analysts. They can see things rationally and are able to look at both sides of a problem. It would be best for them to choose a partner that is a person of action who is honest. They both can become very successful with this combination of personalities.

## Short Second Phalanx of the Thumb

If the second phalanx is short, the person will have a lack of reasoning; they will be neglectful of rules, difficult to handle or manage and hard to work with. They are dull and slow at understanding. The only way that they can really work well is if their jobs are under good direction and their work is routine.

## The Top and Second Phalanxes of Equal Size

Will and logic are equal as the thumb indicates when the two phalanxes are of equal length. It is not common to see this combination. These people live in harmony. Their life is in order with cooperation between logic and will. They will achieve high offices in the various walks of their life. They are very well suited to positions of authority and responsibility.

# The Top Phalanx of the Thumb

Conic- The conic top of the thumb is almost square but tapered at the
end. If the phalanx is long, it is a sign of will power and sensuousness. They
usually are talented at art. If the phalanx is short then the possessor is apt
to react to situations too quickly and with little planning. They can become
emotional and not react logically. They tend to get hurt when dealing with
people because of their lack of self-confidence.

Pointed- The pointed top of the thumb indicates difficulty achieving
their goals. They are too impulsive, have weak will power, lack the will to
resist temptation and make decisions of their own. They need to be guided
not only with everyday life but at work as well. They do not make the
leaders of the world. They can be good routine workers when they are
given good directions but they will take advantage of situations to relax on
the job. The lazy dreamers.

Square- The square or rectangular tip of the thumb indicates a useful
hand. They are reliable workers, with strong will power. This person is
capable of practical, firm and prompt action. They are steady, confident
and sure of themselves. They are reasonable and never obstinate or act
ruthlessly. They make good and reliable friends.

# The Shape of the Thumb

## The Pointed Thumb

The Pointed thumb tip is thin and narrow. Their owners have difficulty achieving their goals. It indicates a weak will. They tend to be idealistic and day dreamers. These people lack decision and the power of resistance. They are opportunity seekers and can wait patiently until the time is right. They have a low energy level and must guard against using it up too freely. If they think someone has done them an injustice, they will never forget the deed and will strive to get even. When they succeed, they will do it in a very mean way. They can be rash, impulsive, impetuous, blaming others for their own failures. These people can be really mean. They are prying, inquisitive and very curious. They cannot stand a closed or locked door unless they know what is behind it. They would make good detectives.

## The Clubbed Thumb

The Clubbed thumb is rounded on the end, bulk shaped, full and tight, resembling a bludgeon. The nail is short and of a coarse structure. Once you have seen it you will never forget it. This thumb has been named the murderer's thumb. Because the person possessing this type of thumb is unreasonable and has a violent temper, they react without logic, carry out their plans regardless of the consequences. They are devoid of self control. This thumb tip has always been associated with violent or criminal nature. When aroused to anger, there is no way to know just what caused the anger to erupt. They lose their self-control and can use physical force blindly, sometimes not even remembering what they have done.

If the tip is very thick it is most likely to be hereditary. If the thumb has not been seen in the immediate family, there is a good chance that someone in the past had it.

Just recently I had a client with a Clubbed thumb on the left hand and a balanced thumb on their right hand, which is very unusual. They were right handed. With this combination, this person can have self control if they learn to use it and understand the temperament they have inherited.

### The Blunt Thumb

If the tip of the thumb is blunt, this person's energy will have a tendency to be all dammed up; they could have a tendency toward an explosive nature. If the thumb has a knot or folds of skin at the joint where the thumb bends or flexes it also may act as a dam to dam up their energies and impair their staying powers.

### The Flat Thumb

The Flat or Nervous thumb looks as though they have been pressed until the substance is gone out of the tips of the thumb. These thumbs are soft or flabby and flat. The person with this nervous thumb is full of nervous energy that can prove too strong for them. This nervous energy they have must be released, otherwise they will be extremely irritable. They put off doing everything and tend to be unromantic.

Physical exercise can help them because they have a tendency to feel tired, to suffer from exhaustion. Their nervous energy seems to be always draining their energy.

### The Paddle-Shaped Thumb

This Paddle shaped first phalanx is often seen when reading hands. The tip of the thumb is broad when observed from the nail side but not thick. The paddle shaped thumb gives strength of will to the first phalanx. With their strong mental will, their owners are capable of standing up under the strain of their energy. They are in control of themselves and handle the problem well, but when it's over and they can relax they often collapse. The strength of will is not always accompanied by robust health.

### The Broad Thumb

The Broad thumb is full, wide and strong. When viewed from the back or nail side, the thumb has a broad look. Both the first and second phalanx are strong and healthy in appearance. These people are usually forceful with good physical strength. They are impatient and often blunt when dealing with others but never deceitful. With slow, strong determination, they can be aggressive and display a brute nature if aroused. They enjoy many activities and interests. Their determination to succeed can bring out their aggressive side. They can become pushy or overbearing.

### The Knotty Jointed Thumb

A knotty joint between the first and second phalanx denotes, as it does with the fingers of the hand an analytical, intellectual person. A knotty joint on a short thumb strengthens the will of the thumb.

## The Waisted Thumb

The Waisted thumb tapers toward the center, producing an hourglass formulation. The second phalanx of the thumb is narrower then the first phalanx, resembling a waistlike formation. These people are brilliant and have an ability to deal with people. They are often very fond of animals. They can be evasive, though they will use great tact. They are not hard to pin down or unwilling to commit themselves. They are gentle, adaptable and good mixers, an intellectual who is impulsive, diplomatic and tactful. They are careful thinkers, believe their opinions are the truth and enjoy expressing them.

## The Spatulate Thumb

The Spatulate thumb increases the force of will causing brutality and strength. You don't often see the spatulate thumb, but when found, it characterizes a leader, a commander. They can be severe disciplinarians. A long first phalanx is a sign of a restless, complaining, fretful person. A short Spatulate Thumbed person can have too much leadership but often they do not apply themselves to the task.

## The Square Thumb

The Square thumb is squarish at the top and sides. The top of the thumb is rectangular or square. This shows a strong will power, common sense, practical and bull headed. They can be blunt and to the point, sure of themselves. They are capable of realistic and decisive action, often tactless but they are neither obstinate or ruthless. They have great endurance and make reliable friends. If the thumb is square, this person likes to work with their hands. Their hands and minds work together beautifully. They tend to be methodical, orderly and business like. They can succeed as a doctor, nurse, in the military, an accountant, an engineer, surveyor, architect, any type of profession or work where the mind and hands work together.

## The Conic Thumb

The Conic Thumb has a cone-shaped top phalanx; these people are good organizers. Their will power is beautifully balanced. They believe in fair play. If the thumb tends to be stiff, they can be conceited, overbearing and even stubborn. If the phalanx is short, the individual is apt to react too quickly without forethought. They are inclined to be too emotional. If the phalanx is well formed, they have lots of will power and are open minded; they are suited to a profession as a painter, and architect, photographer or decorator. With a Conic Thumb any profession connected with beauty woulld be suitable.

### The Set of the Thumb

#### Low Set Thumb

The best way to see the set of the thumb on the hand is to have the client raise their hands to face you in its natural position. It will not only show the set of the thumb but the thumbs' angle. You can easily recognize if the thumb is set close to the root of the forefinger or much lower, almost to the wrist. If the thumb is low set, it indicates a strong love of liberty and an independent nature. Its owner has courage of their conviction, and cannot be restricted. They are ready to fight for freedom and human rights. They are the champions of the underdog and work towards social reform. They have a generous nature and are liberal in their actions. As a rule, the lower the thumb sets on the hand, the greater the intelligence. They are generous and sympathetic people, but can be careless and overgenerous.

#### Medium Set Thumb

The Medium Set Thumb indicates a person who is well balanced, neither extravagant, mean nor obstinate, they are frank, honest, loyal and not weak-willed. They are an adaptable person who avoids extremes.

#### High Set Thumb

The High set thumb is set close to the root of the forefinger. These people want their independence and have a tendency to be mean and selfish. They lack courage and have a restricted outlook on life. They are unable to stand by their convictions - a weak mentality - you wil find them secretive. They show a cautious nature with a tendency to be stubborn.

# Angle of the Thumb

If you extend and stretch your hand out in front of you as far as you can reach, then relax, the hand, still leaving them in the extended position, you wil be able to see the angle of your thumbs.

The best way to see and recognize the Angle of the Thumb on a client have your client face you and extend their hands toward you in an outstretched position that is most comfortable. This will not only show the angle of the thumb but the set of the thumbs, and the flexibility of the thumbs.

## The Average Angle

The Average angle of the thumb is about 45 degrees. This angle shows a good attachment to all normal standards of life. They have good will power and common sense in dealing with life.

## The Narrow or Dependent Angle

The Narrow angle of the thumb angles upwards. It denotes limited will power and selfishness. The owner tends to be narrow minded, prejudiced and even mean.

If the angle of the thumb is extremely narrow, it shows a low degree of intelligence. The owner is unable to show determination or strength of will power. He has a stubborn disposition, not too much chance of becoming successful.

## The Wide or Independent Angle

When the angle of the thumb is wider then 45 degrees it denotes more individuality and strong personality. This person can work alone and prefers individual achievement. They cannot tolerate people resisting their ideas or goals. When the thumb forms a right angle, about 90 degrees from the palm, it is a very unusual occurance. It shows remarkable talent, wonderful will power, never ceasing urge to restore this to a better world. The owner is a leader in life whether it be political, social or religious. They enjoy fighting for causes. They will succeed in life and make unusual contributions to the world.

# The Flexibility of the Thumb

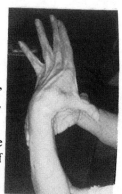

The flexibility of the thumb has much more bearing on a persons' character then that of their hand, therefore, it should be tested separately to check for their variations.

The thumb shows how far will power and logic will be applied to the abilities and talents of their owner which is also indicated by the reading of the hand and palms.

## The Inflexible Thumb

The Inflexible, stiff or straight thumb not only is the angle of the thumb important, so is its flexibility. If the thumb is rigid, firm, does not bend at all, in fact unyielding, it means great rigidity of the character. Their owner is stubborn, stiff necked, have difficulty adapting to new ideas or situations. They have trouble compromising. They are not an easy person to work or live with. They enjoy hard work. People with the inflexible or stiff thumb are not extravagant and they like to hold on to what is theirs. They are thrifty and economical, usually stable, responsible people and can be relied upon for almost everything.

## The Moderately Flexible Thumb

The Moderately flexible thumb bends back slightly under pressure. This is a practical person with a lot of common sense. They have a strong and determined will with a good ability to adapt. They are fairly easy going with an open mind. They like beautiful things but want value for their money.

## The Flexible Thumb

People with Flexible or supple thumbs are broad minded, adaptable, usually tolerant but do not like discord. It generally signifies an impulsive nature, with a lack of discipline. They have a changeable mind. They are generous to a fault, would give you the shirt off their backs. Their money just slides right off their sloping tip. They have extravagant tastes in everything. They are not only generous with their money and material possessions, but giving. of themselves. They are sentimental people but not in all ways, practical. These people are social minded and have a tendency to go to extremes. They will allow others to make decisions for them, willing to go along with the group or their partners' wishes. This does not mean that they are incapable of thinking for themselves, it simply shows an unwillingness to make a decision that would affect others. People with Supple thumbs love a good time and love to entertain. They are often found in politics and like politicians they enjoy talking.

The Flexible Thumb  This supple thumb bends back at the joint. The person owning the flexible thumb is very versatile, easy to adapt and adjust to fit into new situations easily. They are intelligent, very generous, have tact when dealing with others. They have the ability to adjust to people in all sorts of conditions making them good public relation representatives. They are good negotiators, salespersons and make good peacemakers.

When the thumb is extremely flexible backs to 90 degrees or more, these people are generous to a fault. They are extravagant and have very little will power.

## Stiff Straight Thumb

A person with a Straight thumb has a will of iron and can be obstinate. They are reserved, cautious. They are reliable, very loyal friends and partners. They have a great capacity for resistance and are not easily influenced by others, are strongly independent. They will stand by their convictions. Their views are clear and well defined but they will listen to your point of view and will accept correction if you are able to prove your point and logically they will be ready to accept better judgement. This type of person can miss fun in life through their unwillingness to try new situations because of their narrow and limited point of view. They have good self control, budget and control over the flow of their money. A positive quality of the stiff thumb is their ability to concentrate. They do not have a tendency to becoming scattered in long-range plans. Make wonderful brokers-accountants and controllers.

## The Cramped Thumb

The Cramped thumb is held in an intraverted position bending inward closely toward the palm of the hand. This person lacks self-confidence. They are usually cautious and nervous. If the cramped thumb presses against the hand in a confined position, you must add narrow mindedness.

## The Firm Thumb

The Firm thumb shows a person who is practical, cautious, prudent, reluctant and secretive. They are determined, strong and self disciplined. This person is blunt, honest and never seems to give up.

# The Length of the Thumb

The length of the thumb is also very important in the study of palmistry.

## The Average Length

The thumb reaches the middle of the first joint or bottom phalanx of the index finger.

These people have both dignity and high morals, dislike violence, are flexible and have the ability to compromise. They can be firm when it is necessary but always fair in decisions and have good common sense.

## The Short Thumb

The thumb only reaches to the crease at the bottom of the index finger and looks stunted. There people are not too intelligent, with little or no opinions making it difficult for them to reach a decision or set any goals. They can be easily swayed by their emotions and tend to be very impressionable. They can be very abrupt and narrow minded.

## The Long Thumb

The thumb reaches above the crease of the second and third phalanx of the index finger. This is the thumb of a leader, also known as the capable thumb. They are usually intellectual and become successful. These people are of strong opinions, are clear headed, make and carry out their goals. With their goals, common sense and great capacity to concentrate, they can solve any problems.

## The Exceptionally Long Thumb

The leader, the captain, the creator of important things. The possessor of these unusual thumbs are intelligent, strong willed with an ability to influence. They are very successful in politics as well as business, the arts and industry. With their leadership qualities, they can become exaggerated and domineering, demand power, be cruel and ruthless.

# Signs and Markings on the Thumb

A clear single verticle line on the first phalanx of the thumb is a welcome marking. It gives stamina, determination, persistence with the extra energy to accomplish their goals.

When the first phalanx has as many as three verticle lines, it strengthens the will power of the person.

If there are more than three verticle lines on the first phalanx of the thumb, will power will be minimized and scattered. They will have a lack of concentration.

When lines on the first phalanx of the thumb are crossed or cross other lines by themselves, there can be obstacles to success.

Small short lines near the nail of the thumb indicates a bequest or legacy.

A line from the first phalanx of the thumb to the Line of Life predicts death from a metal weapon.

The mark of a Cross near the nail of the thumb with very fine lines on the Mount of Venus indicates unfaithfulness to marriage vows, a person tempted to have affairs, disloyal and lack of moral values.

Two Crosses near the nail of the thumb indicates a love of luxury.

The sign of a Star on the first phalanx and many fine lines on the Mount of Venus indicates a person who lacks the sense of right and wrong, also a sign of immorality, loose character, may even be given to evil instincts.

The sign of two Stars near the nail of the thumb always finds fault and is constantly criticizing.

A Triangle on the first phalanx of the thumb. This marking adds will power to the hand with an interest in science. It is an unusual marking. It gives power of concentration, a wonderful capacity of determination, and they are able to apply all their energies. They will usually succeed and eventually make a name for themselves.

The mark of a Circle on the tip of the thumb indicates a person has a strong will. The Circle adds to the strength of the thumb. It is considered an unusually brilliant sign. It shows great ability for application in their future. This mark is considered a great asset to their owners, special talents.

The Square on the first phalanx of the thumb affects the will power. It may cause the person to be single minded and develop a harsh personality.

The Grille is not a good marking. If it is near the nail of the thumb, you must look for other signs before making any decisions, for the sign adds violence by the hand of another. It can indicate death that is caused by their partner because of unfaithfulness or immorality.

Two Stars on the second phalanx of the thumb indicates these people also can be easily led but they usually have a pleasing disposition and are friendly people.

A Triangle on the second phalanx of the thumb indicates these people are self-restrained. They make good lawyers and are rational and thoughtful. They are logical, can sway crowds. You will see this mark on the hands of preachers, leaders, judges but also can be rabble rousers.

A Square on the second phalanx of the thumb is not a good marking. It adds stubborness. They do have strong logical ability, but with their stubborness, it often defeats their own purpose.

A Grille, this marking on the second phalanx of the thumb is not a good sign to have. It shows lack of moral sense and honest reasoning. Their owners use deception to achieve their ends. Though they have sharp minds, they unfortunately use it in an unhealthy manner.

A line from the second phalanx of the thumb to the Life Line shows troubles in married life.

A Star at the base of the thumb indicates trouble caused from a fall. The fall can be from a ladder.

A Triangle on the side of the thumb on the first phalanx gives power of command and interest in the military.

A verticle line on the second phalanx of the thumb adds clear thinking and sound reasoning power with good logic. Also, if the line is clear cut, it indicates good rationality and logic.

More than three verticle lines on the second phalanx of the thumb shows a quarrelsome and diffuse personality. They have a lack of intelligence and little ability to understand.

Lines across the thumb on the second phalanx means a lack of common sense.

A Forked line on the second phalanx of the thumb indicates this person is slow in making any decisions.

A Cross on the second phalanx of the thumb indicates the person can be easily influenced. Their logic is not always reliable. They have little common sense.

A Star on the second phalanx of the thumb means this person can be led easily in the wrong direction.

## The Family Ring

The Family Ring can be one or more fine lines that circle the second phalanx of the thumb is a good sign. It indicates a sure sign of success and increases their faculty of thinking. It is the mark of exceptional logic which leads to sure success. They will triumph in life through reason and logic.

This ring is found on the joint between the second and third phalanx of the thumb where the Mount of Venus is formed. It is very common and consists of two or three lines that form a chain-like ring around the bottom of the thumb.

It received its name because those who have this ring show a strong attachment to their families. Their family is not just a group of people to them but united by love and affection where they enjoy the comfort and security a family unit provides. They also have a strong sense of responsibility toward each member of their family.

## "Just For Fun"

For fun, check the size of both of your thumbs. If you are right handed, your right thumb will be larger.

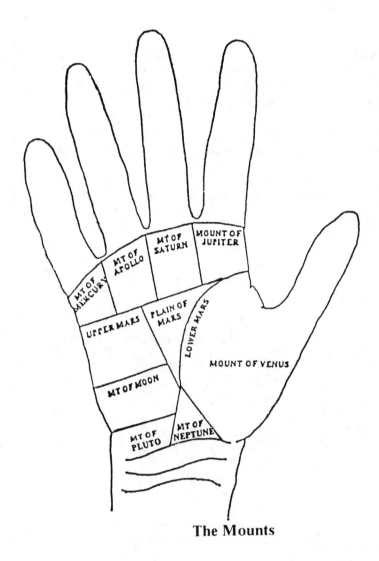

**The Mounts**

# The Mounts

The study of Mounts is very important, each has an individual interpretation of its own. Study each Mount to discover whether the Mount is well developed, over developed or absent. Even hands that do manual labor and have callouses, or rougher and thicker skin it does not depress or decrease the Mounts on the hand.

You must learn where they are located, what they are called and what they will reveal. These Mounts or fleshy elevations have many descriptions. They can be little or big, balls, pads, hills or cushions. Some are high, some are square and some are round. They can be concave or sunken, even flat looking. In your studies you will find the word "Apex" used in reference to the Mounts. The Apex refers to the top or summit of a Mount and can be recognized by the ridges or lines somewhat like a fingerprint. They are usually triangular in design. The Apexes enhance the characteristics when they are found on a Mount. Mounts can be the key to our natural traits and abilities. By understanding them, you will know your client's physical, emotional and moral nature. It can give you and your client an understanding of their character development and show them their energies and how they can be used and chanelled.

In all readings the character of the fingers whether they are long or short, smooth or knotty, round or square are very important; the tips of the fingers must also be studied. The little Mounts known as Droplets or Sensitivity Pads are located on the tips of the fingers.

It is very rare for a Mount to be centrally located, by that, I mean directly under the finger of the same name. If this does occur then your client would be a definite type, such a Jupiterian, Saturnian, etc. Mounts have a tendency to lean towards one another, which can be a good or bad influence. You can read this by studying the Mount they are leaning towards.

You may find a hand completely flat, whith a hollow palm. This will indicate a hard life and hard times. There are other signs you must look for to strengthen this type of hand. In most cases, there will be something in the hand that can counteract a hard life.

There are ten Mounts and only one Valley (The PLain of Mars). I will try to give you an understanding of the positions of each Mount and their meanings, the meaning of each Mount, if they are displaced I will also describe its meaning so that you will have a better knowledge of your client's tendencies. I will be using the old terms for the names of the Mounts. They will have no relationship to Astrological Palmistry. I will not deny that there is a connection, even a great one, but this book will not make any comparisons. So please, when I use the names Jupiter or Mars, they are simply an easier and established way of describing the Mounts. Most of the books I have researched in Palmistry use these names as well. They have always been associated with the Mounts and this simplifies their descriptions.

It is necessary to learn the Mount's exact position and its boundaries to be able to judge whether the Mount is in its proper location or if it is being pulled to one side by the stronger influence of another Mount. This knowledge does not come easily, it takes time and the study of many hands. Being able to recognize the different Mounts and their locations, as they do not have marked boundaries, will become easier as you gain experience. As you become more familiar with the Mount areas and their proper placement you will begin to understand their strength. This will depend upon their size when compared with the other Mounts of the hands. The more directly centered under its corresponding finger, the greater the strength and influence on the personality of your client. To locate the placement of the Mount locate its apex or the highest point of the pad. You will be able to recognize the apex where the skin meets to form a pattern similar to a fingerprint. The Mounts that are pronounced are considered strong. Flat Mounts are considered ordinary and depressed Mounts show weakness and are absent of the Mount"s qualities. When reading a palm, try to find which of the Mounts are the strongest. From this observation you will be able to judge the size of their other Mounts. This makes it easier to read the quality of their different Mounts.

Mounts are generally not formed at their proper places; that is, at the base of the finger or under their apexes. In most cases, they are found toward a neighboring Mount. If the Mounts at the base of the fingers are higher in proportion to the Mounts in the palm of the hand, it indicates an intellectual nature. If the Mounts below the fingers are lower than the Mounts in the palm, it indicates passion. When the Mounts are fairly flat, it indicates a very practical or unemotional nature (the Mr. Spock type from the TV program Star Trek); this person sees everything logically.

What is a good Mount? It should be evenly developed, well placed and firm when gently pressed. What is a not-so-good Mount? When the Mount is encroaching upon other Mounts and if it is soft or if the Mount is absent. A leaning Mount may also be over developed and disrupt the other Mounts. When the palm is ordinary, which of course, can be the hardest to

126

read; look for the Mount that has a deep line on it or is firmer or redder in color than the others. If the Mounts are all similar, look at the fingers of the hand and their length above the Mount. If one is longer or thicker, it can add strength to the Mount. Always examine the character of the fingers, if they are long, short, smooth or knotty. The tips of the fingers as well as the nails and skin, all make up the character of the hand.

Lines, signs and markings on the Mounts are not just formed by opening and closing the hand. They are fundamentally a feature of the palm itself and persistently retain their course against the influx of the other folds. As all people differ, so do these lines, signs and markings that follow their own path. Like an engraving, even if the hand is calloused, it can make it a little harder to read. People such as teachers and secretaries etc., who do a lot of paper work are also a little harder to read; the paper works as sand paper on the hand. It is important that you read both palms before making any statements so that you can give a correct reading.

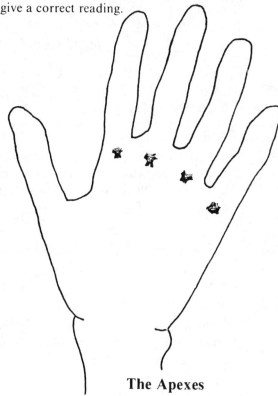

**The Apexes**

# The Location of the Mounts

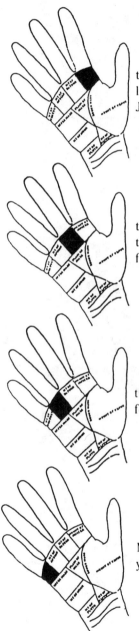

The Mount of Jupiter is located at the base of the Jupiter finger. When the Mount of Jupiter is found full and strong and the apex is centrally located with a Jupiter finger that is long and strong, you have found a true Jupiterian.

The Mount of Saturn is located at the base of the Saturn finger. When the Mount of Saturn is full and strong and the apex is centrally located, if the Saturn finger is longer than the other fingers of the hand, you have found a true Saturnian.

The Mount of Apollo is located at the base of the finger of Apollo. When the Mount of Apollo is full and the apex is centrally located, you have found a true Apollonian.

The Mount of Mercury is located at the base of the Mercury finger. if the Mount of Mercury is full and the apex is centrally located under the finger, you have found a true Mercurian .

The Mount of Venus is located directly under the thumb and is the largest of the Mounts. To estimate the quality of the Mount of Venus, it must be compared to the other Mounts of the hand. If the Mount is very prominant and has good color, you have found a true Venusian.

The Lower Mount of Mars lies between the Mount of Jupiter and the Mount of Venus. The Lower Mount of Mars was subdivided from the Mount of Venus. There is also an Upper Mount of Mars and a Plain of Mars. The Lower Mount of Mars is under the Life Line and above the Mount of Venus. When reading the hand all three Mounts must be analyzed. It is only by combining these three Mounts that we can properly estimate the value of the Mounts.

The Plain of Mars has a separate area of its own, a valley located in the center of the palm. The Plain of Mars has the distinction of being the only valley we have in our hands. In the earlier history of Palmistry the Plain of Mars was considered to be the principle part of our Martian development, but today we find the Upper Mount of Mars to have a stronger influence

The Upper Mount of Mars is located under the Mount of Mercury and Apollo and above the Mount of the Moon on the percussion side of the hand. The terms "Upper" and "Lower" Mars are used because of their location. Using the Head Line as a guide, Lower Mars is located below the Head Line and Upper Mars above the Head Line.

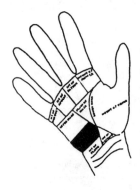

The Mount of the Moon is located on the percussion side of the hand below the Upper Mount of Mars and above the Mount of Pluto at the base of the palm. The Mount of the Moon's strength must be determined by the outward curve on the percussion of the palm and by the size of the Mount it forms on the inside the palm. If the Mount has a decided bulge on the percussion it is considered a well developed Mount. If it is also very thick, forming a large pad on the inside of the palm, it is also considered as a very strong Mount, indicating that this person would be a true Lunarian.

Note: There are two new Mounts I must list, one, the Mount of Pluto and the other the Mount of Neptune.

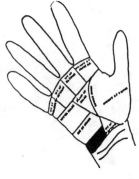

The Mount of Pluto is located at the bottom of the Mount of the Moon. This Mount occupies the unconscious, passive zone of the palm and indicates life, death and regeneration. If the Mount of Pluto is well developed, it emphasizes the power of imagination and interest in the occult.

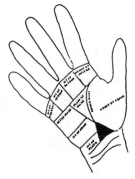

The Mount of Neptune lies below the Mount of Venus toward the lower center of the palm and the Mount of the Moon. If the Mount of Neptune is well developed, it can be seen very easily. The apex or ridge across the lower palm touching both the Mount of the Moon and the Mount of Venus. Because of its location, it is a blend of the conscious and the unconscious of life.

# The Mount of Jupiter

The Mount of Jupiter's name was taken from the chief of the Roman Gods. This is a good description of a Jupiterian with their love of authority and being extremely status-conscious.

The Mount of Jupiter is located at the base of the index or first finger which bears its name. The Mount of Jupiter is one of the most important signs to understand. It can tell you the character and behavior of your client. When you have located the Mount in the palm and its apex or height, this will give you the degree of strength that the Mount will have. If the apex is located below the index finger in a centered position, it deals with success in living. A true Jupitarian, the good personality, the strong one, a guiding light. The good or positive Mount of Jupiter can indicate potential for leadership. They show commanding presence and always have a good opinion of themselves. They enjoy stimulating conversation and have a lot of self confidence. The Jupiterian is always optimistic. Whatever profession they may choose they will do it with a flair and self confidence.

You will find Jupiterians often as politicions or in the military for it gives them an opportunity to hold commanding positions and leadership. They are also found as religious leaders, for they enjoy the high religious rituals. They are teachers, protectors of children and animals. They are hearty characters with a great love of life. One word that sums up a Jupiterian is "Jovial" and very often they are called Jovian in place of Jupiterian.

Individualism is the keynote of a true Jupiterian. Now with the increased emphasis for women to become more independent, the Mount of Jupiter will be found more and more in the palms of our newborn girl-child and in our young women of today.

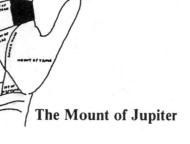

**The Mount of Jupiter**

131

Because this is a reference book, I will name most of the characteristics of the Mount of Jupiter and their meanings. Keep in mind that they can be negative as well as positive but most often, a little of both. They can be an individualist, domineering, organized, enthusiastic, generous, sympathetic, extravagant, honorable, religious, ambitious, natural leaders with a love of command, love of nature, love of display, love of ceremony, desire for fame, desire for power, pride of position. All this in one Mount? Yes, and much more.

With a well developed or positive Mount of Jupiter, the Jupiterian will have a positive outlook on life and a healthy body. They are self assertive and idealistic with a desire to be with people and to help them. You will rarely see a Mount of Jupiter centrally located. If the Mount is centered, these people will conform to a very definite Jupiterian type. If the Mount is well developed it indicates intelligence and logic with an excellent chance for leadership. They have enthusiam and ambition to stand out in a crowd. The Jupiterian generally will marry young and usually makes the right choice. They love to be flattered, are well liked and have a gift for making and keeping good friends. They love to dress up and have a good time; they never overstay their welcome. They take pride in themselves and in their chosen career.

When the Mount of Jupiter is well developed and the index finger is long and sturdy, you will find the qualities of leadership. These people have a tendency to be religious. Their pride, vanity and orderliness can be seen in their appearance. They are always full of energy and the desire to dominate. It also shows their ambition to succeed as an individual.

With a well developed Mount of Jupiter and a long, square tipped Jupiter finger, this Jupiterian likes first place in life. They enjoy lots of confidence in themselves.

When the palm is neither soft nor hard, and the second phalanx of the thumb is long, it adds will and domination to the Mount.

The true Jupiterian will be of medium height, large-boned with a well built body. They will be inclined to be fleshy with an impression of strength. They usually have clear complexions and a healthy look. Their nose is usually straight, of a good size and their eyes nicely expressive with arched eyebrows. They will have large white teeth, a well proportioned mouth, strong chin and perhaps with a dimple in the center. You will find their hair to be thick when they are young. Their voice is clear and pleasing. Their handwriting is usually large, strong and clear with an upward slant.

## The Health of the Jupiterian

With their love of good, rich food and drink in quantity, they tend to suffer from acid complaints. They may also suffer from rheumatism, lung and throat problems, inflamation of the tongue, liver ailments and skin trouble.

## The Negative or Non-developed Mount of Jupiter

If the Mount of Jupiter is deficient or flat, the Jupiterian will have a poor self-image. They have a lack of ambition, feel socially awkward and unable to take advantage of their opportunities. Their negative aspects can be long lasting; they can be lazy, inconsiderate of others and have little or no respect for themselves or others. Carelessness in religion, bad manners and selfishness can be their other problems.

## An Unusually Large Mount of Jupiter

If the Mount of Jupiter is unusually larger than the other mounts on the palm, ambition will play a major role in their lives. These people will tend to have too much pride, vanity and egotism. They are domineering and overbearing, very arrogant, selfish, greedy, bossy, self-centered and extravagant. They try to impress others and draw attention to themselves. They are jealous, very dictatorial and also tend to be gluttons.

## An Excessive and Unfavorably Placed Mount of Jupiter

This type of Jupiterian can be too overconfident and very self-opinionated; they are very vain and act impulsively tending to see things only their way, will go to extremes in all things and exhaust themselves. But, if their Head Line is strong and clear they will have a good chance to reach their goals. If the Head Line is poor or badly formed, it will be a negative aspect for them.

If the Mount of Jupiter leans toward the Mount of Saturn, these people's disposition will be towards serious topics, such as theology, the study of religion, the classics or mathematics. Their temperment can be both proud and sad.

If the Mount of Jupiter leans down toward the Mount of Mars it indicates that this Jupiterian will be self confident, very brave and have talent for a military career.

When the Mount of Jupiter leans toward the Mount of Venus, these Jupiterians will have a pleasant personality and a sociable disposition. They are honest, unselfish, generous, sincere and can be devoted.

133

# Signs and Markings on the Mount of Jupiter

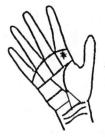

A Star on the Mount of Jupiter can mean a sudden good fortune. This is a very good sign to have on this Mount. The hopes and dreams of this person can be realized when they least expect it.

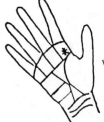

If a Star is low on the Mount of Jupiter it indicates a close association with people of influence.

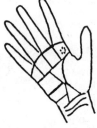

A Circle is a rare sign and is seldom complete, but is usually made up with a number of dots or tiny lines. On the Mount of Jupiter this sign is considered to be a lucky omen for success.

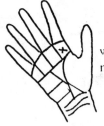

A Cross on the Mount of Jupiter indicates a romantic attachment which will advance this person's wordly prospects and also forecast a brilliant marriage.

A Square on the Mount of Jupiter will protect this person's wordly aims and ambitions against failure and also give this person the capability to be a leader.

A Grille is not a lucky sign. On the Mount of Jupiter it adds frustration to success and lack of energy to this person. They will have disappointments in their dreams and desires which will just be out of their reach. This interference may be caused by others or by themselves for they may become domineering, bossy and selfish and also allow their pride and egotism to interfere.

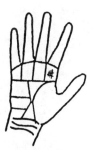

A Triangle on the Mount of Jupiter that is clear is a symbol of good luck and success. This sign gives them the ability to be organized and to handle people well.

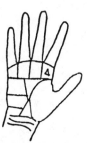

# The Mount of Saturn

The Mount of Saturn, sometimes referred to as the Melancholy Mount, Father Time and the teacher of hard and unavoidable lessons.

The Mount of Saturn is located at the base of the middle finger or second finger. The Mount of Saturn must be carefully read and tested in both palms and must include the finger of Saturn.

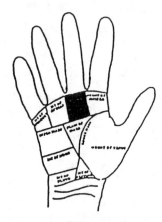

**The Mount of Saturn**

## The Positive Qualities of Saturn

The best development of the Mount of Saturn should be only slight.

The Saturnians, under all circumstances, are lovers of wisdom and will continue to search for it. Although they have always been of a gloomy nature (the messenger of gloom and doom) and they are predisposed to suicide, you must not assume that all Saturnians are bad or always negative, some of the noblest, high-minded and successful people have been Saturnians. Abraham Lincoln was one. But so have some of the most depraved and viscous.

## The Negative Saturnian

The negative Saturnian hand is hard and rough, with rough skin and thick wrists. I have rarely seen a strong development of this Mount together with a strong finger of Saturn. In fact, in most cases, the Mount is depressed when the finger of Saturn shows strength. The longer Saturn finger indicates the possession of some Saturnian qualities. Generally, the Saturnian may be recognized by their straight, upright Saturn finger, the largest in the hand, with the other fingers leaning toward it.

## The Over-developed Mount of Saturn

I always dislike writing anything negative, so let me soften this chapter on the Saturnian by saying that you seldom see a highly or overdeveloped Mount of Saturn with its apex centered. The Saturnian is a peculiar type of person; while the world may need a degree of their sober qualities, we will all agree that we are glad that there are only a few true Saturnian types. The Saturnian is prudent, wise, sober and sometimes called the "wet blanket", "the repressor". You can consider them the balance wheel or the necessary evil, however, the world cannot do without them. Some Saturn influence should be present, but just enough to give the world the balance it needs. For, through sorrow, we appreciate joy and can understand the sorrow of others.

The Mount of Saturn was named for the God Saturn, the Judge. I have heard of Saturn referred to as the planet of fertility and the most malignant of all signs. We must remember that this can be modified by other influences in the hand. It is always better to have a slight influence of Saturn as it gives us gravity and depth of character. A complete absence of the Mount of Saturn shows an insignificant life.

To determine the development of the Mount of Saturn, you must compare it to the other mounts in your client's palms. In most cases the Mount of Saturn is not overly developed. In all readings the character of the fingers, especially the Saturn finger should be studied to see whether the fingers are long or short, smooth or knotty, and the tips of the fingers must also be studied in connerction with the Mount. A true Saturnian usually has long, bony fingers, with the joint of the first phalanx knotted; these are the fingers of the thinkers.

The Mount of Saturn can be used as a check or balance of the other areas of the palm because the mount is less frequently developed than the other mounts, and very seldom found in excess. Markings and signs on the mount are very important to study, as well as all the lines. To give you a nice example before I have to go on to the more negative aspects of the mount, a good strong Fate Line with a small Mount of Saturn is a good indication for success.

If you come across a developed Saturn Mount, this person will be reserved, enjoy solitude and study. Saturnians are catious, weigh all things carefully and are deliberate in their actions. they always consider the bad with the good. They usually are not believers in religion, are born philosophers and love serious literature; have a quietness of spirit, prudence and earnestness at work; enjoy the study of philosophy and appreciates sacred and classical music; have wisdom; loves to act; have good judgement of property and values; and are serious, studious, dutiful at work, good in business, responsible and stable.

The Saturnian, unlike anyone else, is fastidious, particular, even at trifles. They can be very prudent and wise.

The over-developed Mount of Saturn is very rare. If the Mount of Saturn is more prominent than the other mounts on the palm, your client will have the tendency to be sad or morbid, and want solitude; they will be remorseful, with a fear and a horror of death, but with a marked curiosity of death and ghosts. They have melancholy moods and are fearful of the future. They can be suicidal. To help soften or help modify the negative traits of the Mount of Saturn, look for a well-developed Mount of Venus.

The true Saturnian seldom marries; they are the true bachelor, self-centered, self-confident and not really interested in what others think of them. They have a dislike of people, have fits of gloom with unreasonable fears and very little warmth in their personality; they are brooding and introverted. Another Saturn quality is thrift. Prudence, especially in money matters, they can turn to exaggerated meaness, self-criticism and dependency.

A Saturnian will distrust others until they are satisfied of their motives. They are usually individualists. They enjoy being in business by themselves and really do not make social contacts. The Saturnian is pretty much a wet blanket at any social gathering. Their point of view is usually a gloomy one and they will be ready to let you know about it. Being distrustful, they are hard to be around because they are always looking on the dark side. These people tend to be timid and of a nervous nature, cynical and always the doubters. Unsocial, they will not seek the companionship of others. They make good students, enjoy chemistry and are very interested in the occult. You usually find them working the land, with investments in land, mines and houses. They write well and write excellent ghost stories. Rarely do they go into business with others for they mistrust nearly everyone. They are self-reliant, independent and not interested in the opinions of others. They are saving to the point of being miserly.

They have a great love of music and are often fine performers and composers. Their choice of music will be severely classical with a strong tendency toward sadness.

In the study of criminology, they have found more real crimes from the Saturnian and Mercurian types than from any of the other types. It seems that these two types have a dislike toward mankind, even if they have only a slightly over-developed Mount of Saturn. These people want to invade the rights of others.

## The Under-developed Mount of Saturn

The apex is almost always centered under the Saturn finger when the Saturn Mount is under-developed, while the apex of the other mounts all lean toward it. If you look at your own palm you can understand why. It is the Mount that is usually undeveloped. With a small Mount of Saturn your client will have little or no interest in the occult or the mysterious. They are free with their opinions and prefer to discuss cheerful subjects. They are social and really do not care to be alone, except perhaps when working.

It must be remembered that the lines and other signs below the Saturn finger will be very important and must be considered. The under-developed or small Mount of Saturn, if favorable, gives these people prudence, wisdom and patience. What they earn in their lifetime they will keep. They like a quiet life and do not seek great fortune. They enjoy sacred, serious and classical music and fine art. They do well in agriculture, gardening, mining and all things that pertain to the earth.

With a slightly developed Mount of Saturn, your client will enjoy solitude, quietness and will always be cautious. They are sincere and earnest at their work. They have prudent characteristics, which enable them to become successful. They have an interest in the occult and philosophy.

As you see, the Mount of Saturn can be favorable if it is small or under-developed. With this influence, they can choose to become teachers, and can bring depth to their character.

# Absent or Flat Mount of Saturn

People with a flat or absent Mount of Saturn tend to lead a haphazard life style. Some Palmists will go to the extreme and say that these people will have a negative existence or insignificant life. But you must be careful when reading these palms and look not only to both hands, but the lines and other mounts, before you start any reading and make any statement. The absence of the Mount of Saturn denotes a poor life. These people are almost too easy going. Life just seems to pass tham by. They do not take life seriously and have a frivolous, trivial way of looking at things. They can be continually oppressed by a sense of misfortune, and are continually being plagued by misfortune. A good Fate Line can temper this.

# Signs and Markings on the Monut of Saturn

A Star on the Mount of Saturn is a very good sign; it indicates a dramatic success in business or in the arts.

A Triangle on the Mount of Saturn indicates a great aptitude for the occult sciences. These people have a good mind and are very suited for research careers.

A Square on the Mount of Saturn adds job protection and protects against any financial worries.

A Cross is not a good sign on the Mount of Saturn. Some Palmists call this marking the "Sign of the Scaffold", sudden death or sudden endings

A Circle on the Mount of Saturn will cause this person to be isolated and be alone.

A Dot on any mount is not a good sign, it indicates illness.

A Grille on the Mount of Saturn is not a good sign, it indicates and intensifies this person's depression and brooding tendencies; it can also indicate a misfortune.

# The Mount of Apollo

The Mount of Apollo is also known as the Mount of the Sun. When the Mount is large and well developed it is considered to be a good sign; it indicates glory, publicity, brilliancy, artistic, dashing, happy, successful with a desire to shine. This mount gives enthusiasm; they see beauty in all things. People with a large Mount of Apollo love to build and enjoy beautiful homes and want their surroundings to be artistic and beautiful. They usually are generous and love luxurious things. They have a bright and happy personality. People with a Mount of Apollo developed, always have a word of brightness, gaity and love to entertain you. A highly developed Mount of Apollo can produce a person of true enchantment, whether they are famous or not. An Apollo Mount will give your client versatility at home as well as in business. They love the arts and they often become patrons of the arts.

**The Mount of Apollo**

## The Normally Developed Mount of Apollo

A normally developed Mount of Apollo indicates that this person will be lucky. They will have a pleasant, sunny disposition with a love of beauty, refined tastes and artistic abilities.

142

## An Over-developed Mount of Apollo

People with an over-developed Mount of Apollo have natural intuition; they seem to have knowledge beyond their experience. They love to expand and show fearlessness leading them to colorful and spectacular achievements. Although sometimes they must 'Pay the Piper', even their critics will forgive them. The developed Mount of Apollo has amazing gifts of talent.

## The Positive Aspects of the Mount of Apollo

With a well-developed Mount of Apollo, these people love art, artistic things and beauty' though they are not born artists themselves, they always encourage the arts. With intelligence and brilliant minds for success and the ability to make their fortune. They love fame and fortune and usually enjoy a successful life. They have a natural knowledge, usually are intuitive, sensitive and very perceptive. They are not workaholics, but rather rely on their brilliant and agile minds. They tend to be versatile, quick thinkers and can be surprisingly inventive. They can make good use of any idea that may come along. They love to attract attention and usually get credit for more than their worth. They have the ability to shine in any field or group of people.

## The Absent or Flat Mount of Apollo

People with a flat Mount of Apollo have little or no interest in art, beauty or culture. They have a taste for low type pleasures. They tend to lead a dull and aimless existence.

## The Negative Aspects of the Mount of Apollo

When the Mount of Apollo is excessively high or large, these people will enjoy good taste, have money and attention, however, they like to boast about themselves and their capabilities, which they will tend to exaggerate. They are extravagant spenders and love to display their possessions and surround themselves with luxury.

# Signs and Markings on the Mount of Apollo

A Star on the Mount of Apollo is a good sign; it indicates wealth, prestige, high social standing and success. These people will gain their success through their own talents, plus the help and good will of influencial people.

A Triangle on the Mount of Apollo is a lucky sign and adds success to this Mount; these people will obtain prosperity and fame.

A Cross is not a good sign on the Mount of Apollo, it symbolizes the end of ones hopes; however, if a Success Line continues beyond the Cross this person may be able to regain their success.

A Circle is a very rare sign. It is a symbol of the Sun or Apollo, and when found on the Mount of Apollo, it forcasts fame, glory and success.

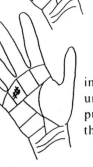

A Grille on the Mount of Apollo is really not a very good sign, it indicates that this person will be striving after glory which will be unobtainable because of their vanity or errors. They are always seeking publicity and it doesn't matter to them what method they use as long as they can make a name for themselves.

# The Mount of Mercury

The Mount of Mercury is located in the active, unconscious zones of the hand; it lies beneath the Mercury or little finger. The Mercury finger is known as the money or business finger and covers the traits that are successful for making money. The Mount of Mercury indicates the ability to accomplish and put together what it will take to make it happen. These two characteristics when combined, will indicate how well the Mercurian will succeed in the world of money and business. Mercury in mythology is known as Hermes, the winged messenger of the Gods. The true Mercurians can communicate well and are interested in the occult sciences and healing, and are very successful in business. They are also lawyers, scientists and physicians.

**The Mount of Mercury**

The Medical Stigmata is located on the Mount of Mercury. These are small vertical lines under the Mercury finger. If the Mercury finger is longer than normal and strong, it increases the talent for medical studies. This marking will be found on the palms of prominent and successful physicians. The Medical Stigmata also includes people with the talent of a surgical nurse, diagnostician and the person studying the occult sciences with a special aptitude for making money.

Children Lines are also located on the percussion side of the Mount of Mercury.

Because of all the activity on the Mount of Mercury identifying all the different markings, lines and signs is very important and they must be carefully confirmed.

Although Mercurians are fine writers, excellent speakers, shrewd in business and in the professions of law and medicine, they are in an element which shows their good side, but there is a bad side - a very bad side. There are also no greater liars, swindlers and cheaters than a bad Mercurian; for this reason careful examination of all the elements of the hand must be considered. The Mercurians are usually successful because of their shrewdness and unusual ability to judge human nature.

The Mount of Mercury should always be considered with the kind of Head Line found in the palm of the hand. If the Head Line is long and strong it will increase all the positive mental aptitudes and indicate a combination of success and clear thinking. If the Head Line is weak or badly marked, it will add to the weakness of the Mount and all its bad aspects.

## Displaced Mount of Mercury

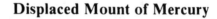

If the Apex of the Mount of Mercury is near the base of Mercury, or little finger, this indicates an excellent sense of humor and an eloquent speaker. They will express themselves very well.

If the Apex is close to the Mount of Apollo, money will not be important. They will not be interested in finance, only what it will buy; there is a blend of business and art. This combination is found in the hands of polititians, lawyers and religious leaders who use their ability for communication in business. They have a great love of animals and would rather love and tend to them rather than they would children.

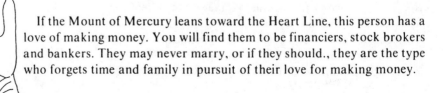

If the Mount of Mercury leans toward the Heart Line, this person has a love of making money. You will find them to be financiers, stock brokers and bankers. They may never marry, or if they should., they are the type who forgets time and family in pursuit of their love for making money.

146

If the Apex of the Mount of Mercurey leans toward the percussion side of the hand, these people will be very successful in business. They will be wealthy if they follow their instincts. They can be very dashing and courageous, never shirk their responsibility, and are dauntless and quick in their actions.

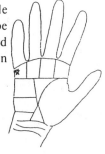

## Health of the Mercurians

Everything that can affect the nerves and nervous system will have an effect on a Mercurian. They suffer from indigestion caused by nervous worry and anxiety, hysteria, schizophrenia, paralysis and stuttering. They also may suffer from insomnia, have trouble with their bronchial tubes, throat, nose and eyes.

## Over-developed Mount of Mercury

A Mercurian with an overdeveloped Mount of Mercury has a strong materialistic streak and a desire for easy money. They can be light fingered, a liar, a cheat, and use their natural astuteness and gift of gab to fleece the unsuspecting public. You will find them to be card sharks, thieves, gold-diggers, con artists and unscrupulous business people.

People with an over-developed Mount of Mercury are schemers and have an evasive nature. They can be very superstitious in a very objective way; they will believe in hunches and luck. They will exploit almost anything that will offer them a quick return.

With an over-developed Mount of Mercury they can be too enthusiastic in promoting new ideas. They think in terms of maximum gain instead of minimum where cash return is concerned, and often overshoot their marks. These people will use any advantage to get what they want, and will even use sentiment to gain a personal goal. They are unpredictable and know it, they are over-confident and believe that no matter how outrageous they are, they can always think their way out of a situation. They are unscrupulous and scheming.

## A Flat Mount of Mercury

People with a flat Mount of Mercury are usually failures in any business venture, and tend to be gullible with a little or no head for business. They are dull, humorless, long-winded and boring.

With a flat or absent Mount of Mercury there is no intellectual talent, nor scientific potential; their mentality is poor, they dislike keeping accounts, are careless in financial matters and lack sales ability.

## Well-developed Mount of Mercury

With a well-developed Mount of Mercury, these people will have a quick mind and good comprehension, and are agile on their feet. They make good teachers, reporters, writers, photographers and love to travel. They will have good business sense and are interested in all the sciences. Many Mercurians are into the occult sciences and have become mediums and healers. They handle their money well, as well as other people's money. They speak well with a large vocabulary and have a good sense of humor.

# Signs and Markings on the Mount of Mercury

There are many signs and markings on the Mount of Mercury. The Children Lines, Marriage Lines and even the Medical Stigmata are all located on the Mount of Mercury. All these lines and signs make it a very difficult area to read accurately.

A Star on the Mount of Mercury is a very good sign to have. It indicates success in a professional career, as an inventor, scientist or writer.

A Cross under the Mount of Mercury protects a change in profession or business and is generally favorable.

A Cross on the Mount of Mercury indicates that this person will have finesse and diplomacy.

A Cross on the Mount of Mercury can indicate an overly accomodating nature. These people might often use a polite lie in order to avoid any confrontation.

A Cross on the Mount of Mercury can be a warning against the dishonesty, deception or double dealings of others.

A Square on the Mount of Mercury indicates an aptitude toward a teaching career.

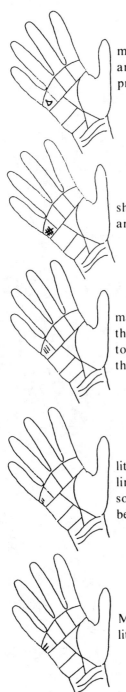

A Triangle on the Mount of Mercury confirms and strengthens the mental abilities of this person and also indicates their ability to influence and get along well with people that will help them to succeed in their profession.

A Grille on the Mount of Mercury is not a good sign; it indicates shrewdness and extreme nervousness. This person's character is cunning and can be dishonest in business.

The Medical Stigmata sign is located on the Mount of Mercury. This marking consists of short, straight, vertical lines placed close together on the Mount of Mercury at the base of the little finger. It indicates the ability to care for the ill, and, as the name of this sign implies, it is often found on the palms of doctors, nurses and healers.

Children Lines can be found on the Mount of Mercury at the base of the little finger. These are tiny vertical lines near the Marriage Lines; a strong line indicates a boy child, a fainter line a girl child. These lines can sometimes be found in the palms of people who are childless and who have become very attached to a child or children belonging to someone else.

Marriage Lines or Lines of Affection can be found on the Mount of Mercury on the edge of the hand or Percussion between the base of the little finger and the Heart Line.

# The Mount of Venus

The Mount of Venus is the largest Mount on the palm and should take up approximately one-third of the palm's surface. When normal it covers the third phalanx at the base of the thumb that is encircled by the Life Line. Doctors call it the "thenar eminence," thenar meaning the palm of the hand, eminence meaning hill or elevation. The science of physiology indicates that this mount covers one of the most important blood vessels in the palm, the Great Palmer Arch, which gives good blood supply and active circulation to a well-developed mount.

The Mount of Venus is named after the Goddess of Love and Beauty, which designates the capacity for love, passion, friendship, attachment to family, children, sympathy and love of music. Sometimes referred to as the Mount of Melody.

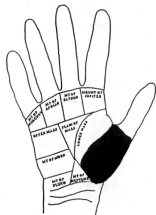

**The Mount of Venus**

The Mount of Venus can be divided into two parts. The upper section nearest the Head Line is referred to as having spititual aspects and the lower section, particularly if the mount is well developed, indicates artistic abilities and sensuality. There is seldom an apex found on this mount, so the center of the mount will have to be estimated. Its normal appearance is well-rounded and smooth. These people will be attractive to the opposite sex. They will enjoy good health, optimistic spirits, gaity and love of music.

The Mount of Venus should be well placed, padded and firm to the touch, not too soft nor too hard. This will indicate a strong, healthy person of sympathetic nature with understanding for the welfare and happiness of

151

others. They have a loving disposition with a fair amount of passion. This produces a happy home and a well rounded life. Its other attributes are a possession and admiration of beauty, grace, melody, dancing, gallantry, tenderness and benevolence, with a constant desire to please and to be appreciated. The Mount of Venus is found on the hand of all singers.

People with a strong Mount of Venus have similar traits to a Jupiterian, only the Venus influence adds beauty and a softer, more feminine quality. These people have beautiful complexions with lovely color to their cheeks and dimples. Their eyes are large and clear with long lashes. Their noses are usually small and well-shaped with a small mouth, round chin and small shell-like ears. Their hands are usually very fair, soft and dimpled. Their fingers are short with a small thumb.

Very often the size of the Mount of Venus can change. A strong love affair has been known to increase the size of the Mount, but a prolonged period of loneliness can decrease the mount.

## Well-developed Mount of Venus

A well-developed Mount of Venus can make a man effeminate or unmanly, which some people consider a weakness or self indulgent trait, but the Mount of Venus also softens the malignities or harmful tendencies of other Mounts which may be bad.
When the Mount of Venus is well-developed, these people are lovers of pleasure, applause, poetry and music.

A highly or well-developed Mount of Venus which is deeply colored or fleshy, indicates a passionate person with a sense of music and artistic appreciation. They will have a zest for life and physical vitality.

A high soft Mount of Venus indicates that this person is easily aroused and excitable. They can be caught up in a sudden, mad infatuation and will swear to their love and devotion eternally, however, this type of high soft Mount of Venus will make these people fickle and their romances end as quickly as they begin.

A man or woman with a high firm Mount of Venus is highly sexed. To them the physical side of love and marriage is all-important. Throughout their lives the urge to love and possess is a compelling force.

## Over-developed Mount of Venus

An over-developed Mount of Venus brings out animal instincts and passions and will be predominant in this person's life.

If the Mount of Venus is excessively large this person has an abundance of physical passion and a large appetite for sex.

## Under-developed Mount of Venus

A small, flat or weak Mount of Venus indicates a lack of vital force and physical passion. This person's personality will tend to be sluggish, indifferent and cold, especially if the Mount is intersected by the Life Line down toward the wrist.

If the Mount of Venus is small and flat, these people usually have a delicate health condition. They will have a weak sexual drive and a cold nature. They seem to be self-contained and detached. They seem to find love and devotion of others quite boring and a burden; they do not like encumbrances and would rather be without any commitments. If they marry, it will be for practical reasons. If their partner also has a cool temperment, the union can be a happy one.

If the Mount of Venus appears to be flat and pale this person will have very little sex drive or passion; they may be frigid. This type of Mount is not a good sign, these people may get their satisfactions by being hurt or hurting others. If the hand is also thin with red splotches, they could have the tendency to bite, scratch or beat their sex partners. They can be unethical and lack a sense of right or wrong.

If the Mount of Venus is flat, it indicates that this person will be hard to deal with in business and is usually indifferent in their home life.

## Negative Mount of Venus

If the Mount of Venus is reddish and hard to the touch, this person can easily become sexually aggressive and brutal, especially if the texture of their skin is course.

If the Mount of Venus is hard, high and red, it indicates that the emotions of this person will be intense. Depending upon the rest of the hand, this person can be dangerous too. They will not take "no" for an answer; they are willing and ready to fight for what they want, and they may become angry or furious when thay cannot satisfy their sexual desires. When in love they can be insatiable and untrue as a lover. These people are often bigamists. If a man, they will have a mistress or two on the side.

## Absence of the Mount of Venus

The absence of the Mount of Venus indicates coldness and dullness. If the Mount of Venus is void of any lines, it increases the coldness of this person and in many cases indicates a short life.

The hollowing out of the Mount of Venus after the age of fifty indicates a loss of vitality.

# Displaced Mount of Venus

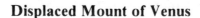

When the Mount of Venus is displaced toward the thumb forming a large, elevated area close to the base of the thumb, this indicates that this person will be ruled by their emotions.

When the Mount of Venus is fullest close to the area of the Life Line and the flesh looks as though it is bulging along the inside of the Life Line close to the center of the palm, it indicates an intense sexual desire.

If the Mount of Venus is displaced toward the Life Line, it adds sensuality to this person; they will be very fond of luxury and comfort.

If the Mount of Venus is displaced toward the Mount of the Moon, it is not a good sign; this person will be sensual to an extreme and will be incapable of self-discipline and only interested in their own sexual pleasures.

If the Mount of Venus is displaced toward the wrist of the hand it is also not a good sign. These people are sensuous and seek only pleasures that will satisfy their own sexual appetite with animal instincts.

When the Mount of Venus forms an angular formation it gives this person an ability for rhythm, and an interest in music and dancing, usually a talent for both.

If the Mount of Venus is well developed and falls toward the Mount of Jupiter, it indicates a deep affection for family. These people will sacrifice anything for their family. Many mothers and fathers have this type of Mount of Venus

## Signs and Markings on the Mount of Venus

A Cross, Grille, Island or Dot indicates defects on the Mount of Venus, while a single combination of the Triangle, Circle, Square or single vertical lines strengthen the Mount of Venus.

A Cross on the Mount of Venus indicates that this person will find true love and have a happy marriage. Look to the Lines of Affection, if the Marriage Line is strong and long it will add significance to the Cross.

A Cross between the Mount of Venus and the Mount of the Moon near the base of the hand will indicate a change in this person's career.

If a Triangle is on the Mount of Venus, it indicates that this person will have a calculating personality and often marry for money or position.

A Star at the base of the Mount of Venus close to the wrist will be a bad influence; it is called the mark of the "Star-crossed lover" and indicates that there will be difficulties and delays in the path of true love.

A Star in the middle of the Mount of Venus is a symbol of great charm and sex appeal and indicates that this person will be lucky in love.

A Star just under the second crease of the thumb on the Mount of Venus indicates a marriage that will last this person's whole life.

If a Star on the Mount of Venus sends lines to the Life Line, it indicates a death of a relation or a dear friend. The location of this line will indicate the time of their loss.

A line from the middle of the Mount of Venus to the base of the hand and rising to the middle of the Mount is a sign of good luck.

Lines on the Lower Mars touching the Mount of Venus, parallel to the, Life Line, are a good sign, and add strength and protection to the Life Line.

Horizontal lines on the Lower Mars across the Mount of Venus are referred to as Worry or Stress Lines and indicate problems with loved ones or family.

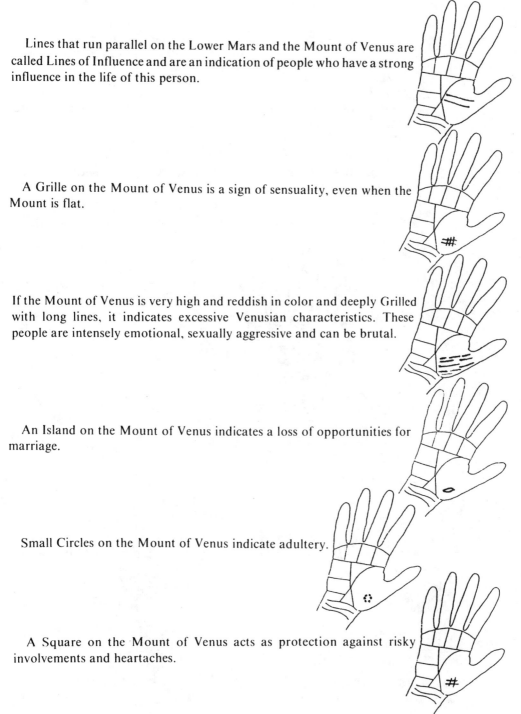

Lines that run parallel on the Lower Mars and the Mount of Venus are called Lines of Influence and are an indication of people who have a strong influence in the life of this person.

A Grille on the Mount of Venus is a sign of sensuality, even when the Mount is flat.

If the Mount of Venus is very high and reddish in color and deeply Grilled with long lines, it indicates excessive Venusian characteristics. These people are intensely emotional, sexually aggressive and can be brutal.

An Island on the Mount of Venus indicates a loss of opportunities for marriage.

Small Circles on the Mount of Venus indicate adultery.

A Square on the Mount of Venus acts as protection against risky involvements and heartaches.

# The Mounts of Mars and the Plain of Mars

Mars is the fury God of War. These two Mounts of Mars indicate fighting, courage or cowardice, with a strong resistance or weak surrender in the face of danger. The Lower Mount of Mars, located beneath the Mount of Jupiter, indicates physical courage, the aggressive spirit that is always ready to attack and strike the first blow. The Upper Mount of Mars, above the Mount of the Moon, indicates moral courage and passive resistance. The Plain of Mars, which separates the two Mounts, indicates judgement; it shows how much thought and concern will be taken.

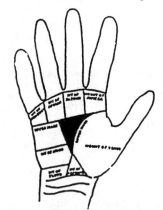

The Plain of Mars

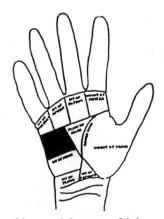

The Upper Mount of Mars

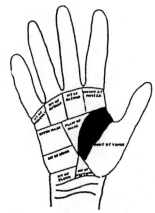

The Lower Mount of Mars

# The Upper Mount of Mars

The Mounts of Mars are the most difficult of all to study for they are made up of three sections. The Lower Mount of Mars or positive Mount is located under the Mount of Jupiter and above the Mount of Venus. The Plain of Mars is in the center of the palm between the Upper and Lower Mount of Mars and under the Mounts of Saturn and Apollo; it indicates a combative spirit. The Upper Mount of Mars, or negative Mount, under the Mount of Mercury and above the Mount of the Moon indicates a most pugnacious spirit and quarrelsome quality; but also bravery.

In almost all hands some Martian development is seen.

The Upper Mount of Mars is located on the percussion side of the hand between the Mount of the Moon and the Mount of Mercury. Its boundaries are determined by the two major horizontal lines, the Heart Line and the Head Line. The palm is divided into two halves. The thumb side of the hand is known as the positive half, and the percussion as the negative half.

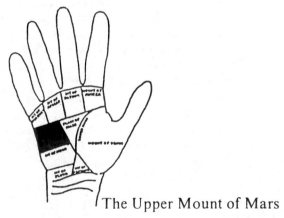

The Upper Mount of Mars

People with a normally developed Mount of Upper Mars have true courage, moral as well as physical. They have good powers of resistance and stamina. They are endowed with calm courage and maintain excellent control. They resist any attempts by others to impose on them. They will push themselves over any and all obstacles and will not allow anyone to stop their progress. They will not recognize defeat. They are not people who fight physically, but ones who meet adversity with calm defensive opposition. They are the soldiers, the explorers, the martyrs and mothers of the world. They are capable of a great deal of staying power and do not

159

yield to circumstances easily. They are generous and forgiving. They will not go to pieces in a crisis, and have a certain kind of bravery that keeps them from becoming dismayed or upset when things do not go well. They simply do not scare easily.

The very negative personality of a Martian can be lascivious, wanton and lustful and they can become an alcoholic and a criminal.

To distinguish the varied qualities of the Mounts of Mars, all aspects of the hand and palm must be studied.

## Absent or Flat Upper Mount of Mars

If the Upper Mount of Mars is absent or flat, this person will be good at bluffing, but will back down if pressed; they do not have the power of resistance. It is an indication that they are cowards and tend to be rather childish; they never seem to grow up. They are hasty and lacking in stamina and will have problems, and will be unsuccessful in life for they lack self esteem.

An absent Upper Mount of Mars also indicates that this person will most likely have a wrecked life, become a drifter or transient because they are easily discouraged. They will go under in their struggle for their existence, no matter how gifted or talented they may be.

A person with a flat or absent Upper Mount of Mars will be timid and cowardly, and become submissive and docile to save their own skin. Because of their fearful nature, when faced with something new, their initial reaction is fear or the feeling that they will be unable to cope with the situation. They would rather not put up with life's irritations. A partner can help this person with their endeavors.

## Over-developed Upper Mount of Mars

A person with an over-developed Mount of Mars usually has a bad temper, but they will rarely resort to physical force to express their temper; instead they will use sarcasm and mental cruelty.

# Displaced Upper Mount of Mars

When the Upper Mount of Mars leans toward the Mount of Mercury it indicates a fortitude and fearless spirit. These people are capable of tremendous powers of endurance and unusual staying power, and will succeed in their aspirations.

When the Upper Mount of Mars leans toward the palm of the hand and can be visibly seen bulging toward the center of the palm, it changes the passive qualities of the Mount and undergoes a complete change. This person will be able to show an aggressive spirit. Besides maintaining their quality of resistance, they also take on the characteristics of an aggressive and courageous personality.

If the Upper Mount of Mars leans toward the Mount of the Moon it indicates that this person will have a meekness of spirit, tremendous patience and a tranquil nature. They will be endowed with hypnotic powers that enable them to influence others, even though they are not aware of those powers. They are often very independent.

If the Upper Mount of Mars is over-developed and leans toward the Mount of the Moon, they may not fight physically. This is a mark of intelligence; they will not be afraid but will stand up for their rights. They are our inventors, pioneers and they love gambling.

# Signs and Markings on the Upper Mount of Mars

If there is a Cross on the Upper Mount of Mars, this person must be careful not to let their aggressive instincts get out of control and cause trouble.

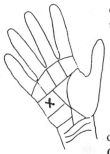

A Cross on the Upper Mount of Mars indicates that this person will never forget an injustice done to them. Theirs is a passive resistance. They are the sit-down strikers for justice.

A Cross on the Upper Mount of Mars indicates a quarrelsome disposition. This person is inclined to fight, especially if there is a second Cross on the Plain of Mars.

A Cross on the Upper Mount of Mars warns against physical danger. If the Upper Mount of Mars is over-developed, then the danger will come from their own quarrelsome and stubborn nature.

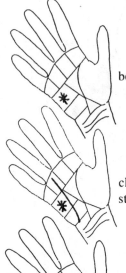

A Star on the Upper Mount of Mars indicates that this person can become violent.

If there is a Star on the Upper Mount of Mars, this person should pay close attention their health. If they have a strong Line of Success, their strong character will enable them to achieve success.

A Triangle on the Upper Mount of Mars indicates erratic courage and this person will suffer from imaginary injustices.

A Triangle on the Upper Mount of Mars indicates that this person would do well in a military profession.

If there is a Square on the Upper Mount of Mars, it indicates protection from bodily harm.

A Square on the Upper Mount of Mars adds protection from enemies.

A Square on a flat or normally developed Mount of Mars will add protection from bodily harm.

If there is a Square on an over-developed Upper Mount of Mars, it is a good sign that this person does their best to keep their temper under control.

A Grille on the Upper Mount of Mars is not a good sign; some Palmists believe it indicates a violent death or a violent person.

A Grille on the Upper Mount of Mars indicates a risk to this person of a violent death, and they must take precautions to avoid accidents. It can also indicate a tendency for holding anger. These people need some kind of physical outlet, such as a sport of some kind.

A horizontal line that runs across the Upper Mount of Mars from the percussion side of the hand symbolizes an enemy and warns that this person should be on guard. They may cause their problem due to their temper and irritability.

A vertical line on the Upper Mount of Mars indicates a constant irritation. These people have excessive energy.

# The Plain of Mars

The Plain of Mars is located in the portion of the palm called the hollow of the hand, and is crossed by almost all the major and minor lines. If the palm of the hand looks flat, the Plain of Mars is called "high". If the palm of the hand is saucer-like, then it is called "normal". If the palm of the hand is very deep, it is called "low". The Plain of Mars connects the Lower Mars near the thumb, which indicates the combative side of our nature; if we will defend ourselves in physical combat. The Upper Mars on the percussion side of the hand indicates courage, along with the Plain of Mars which separates the two Mounts indicating judgement. It shows how much thought and concern will be taken. It is the Plain of Mars that will make us consider our actions before we act upon them.

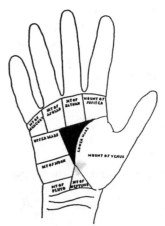

**The Plain of Mars**

## Variations on the Plain of Mars

If the Plain of Mars is high, the palm will look rather flat and will indicate that this person will act impulsively. They will be given to action without thinking out their actions carefully.

If the Plain of Mars is very hollow, this person will pause a long time. They are slow to act and will not be interested in physical combat.

If the Plain of Mars is concave like a saucer, it is considered normal and this person will have normal reactions to combat.

A Plain of Mars that is highly developed and covered with lines indicates a love of constant struggle and war, especially when their nails are short and a Cross is found on the mount. This network of little lines always indicates obstacles in the way of good fortune.

If the Plain of Mars is flat-looking or slightly concave, the Plain of Mars is high. This person will be impulsive, often overbearing, conceited, proud and extroverted with little or no concern for others.

If the Plain of Mars looks hollow like a bowl or valley, then it is considered low. This person will be melancholy, an introvert, slow to act, overly concerned with what the world will think of them. They are apt to bite the hand that feeds them and tend to be defensive. If the Plain of Mars is very hollow, look for signs of weak internal organs, as the center of the palm often becomes flabby before an illness; the Plain of Mars is an indicator of a person's health and well being.

The Plain of Mars is a very sensitive area of the palm of the hand. When stroked it can cause sexual excitement.

The Plain of Mars indicates whether a person will stop to consider their actions before acting impulsively.

The average Plain of Mars is neither high nor hollow, and is concerned with the well-being of others. It intensifies the debate between good and evil.

The Plain of Mars when well developed or crossed with many horizontal lines indicates a person with a sudden violent temper and abusive outbursts.

If the Plain of Mars is very high and hard, these people enjoy great combativeness and are eager to fight.

If the Plain of Mars is hollow, these people will be submissive and may have poor health.

If the Plain of Mars forms a hollow or valley under the Life Line, there will be domestic problems.

If the Plain of Mars forms a hollow or valley under the Fate Line, these people will have disappointments in business.

If the PLain of Mars forms a hollow or valley under the Line of Success, these people will have failure in their artistic work or profession.

If the Plain of Mars forms a hollow in the top of the Quadrangle and under the Heart Line, it indicates disappointment in a love affair.

## Signs and Markings on the Plain of Mars

Cross lines, Stars, Crosses or Grilles seen on the Plain of Mars increase the inflammibility and temper of this person.

If the Plain of Mars is well developed and is crossed with many fine lines it indicates that this person will have sudden temper outbursts.

A double Trident on the Plain of Mars to the Mount of Apollo promises honors in art, but this person must overcome their problems.

A Cross on the Plain of Mars adds a quarrelsome personality to this person.

The Psychic Cross lies in the Plain of Mars in what is called the Quadrangle. The Cross must be independent and clear, not touching any of the Major Lines. The Psychic or Mystic Cross indicates an interest in the Occult and Metaphysical science.

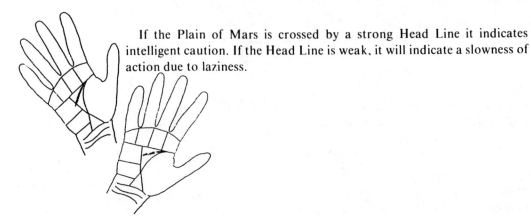

If the Plain of Mars is crossed by a strong Head Line it indicates intelligent caution. If the Head Line is weak, it will indicate a slowness of action due to laziness.

# The Lower Mount of Mars

The Lower Mount of Mars is also called the Mount of Active Resistance. It is the triangular cushion that lies between the beginning of the Life Line-Head Line conjunction and the Mount of Venus, following along side the Life Line. It indicates a person's fighting ability, their strength, skill and courage, especially in battle, their active resistance or hostility. It indicates whether the person will fight physically and it reveals the aggressive side of their personality.

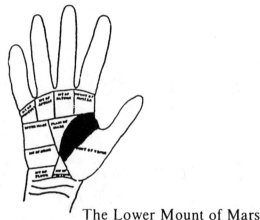

The Lower Mount of Mars

If the Lower Mount of Mars is not cushioned and looks wrinkled, this person is no fighter; they will never pick a fight. They are peace loving souls. Be sure to look at their thumbs; if they are strong, when forced to fight this person can become fierce.

The Martian is usually of medium height, strongly built, very exact in their ways, and always look as though they can take care of themselves and be able to force their way through the world. They would prefer to do so mentally if they have a choice, but will be physical if they must. They enjoy good health and are always energetic. They are generous, like to form lasting friendships and they have congenial spirits. Although determined, they can be amenable to reason and can be fairly easily led, but do not try to make them do anything for they will resist. They are intense in everything they undertake, but opposition can arouse their fighting spirit They are always best handled with tact and diplomacy. They are always ardent, steadfast and persevering people with a strong pride and love of show.

# Displaced Lower Mount of Mars

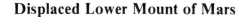

If the highest part of the Lower Mount of Mars is located near the second phalanx of the thumb, anything that angers these people will also arouse their sexual drive.

If the center of the Lower Mount of Mars leans toward the Mount of Venus, these people will be overly protective of their children, spouses and possessions.

If the highest part of the Lower Mount of Mars is displaced near the Mount of Jupiter, these people will fight for people in high places.

If the Lower Mount of Mars is displaced toward the Mount of Jupiter, it indicates that these people have the power of initiative action and ambition, due to their personal dignity and pride.

If the Lower Mount of Mars leans toward the Mount of Venus these people will have power of endurance and courage due to their affections.

When the Lower Mount of Mars leans toward the base of the thumb, it indicates that this person's courage will come through their will power and determination.

When the Lower Mount of Mars leans toward the Plain of Mars, it indicates a tremendous potential for a daring and bold life. This person loves danger, shows no fear and has combative instincts. They love an exciting and dangerous life.

## Over-developed Lower Mount of Mars

People with an over-developed Lower Mount of Mars seldom feel any pain when they are fighting and they have a very high tolerance to pain. Look to the thumbs to see if there is a strong bar of temper on the second phalanx of the thumb. This type of Mount indicates a violent, quarrelsome bully; they are cruel individuals who are aggressive with a sharp tongue and usually have a disturbing effect on the lives and happiness of those around them. In all fairness, however, it must be noted that they are never afraid of taking risks and in an emergency will act bravely.

This person with an over-developed Lower Mount of Mars would rather punch another person than listen. They are born fighters and this could make them good boxers or athletes.

If the Lower Mount of Mars is excessive, it will show a cushion when the hand is closed. This person can be cruel.

## Flat Lower Mount of Mars

If the Lower Mount of Mars is flat it indicates that this person is a coward and can neither fight or put up strong resistance. They are born losers.

People with flat Lower Mount of Mars do not care for arguments; they will back up when cornered. These people have to be pushed to complete their tasks.

People with a normal Lower Mount of Mars have a combative spirit, fortitude, determination, courage and strong resistance. They have good self control and coolness in tough situations. They have the ability to carry out orders no matter how dangerous they may be.

# Signs and Markings on the Lower Mount of Mars

Crosses on a high Lower Mount of Mars indicates tragedy from an accidental killing in a fit of temper; with am additional Cross on the Mount of Saturn, this person will go to jail.

A Cross or Grille on the Lower Mount of Mars warns against a risk of sudden death.

A Grille on the Lower Mount of Mars indicates a war-like spirit and a tendency to be quarrelsome and have an aggressive nature.

A Triangle on the Mount of Mars indicates fame from a brave deed.

A Triangle on the Lower Mount of Mars gives this person cool courage and enterprise in the face of danger and promises distinction or promotion in a military career.

A Star on the Lower Mount of Mars indicates that this person will achieve their goal through their own strength and will,

A Star on the Lower Mount of Mars indicates a person who will fight against all odds in order to obtain their goals.

172

A Vertical Line on the Lower Mount of Mars indicates courage and aggressiveness.

A Double Trident from the Mount of Venus to the Lower Mount of Mars is interpreted as a joining of the two Mounts which indicate ties in previous lifetimes.

A Square on the Lower Mount of Mars indicates a person who can be exposed to danger in their occupation but will receive added protection in any perilous situation and they will be unharmed.

# The Mount of the Moon

The Mount of the Moon is a fleshy elevation covering an area close to the wrist and alongside the percussion side of the palm, roughly between the area of the Fate Line and the Head Line, toward the outward edge of the palm. The Mount of the Moon compliments the Mount of Apollo, because it informs us of the regenerative organs and most important, a creative imagination and creativity.

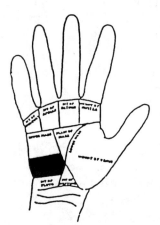

**The Mount of the Moon**

The Mount of the Moon is usually high since the base of the hand is used in all types of work. The cushion usually flows into the Mount of Venus which is separated by the Life Line.

The Mount of the Moon is a very interesting Mount. It falls in the unconcious and passive zone of the palm. This is appropriate, for the function of the Moon is a storehouse of our memories. The Mount of the Moon is traditionally associated with writing ability and imaginative creativity. These people have a love of water, to travel and visit strange places, with a yearning for the mysterious. If they are unable to travel or experience the unusual, many of them become obsessive readers. They like to be with people who interest them, and are often rude by ignoring others. They change their friends with their different moods and are quite fickle. They do not like to be alone, but since they have such a creative imagination, they are never bored with their own company, and often travel alone. They have a tendency to concentrate very seriously and will exclude everyone else and go off by themselves in order to work or complete their plans. They are great worriers and this can cause them their greatest problems.

## Over-developed Mount of the Moon

When the Mount of the Moon is over-developed, these people become discontented with their lot in life. Their urge to travel is uncontrollable. Those who have a heavy outward bulge prefer to travel by sea and to live near water. They shrink from society because they feel that they are different from other people or that they are misunderstood. They are worriers and this often takes the form of imaginary ailments.

The Lunarians can be under the control of both the thumb and the Mercury finger; a strong thumb will bring out the best in a developed Mount of the Moon and can modify or temper an over-developed area. A weak thumb will lack will power or logic and will leave a Lunarian very much the prey of his own imagination.

If the Mount of the Moon curves outward on the edge of the palm, it indicates a love of water. These people will be drawn to live by the ocean, lakes, rivers or streams. This type of outward curving is found on captains and navigators.

A crease line on the Mount of the Moon indicates love of voyages.

## Flat or Absence of the Mount of the Moon

If the Mount of the Moon is totally absent or flat, it indicates a sign of complete materialism. This is an extremely rare hand.

If the Mount of the Moon is very slight, which looks straight-sided, cramped or almost bony, it indicates that these people are cold, matter-of-fact and lack sympathy. They are impatient with anyone with new ideas, dislike strangers and lack enthusiasm.

# A High Mount of the Moon

A person with a high Mount of the Moon has a restless nature and tends to be fickle, untrustworthy. They can be selfish, melancholy, superstitious and unwilling to work. They have a very vivid imagination and are born travelers, unable to settle down. They make poor lovers or marriage partners. They enjoy music, poetry and art. Their reading material tends to be travel, romantic novels or materials of an imaginative nature. They are not interested in facts or reality. They do not have a robust nature and tend to be changeable, unreliable and weak.

# Negative Mount of the Moon

If the Mount of the Moon is high and very full, it indicates a large imagination; psychics and spiritualists have a very high Mount of the Moon. The negative side of this very full Mount is that psychotics and schizophrenics also have this type of Mount, so a high Mount of the Moon is not always an asset. A person who cannot tell a daydream from reality will have an abnormally high Mount of the Moon. Again, you must look at the whole hand and palm before making any descisions as to the character of this person.

# Displaced Mount of the Moon

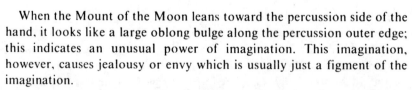

When the Mount of the Moon is displaced toward the center of the palm to the Plain of Mars, it adds aggressiveness to this person's imagination and gives them the power to influence people and situations. It can be a good aspect as well, for they will have an alert mind, and with a good imagination it will help them toward making a success of their life.

When the Mount of the Moon leans toward the percussion side of the hand, it looks like a large oblong bulge along the percussion outer edge; this indicates an unusual power of imagination. This imagination, however, causes jealousy or envy which is usually just a figment of the imagination.

These people will have a wonderful opportunity to become wealthy, especially if they follow their natural instincts in business.

If the Mount of the Moon is very displaced and encroaches upon the boundary of the Mount of Venus, this person becomes very emotional and their imagination causes fantasies which they will be unable to control.

When the Mount of the Moon is displaced toward the Upper Mount of Mars, it indicates an active imagination, creative talent and the love of harmony. These people have inventive ability and have control of their creative and imaginative minds.

## Health of the Lunarian

The health of Lunarians is not endowed with too much stamina. Sluggish and indifferent by temperment, they are unable to stand hard work or long hours. They are constantly reminded of their need to preserve their energy and to take care of their health and well-being. They suffer from nervous fears usually caused by matters concerning their health, and in extreme cases they can be given to hallucinations and acute forms of anxiety.

They have a tendency to suffer from intestinal, rheumatic and bladder problems.

The color of the Mount of the Moon is important. If the color of the area should be mottled, marked with spots or streaks of different colors, or blotched, it will reflect any abnormality of the sex organs and any abnormal enlargement of the pelvic area; this will inflame the Mount.

# Signs and Markings on the Mount of the Moon

A Star on the Mount of the Moon indicates a brilliant imagination.

A Circle or Cross on the Mount of the Moon is a warning against the risk of danger or accidents while travelling especially by water.

A Cross on the Mount of the Moon also indicates that this person will go to extemes easily, they are excitable and have exaggerated views of most things.

A Square is a good sign to have on the Mount of the Moon, it protects against travel risks, and if it appears to cover a Circle or Cross it helps greatly to lessen its harmful effects.

A Grille on the Mount of the Moon is considered very bad; it is a sign of illness, this person tends to be worrier and has imaginary fears.

If there is a Grille on the Mount of the Moon and also on the Mount of Venus, the combination will make this person very sensitive and always in a state of nervous irritation. These people are sad and discontented without cause, and tend to magnify any trivial annoyance into gigantic troubles making them difficult to live with.

A Triangle on the Mount of the Moon is a good sign. It indicates that these people are creative and will have success in their lives, especially if they are writers or artists.

If a Whorl is seen on the palm near the joining of the Mount of the Moon and the Upper Mount of Mars, these patterns which are often seen, have a pattern or ridge that resembles a fingerprint. If one of these whorls is  present, this person will have an understanding heart. This mark is nearly always found on the hands of ministers, counselors and doctors. This apex or ridges join the characteristics of the two mounts it touches and gives it added power.

# The Mount of Pluto

The Mount of Pluto has been recently recognized and studied. It makes up the third section of the Mount of the Moon located between the Bracelets and the lower area of the Mount of the Moon at the base of the palm on the percussion side of the hand which represents the deep subconscious area of the mind. It indicates life, death and regeneration. They have a reserve strength and memory of ancient truths or ancient knowledge. It can signify an interest in the occult and the metaphysical world. If the Mount of Pluto is flat, this person may be creative, but have no interest in the occult or metaphysics.

If the Mount of Pluto is well-developed, it emphasizes the power of imagination and the talent for the occult.

A highly developed Mount of Pluto is rare. The mount must bulge upward and outward in order for it to be considered highly developed. If found, it indicates qualities of mystery and secrecy. This person's love for intrigue is very strong; they could easily become involved with spying. They have a great imagination and sexual fantasy.

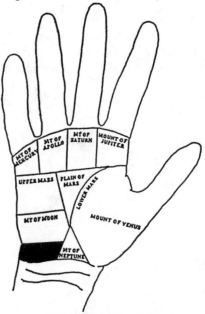

**The Mount of Pluto**

# Signs and Markings on the Mount of Pluto

A Triangle on the Mount of Pluto adds to the power of imagination and creativity in the occult.

A Grille on the Mount of Pluto could indicate the inherent psychic power and the need to develop their own inner security.

The Line of Intuition on the Mount of Pluto indicates a true psychic person.

The psychic hand will have a high Mount of Pluto and a high Mount of Neptune , with the Ring of Solomon, the Mystic Cross, a Bow Line of Intuition

# The Mount of Neptune

The Mount of Neptune has been recognized only recently. The Mount does not have any true boundaries. It is shaped like a triangle in the center of the lower area of the palm next to the wrist, with a distinct hollow between the Mount of Venus and the Mount of the Moon touching the Mount of Pluto. Its effect when present is strong. The life forces seem to flow freely through owner, that a magnetism is given out. These formations are found on the hands of doctors, nurses, and less orthodox healers, and all who make people feel better when they enter the room. No public speaker can project themselves across the footlights without the Mount of Neptune. When the Mount is very prominent, the person can give pleasure, no matter what they are reciting.

The Mount of Neptune represents the dividing line between the conscious and the unconscious zones of the hand. When the mount is well-developed, these people are very interested in mysticism, extra-sensory perception, spirituality and psychic power. Their instinct, rather than logic, will guide their lives. With their love for mysticism and spirituality, you will find their library filled with well read books on these subjects. They have psychic talent and a good ability to communicate on the extra-sensory level. They love speaking to groups and giving lectures, and they will captivate their audiences. They make good actors. By reading both palms, you can determine the degree of the Mount's strength.

There is a negative side to the Mount of Neptune; it can be camouflage and deception.

**The Mount of Neptune**

182

# Signs and Markings on the Mount of Neptune

A Circle, Star or Triangle on the Mount of Neptune adds intuitive musical and artistic talents to this person's abilities and are good signs to have on this Mount.

A Cross or Grille are not good signs. If either sign is on the Mount of Neptune, it indicates that this person may have problems with drugs or alcohol. They should be advised to seek counseling for themselves and with their unusual talent they should help other people in rehabilitation programs.

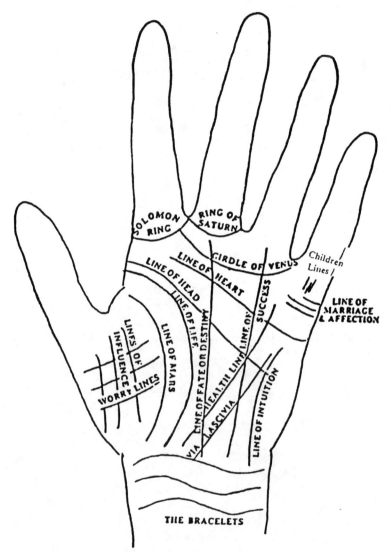

**Lines on the Hand - Cheiromancy**

# Lines on the Hand - Cheiromancy

**CHIEROMANCY** is the study of the Lines of the Hand; The Map of Our Life. It has been proven over and over again that certain marks and lines on the palm of the hand with other signs, indicate past, present and future.

I do not believe the lines on the hand appear by accident nor are they caused by the constant folding of the hand. Books on anatomy call them "Flexure Lines," and suggest that they are simply the folding of the flesh of the palm. You can have fun challenging such a statement by asking for a demonstration of the movements causing them, such as, a Star in the palm. I believe that the flesh of the hand folds where the lines have made an easy path; The Map of Our Life. Every line, sign or marking on the palm has its own meaning.

Palmists believe that there is a natural position for each of the lines and any change in their natural position must be read very carefully. It is important to understand that the lines on the palm of the hand are the energy level and potential of their owners life. Generally the more lines a person has on their palm, the more interesting life that he or she will have. The condition and position of the line must be taken into consideration. If there are only the three basic lines on the palm of the hand, the Heart, the Head and the Life Line, their owner will lead a basic life with little or no great ambition. If these people, however, find a partner with great potential, they can achieve great things together. You've heard about the "woman behind the man" and, of course, the "man behind the woman"

The lines on the palms of the hands form a natural guide to our lives. They can help us choose our direction. We can protect ourselves when we see problems in our future. They can help us understand our physical constitution, our mental and emotional characteristics, sexuality, creative ability, relationships, healing ability and psychic power; our past, present and future.

The lines and markings in the palm of our hands can change. They can be affected by our attitude and behavior. Learning to meditate can help our nerves. Stopping smoking can help our heart and general health. Changing our diet we all know will help us live longer and better. Taking the time and energy to communicate with our loved ones can help us to work out problems in a relationship. It can help us to learn to control our temper. All these things and more can change the lines on our palms. We will always have free will but we must also take personal responsibility for our life and its direction.

No two hands are alike. Each and every variation has its own meaning. For me to attempt to draw diagrams of all the variations of the lines and their meaning would be an impossible task. I will, however, try to illustrate as many as possible in hopes that this reference book will offer you all the help you will need.

When reading the lines of the palm, you will first notice the character, strength of each line, its clearness, color, depth and, eveness. The lines should be of medium depth and width, for example, deep lines denote intensity, wide lines denote overactivity and very fine lines indicate a lack of physical strength. Few lines indicate an ability to work without worry. Many lines denote many interests, but can also mean nerves, tension and conflicts. A frayed line with little lines on it weakens the value of the main lines. A chained line will show a period of an illness. A broken line can mean a change. A forked line can be at the beginning or end of the line and can draw help from the area of the mount at which it is located. A split line shows weakening influence. Think of the lines as electric currents flowing in and out through the finger ends. The cleaner the lines are the easier for the currents to flow.

## Changing Lines

Can lines change? Yes!
There are thousands of cases on record where people have decided to change their lives and the condition of their health. While they are accomplishing their goals the lines change.

# Basic Lines

The lines of the Heart, Head, and Life are Major Lines. They are the three basic lines on the palm of the hand.

**The Heart Line**

**The Head Line**

**The Life Line**

These three lines are not only found on almost every palm but represent the three fundamentals of our existence. However there are palms which have only two lines. The Heart and Head Lines have combined to form one, called the Simian Line, which I will explain later in this book. Palmists believe that the basic lines and the other major lines are developed in the first sixteen weeks of conception. They are our genetic record and reflect all that comes with us, our coloring, the shape of our body, hands, vitality, health, temperament and intelligence.

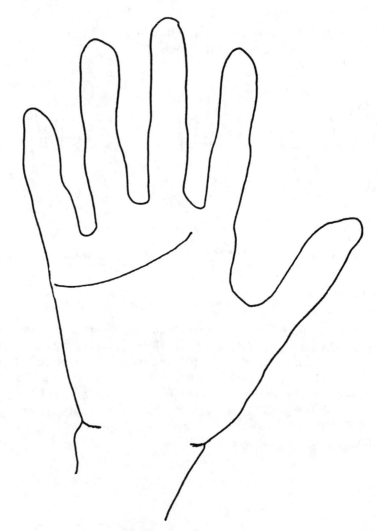

**The Heart Line**

# THE MAJOR LINES

## The Heart Line

In my efforts to make this book live up to its name, I will try to bring you up to date on all new discoveries in my research of Palmistry. The Heart Line is also known as the Line of Emotion. Until recently Palmists have realized that the line should start under the little finger by the Mount of Mercury and travel horizontally across the palm toward the Mount of Apollo, Mount of Saturn and sometimes to the Mount of Jupiter. I was always confused about this line when studying Palmistry, for I did not agree with the older studies. I am now happy to be able to state that the modern version is acceptable not only to myself, but to my colleagues. The older versions have the Heart Line starting on the opposite side of the palm by the Mount of Jupiter under the index finger. You will still see this reference in some books.

As its name suggests the Heart Line gives us information accurately about the condition of the heart as an organ as well as the nature of our feelings, our sensitivity, our moods, emotional life, sex life, and our generosity to others. I am not speaking of material things but of ourselves and the help and love we give to others willingly.

Although the Heart Line is one of the three basic lines, it is not always present. The line can be faint and broken, or it can merge completely with the Head Line. This merging line is called the Simian Line which I will discuss and illustrate later in this chapter.

The quality of the Heart Line is, of course, very important. The formation of the Heart Line should be clear, deep, neither too broad or too narrow and of good clear color. This indicates, love of family, human sympathy, sexuality and jealousy, affection, loyalty, emotional and good physical qualities - A healthy heart with a good blood supply.

# Variations on the Heart Line

The Heart Line starts at the percussion side of the palm under the Mercury finger, on the Mount of Mercury, and runs across the palm of the hand towards the Mount of Jupiter and under the Jupiter or Apollo finger

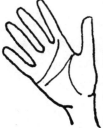

The Heart Line can be absent. Some hands have a Heart Line and Head Line joining as one line. You will never see a hand without a Head Line. When the Heart Line is missing, it indicates a lack of sympathy and affection, and shows a person who can be cold-blooded, selfish and who desires personal success, even at the expense of others. It is not known as a good marking. Be sure to look at both hands before making any statements.

When the Heart Line curves up toward the Mount of Jupiter under the base of the Jupiter finger, these people love too much showing an adoration toward their loved ones. They are very giving, not only of material things, but of themselves. They will always be there when needed and give of their time and energy to help others.

When the Heart Line curves up between the Mount of Jupiter and Saturn at the base of these fingers, this indicates a sentimental person, but one who shows a little more common sense when dealing with loved ones. The curve of the line is still an exaggeration of the Heart Line, which also makes them generous and caring.

When the Heart Line curves up toward the Mount of Saturn under the Saturn finger, it indicates sensuality. This person is interested in the pleasure from sexual relations and physical desires rather than love.

When the Heart Line has three branches, one running to the Mount of Jupiter, one to the Mount of Saturn, and one between the Mounts of Jupiter and Saturn, it indicates the union of sentiment, sensuality, common sense and passion, also indicating that this person will be ruled more by their emotions than their head.

When the Heart Line ends close to the Head Line, this indicates the Head Line is too powerful and when it comes to a decision or judgment, their head will dominate. This is especially true if the Head Line is deeper and clearer than the Heart Line.

The length of the Heart Line is important. It will indicate too little or too much heart. If a Heart Line runs only a short distance and stops, it indicates that this person will have serious difficulty at the time the Heart Line ends, even if all the other major lines go on to their normal length. This abrupt termination of the Heart Line means either that the heart will stop beating or else that this person has little heart or affection for others. It is a poor sign. You must look at both hands before making any statement.

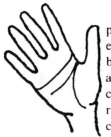

If the Heart Line crosses the entire palm of the hand, it indicates that the person has too much heart and will allow sentiment to guide them in everything. In business they will hire someone because they need a job, not because they would be suitable for the work. They become jealous easily and love too much. They suffer if this love is not returned. This is not considered a really good sign because of its extremes. These people are ruled by sentiment and cannot cope with or understand schemers. They are considered impractical; they have too much heart.

If the Heart Line curves upward to the Mount of Mercury, then continues across the palm, this indicates the influence of the Mount will be very strong at that age and time, and they will love the qualities of a person belonging to this Mercury type. In this case a person with good business sense, who loves to communicate, is interested in medicine and science.

If the Heart Line curves upwards to the Mount of Apollo then continues across the palm, this person will love the qualities of a person belonging to the Apollo type at that point in their life; a creative successful person with a love of art and a happy personality.

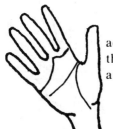

If the Heart Line curves upwards to the Mount of Saturn, then continues across the palm, this person will love the qualities of a person belonging to the Saturn type at that point in their life; a serious, wise, superstitious and ambitious person.

If the Heart Line curves upward to the Mount of Jupiter, this person will love the qualities of a person belonging to the Jupiter type at that point in their life; a religious, ambitious and philosophical person with a love of nature.

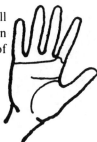

If the Heart Line dips downward toward the Head Line, it indicates that this person will make decisions mentally rather than emotionally, as the Head Line will have a strong influence. At the time the Heart Line dips toward the Head Line, it can cause indifference, greed, selfishness and cold heartedness towards others.

If the Heart Line ends in the Head Line, it indicates that the Heart Line has lost all of its values and this person will be totally dominated by their head.

If the Heart Line deflects down to the Head Line and regains itself and continues on its course, it indicates that there is still left a portion of their former affectioinate personality and that mental and wordly interests have not entirely overcome their heart and sentiment. However, these people will always be strongly influenced by their head rather than their heart.

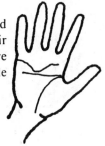

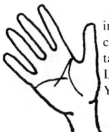

If the Heart Line deflects downward and cuts the Head Line in two instead of merging with it or going back to its original course, this will cause serious injury and damage to the Head Line. Such a marking can not take place without disaster. It indicates that the time the line cuts the Head Line, it will cause a mental breakdown, serious brain fever and even death. You must look at both hands before making any statement.

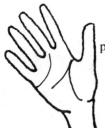

If the Heart Line ends under the Line of Saturn, it indicates that this person tends to have a cold nature and a dislike for mankind.

If the Heart Line ends under the Mount of Apollo, it indicates that this person is strongly attracted to someone with Apollonian qualities, and would be happier with this type person in marriage.

If the Heart Line begins high on the Mount of Mercury, it indicates that this person's affections are influenced by finances. They must always have money in sight before love is recognized.

If the Heart Line is defective and does not run its natural course on the palm, both hands must be studied. When you see a Heart Line that attaches itself to the Head Line in a short line, it indicates that this person tends to be cold and heartless and the line should be read as if the Heart Line is absent. This line going to the Mount of Jupiter indicates a very ambitious person who will never worry about the welfare of others when furthering their own ambitions.

If the Heart Line is defective and does not run its natural course on the palm, and starts on the Mount of Jupiter and attaches itself toward the middle of the Head Line, it indicates this person will not become extremely cold or heartless until the middle of life.

If the Heart Line leaves too wide a space under the mounts, this person will be attracted to the Martian type lover. They will love ardently with a strong, curt and blunt manner. This line also produces a narrow quadrangle, giving this person a secretive nature.

If the Heart Line starts low on the Mount of the Moon it indicates an extremely jealous nature. By starting in this unusual area on the Mount of Moon this persons imagination will magnify every act of the one they love, imagining unfaithfulness. This is not a good sign to have.

If the Heart Line forms a curve that ends on the Plain of Mars cutting the Head Line, it can be a serious problem. The Plain of Mars shows temper and excitability and will endanger life by cutting the Head Line. This person will be extremely irritable and changeable in their affections, constantly looking for excitement; they are hard to get along with.

If the Heart Line curves and ends on the Mount of Venus and cuts both the Head and Life Line, it is a serious threat to life. This is a rare marking. Carefully note the condition of the lines where the Heart Line was cut and the condition of the Head and Life Lines afterwards. If there are defects on either of the lines, you will know damage has been done. If the Life Line ends or fades soon after, you will know that life will terminate. Again, I must caution you about making any statement of death at any time.

If the Heart Line has a branch rising from it to the Mount of Jupiter, it indicates that this person's ambition will guide their love and they will be attracted to someone with Jupiterian qualities, they would not necessarily have to have money, but someone with a promising career.

If the Heart Line has a branch rising to the Mount of Saturn, it indicates that this person will be attracted to someone of Saturnian qualities such as, scholarly, scientific, mining or horticultural aptitudes. They love a person who is sober, cautious and has wisdom.

If the Heart Line has a branch rising from it to the Mount of Apollo, they will be drawn to a person with Apollonian qualities such as an artist, one who dresses in a showy fashion or one who has a talent for making money.

If the Heart Line has a branch to the Mount of Mercury, this person will love the qualities of the Mercurian such as, an eloquent speaker, someone who can make money, and they will be influenced by the amount of money their lover has or has the ability to make.

If the Heart Line has small descending lines that fall from it, it indicates a conflict between the heart and the head. The Head Line will became a very strong influence. These descending or falling lines were read by old Palmists as an indication of "love-sorrows and disappointments" I can understand this reasoning, for if one loves, but allows the head to rule and reasons that the one they love is not as good a match as someone else they will have "love-sorrows and disappoitments", for their calculations of the head has stifled their sentiment.

If the Heart Line has a large, strong branch line falling to the Head Line and merging itself into the line, this indicates that the heart has surrendered and this person will be ruled by their head. The age or time is indicated at the point the branch splits away from the Heart Line and merges into the Head Line.

Breaks in the Heart Line even though small must always be considered serious When they are wide or end in a broken line and are far apart or unrepaired, they become serious enough to indicate a fatality. When there is a break of any size always look for a repair sign.

If there is a break in the Heart Line under the Mount of Jupiter, it indicates health problems to the heart will be caused by overeating that will produce a functional heart disturbance. If not a health problem, then the break in the Heart Line will indicate a problem of too much ambition or pride.

If there is a break in the Heart Line on the Mount of Saturn, first look for health defects. this break in the Heart Line could mean gout or rheumatism complicated with a heart problem. Look to the Life Line to see how serious this may become. If the break is not a health problem, this person's depression, negative attitude and restrictions will be the cause of their problem at this time in their life.

If the Heart Line breaks under the Mount of Apollo, it will be nearly conclusive proof that the break on the Heart Line will be a heart problem. This defect is an Apollonian trait. If it is not a health problem, the break on the Mount of Apollo will indicate a lack of self respect, lost potential or dependence on others.

If the Heart Line has many breaks, this person has either had constant recurrences of weakness to the heart or they have suffered from many broken love affairs. If the breaks are close together, they will most likely have heart failure.

If the Heart Line has breaks that are close together and these broken lines turn down instead of rising to the Mounts, then the Head Line of this person will have a strong influence at the time the breaks occur and cold reasoning will fight against warm, loving sentiment. If the broken ends are short, the Head Line will not rule completely.

If the Heart Line has breaks that merge into the Head Line, reason controls sentiment. If the break is wide at the time, this person never entirely overcomes it; if the break is narrow they can overcome the coldness, however, they will be unhappy at this time. By noting each break, you will be able to estimate the age these events occur, and by noting where the end of the broken line merges into the Head Line, you can tell what has caused the problem.

When the Heart Line has a broken line that drops and sharply cuts the Head Line, the cause of the break can be from either health or emotional problems; this break will seriously impair the Head Line at the time the Heart Line crosses it.

# Signs and Markings on the Heart Line

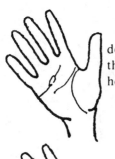

If there are Islands on the Heart Line, they are always considered a defect. They obstruct, weaken and often indicate a weak physical action of the heart. The size of an Island will indicate how serious the problem is and how long the problem will last.

When an Island is located under the Mount of Apollo it becomes more serious than any other location on the Heart Line.

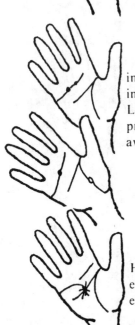

Dots on the Heart Line are generally health defects and their size will indicate the degree of seriousness of the health problem. If there are no indications of health problems on both hands but a small Dot on the Heart Line, it will not be considered serious. However, if there are health problems it becomes a serious difficulty and this person must become aware of impending problems and take better care of themselves.

When the Heart Line has a break and drops down and sharply cuts the Head Line and if the line has a Star at the junction of the two lines, an explosion will occur in the head which can be caused by either an emotional upset or ill health.

If the Heart Line has a break and drops down, sharply cuts the Head Line and if the line has an Island at the junction of the two lines this person's head will be left in a weakened condition afterwards; the length of this weakness will be determined by the size of the Island and at the time or age the Island appears in the Head Line.

If there is a break in the Heart Line and the line becomes Chained, it indicates that the heart will never fully recover from whatever caused the break.

If after there is a break in the Heart Line, and the line has an Island or Islands, it will indicate that this person will be weak and in delicate health during the time the Islands appear on the Heart Line.

When the Heart Line has a break and a Star is filling the break area, this person will die suddenly or have a very serious heart attack at the age the Star appears. This sign will be more dangerous if the Star is under the Mount of Apollo.

When the Heart Line has a Star and the line continues with a Chained Line these people will have a severe heart attack from which they will never recover.

When the Heart Line has a Star and after the Star the Heart Line becomes thin and narrow, the illness or emotional problem shown by the Star will destroy the vigor of this person's heart. The heart will always be weak and their affections will become cold and their views selfish and narrow.

When the Heart Line has a break and is cut by a Cross-bar at both ends of the line, which is a very serious defect, it can have a repair marking helping it. A Square can make this repair by forming a box on the line. Though a heart attack will be serious, the Square during the time of the break will help the Heart Line repair itself and the Cross-bar becomes less of a threat.

If the Heart Line has a break and is cut by a Cross-bar at both ends of the line, death from heart disease will occur.

When a Heart Line has a break and is cut by a Cross-bar, it is a bad sign and a sudden death or heart failure will occur in most cases.

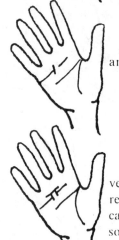

If the Heart Line has a break and is cut by a Cross-bar on both ends it is a very serious defect, however, it can be helped or repaired. One of the best repairs would be a Sister Line joining the ends of the Cross-bar. In this case, this would be danger of a heart attack, but the Sister could help repair some of the damage to the Heart Line.

Cross-bars cutting the Heart Line can cause constant heart irritation, either illness or worries over the affection of their loved ones. To understand the problem, look to both hands to see if you can locate any health defects. If not, the Cross-bars will apply to their affections. If the Cross-bars are little lines they indicate temporary heart problems of a functional character; if they are very deep, they become serious. If the Cross-bars cut the Heart Line in many places, it shows that the trouble will be continuous. If there is heart disease, it indicates palpitations and valvular difficulties. This is not a good sign. If the Cross-bars do not relate to disease, then there will be constant problems with this person's affections at the time and age the Cross-bars show on the Heart Line.

When a Heart Line has a break with a Dot at the end of the break, it indicates a serious heart attack will occur at the time the Dot appears. A very large, deep Dot indicates a fatal attack; a small Dot indicates a serious illness which can be overcome.

When a Star is seen on the Heart Line, you must understand its location before making any statements. It can be caused by illness or emotions. If illness, then it will be heart disease; a severe attack if the Star is small but poorly formed. If the Star is under the Mount of Saturn, it will add the complication of rheumatism of the heart. If the Star is large and well formed with the center exactly on the line, it will cause an explosion, sudden heart failure, at the age or time the Star appears.

When the Heart Line has a Star and the line continues with an Island on it, this person will have a severe heart attack with a weakness and delicacy afterwards. Only when the line becomes strong again will they overcome the heart attack.

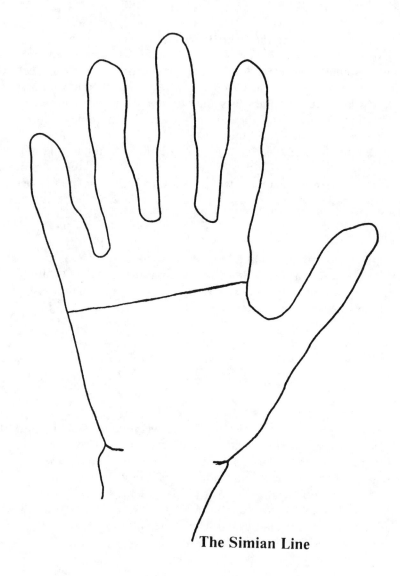

**The Simian Line**

# The Simian Line

When the Head Line unite into one line with the Heart Line above and then forming one line accross the Palm toward the percussion side of the hand. This formation is called the Simian Line. This is a rarely seen sign and not a good sign to have. One of the more clearly visible and easy to be seen signs in a persons hand is the development from two lines in the palm of the hand of the Ape or Primates palm, to the three lines of the palm in our hands. It would be wrong to state that the Simian Line in our hand eliminates the Heart Line on the contrary both the Heart Line and the Head Line have joined.

The first scientist to notice this peculiarity or irregularity in our lines was F. Wood Jones who is responsible for naming it the "Simian Line" pattern.

In most cases the Simian Line is seen in one hand only. When it does occur in both hands. They can expect its effect to be doubled and reinforce the qualities of the line. This line is by no means seen in the hand in only one race or personality. The line is called a "Sacred Line" by the Chinese and Japanese. Because the Simian Line is rarely seen. The line can be on intelligent people although they are just a little different.

Some of the typical characteristics of this line can be a violent temper, lack of self-control and an inability to fit into any community.

Although many of my fellow Palmists believe the Simian Line indicates suicidal tendencies. I do not totally agree in all the negative aspects of the line. They can be erratic and unpredictable, lack self control but they are not necessarily violent to others or themselves.

The Simian Line shows concentrative power. A person with this line expends all their energy on one thing at a time. Once they have decided that they want a thing they will not rest until they have obtained their ambition. If interested in a task they will appear to forget everything else until they have completed their task.

Their desire for personal gratification is unlimited. Their sexual tendencies are both physical and sensuous. They love with the same intensity, so their partners must identify themselves with their careers and hobbies in order to find any companionship or happiness. At times they are either very sentimental or emotional. At other times very practical even to the point of rudeness.

# Variations of the Simian Line

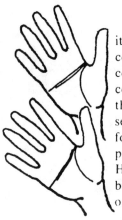

If the Heart Line leaves its natural place and unites with the Head Line, it becomes a Simian Line. This person will have great powers of concentration. They will have great intensity of purpose, but very little compassion. This Simian Line is not a happy sign. Because of their lack of compassion, they will have little or no companionship, which will cause them to be lonely and feel isolated from others. They are usually very sensitive and have their feelings continually hurt. It is not a sign of success for they tend to be loners and do not get along with others in their professions. Because of the Simian Line location, close to or joining the Head Line, this person has very little heart or emotional feelings. Look at both hands before forming any opinions; the Simian Line may be in only one hand.

If the Heart Line leaves its natural place and the Head Line joins the Heart Line in a higher position more toward the base of the fingers of the hand, the Simian Line can be tempered and this person can have a little more compassion and be able to show emotions, affection and feelings, and their mental control will be less intense.

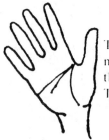

The Simian Line, if joined to the Head Line, adds great determination. These people want their own way and they can be very stubborn. Once they make up their mind they want something, they will not rest until they attain their ambition. Their sexual tendencies are both physical and sensuous. They have great desire for personal gratification.

When the Simian Line joins the Head Line, these people have a definite control of their decisions and ambitions. These people are logical and have good forethought and calculations, although they do have the ability to act on sheer impulse without forethought.

Children with the Simian Line are often thought of as difficult. These children are inclined to have unexpected changes. They do not find it easy to compromise. Their personal desires are more important to them than the acceptance of their peers. It can cause them emotional inner conflicts and clashes at home and in school.

When the Simian Line is seen on the palm, these people can make a decision and stick to it tenaciously; they can be tough to live with. They are "a law unto themselves", you either go their way or they will leave you behind.

When the Simian Line joins the Head Line at the center of the palm, it makes it very difficult for this person. Their Head Line has overtaken their emotions and they will have a tendency to become cold towards their loved ones with their own gratification becoming more important.

At times the decisions and ambitions of these people are calculated and logical while at others times they are emotional, impulsive and without forethought. They often change their minds and reverse their decisions. They are the most difficult people to deal with and just as difficult to live with; they are a law unto themselves.

The word "Simian" from the Dictionary pertaining to, resembling or characteristic of apes and monkeys.

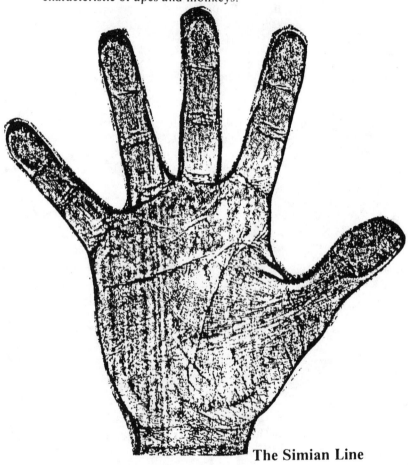

**The Simian Line**

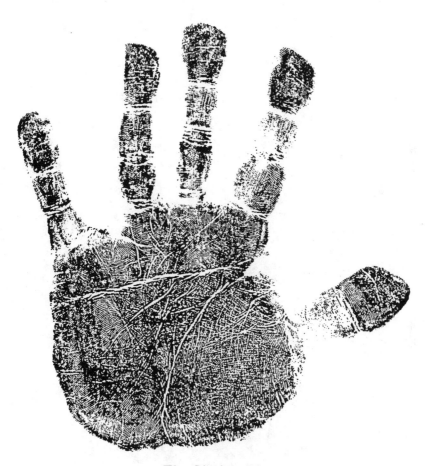

### The Simian Line
Note: The Girdle of Venus on these hands

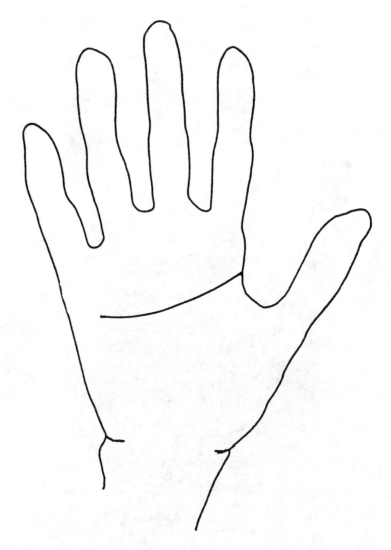

**The Head Line**

# The Head Line

The Head Line also known as the Mentality Line or Cerebral Line will be found at the beginning of the Life Line under the index finger, at the thumb side of the palm, and runs horizontally across the palm towards the percussion edge or edge of the palm of the hand under the little finger. The most common beginning of the Head Line is interlocked with the Life Line, because of the controlled environment we usually live in as an infant and young child.

The Head Line is one of the most important signs on the hand. Your client may have a good Fate or Success Line but unless the Head Line is strong and clear they may not be able to carry out their destiny.

The Head Line is the indicator of the mental balance, control, interests and the depth of our lives. Our ability to concentrate, the degree of intelligence, creative imagination, including memory. This line is also a great controller of our nature.

When reading the hands you must always pay attention to the lines in both palms of the hand. They must be compared. The left hand showing their inherited tendencies, the right hand the development and cultivated qualities, assuming your client is right handed. Any differance or even the slightest change in the lines should be read and discussed with your client.

Let me mention here and will repeat through out the book I will endeavor to illustrate as many variations as simply and clearly as possible so you will be able to recognize the lines signs and markings, and understand their meanings. When reading the lines in the hand of your client, you must remember if the lines, signs or markings are different in their hands. They then have a decision to which path in life they will choose to take.

When reading the Head Line study the quality of the line. The best Head Line is clear, reddish in color and deep. When you find the line in this good condition it will indicate an ability to concentrate, sound judgment, a good memory, vigorous and clear thought.

I have never seen a hand without a Head Line. Even in the hands of the retarded, the mongoloid or those with learning disabilities there is always a sign if only a brief Head Line. You must remember the Head Line not only tells of mentality and intellectual development, but of illness and disease that may effect the brain or head.

# Variations of the Head Line

The Head Line should not run to the percussion, but toward that side of the hand. The length of the line indicates the mentality of the person, the shape and character of the line will indicate the person's mental abilities and the condition of their mental health or any accident to the head.

When the Head Line is short it indicates that this person does not have a strong mentality. You must look at both hands before reading any futher. Look at the Life Line if it also is a short line it will indicate a short life. It may also show up on the Heart Line.

If the Head Line is short and the Life Line is the same length as the Head Line, death is certain.

When there is a wide space between the Head and Life Lines the person is born self-reliant. They can be anti-establishment or even a rebel if the Head Line is half way or more to the base of the Mount of Jupiter. This persons independence is carried to the extreme. Instead of being independent this can make them cold, selfish and even deceitful. They do not enjoy the company of others or even animals and have little sensitivity of the little pleasures of life.

When the Head and Life Lines show a small gap between them, it indicates that this persons independence comes early in life. They are not afraid to stand alone. They are self contained and self starters. If they have an ambitious nature they are likely to achieve it without outside help.

If the Head Line does not leave the Life Line until past twenty it indicates that mental activity begins later in life: this also indicates a person whose perception may be dull. They don't understand when people slight them. Study the shape of the fingertips, if they are square or spatulate and the fingers and the palm of the hands are thick and red, this person will be very dense. If they have only the three basic lines, Head, Heart and Life, it indicates an elementary heaviness of intellect. These people will be cautious, non-committal, dependent on others, lacking an ability to command, blunt and at times tactless.

When the Head and Life Line are joined at the time of birth it indicates early timidity, shyness and overly dependent on their parents and always wanting to please them.

When the Head and Life Lines are joined past infancy into the twenties it indicates parental domination to the time showing on the Life Line. You must read both hands and all other signs to determine whether this is good or bad for them.

If the Head Line extends across the entire hand toward the percussion in a straight line. With a normal Heart Line, it shows a superiority of the mentality and this person will be out of balance. They will be greedy grasping and stingy. They view all things from a totally mental standpoint, they are not sentimental but practical in all things.

When the Head Line is distinctly separated from the Life Line it indicates self reliance. These people are original, not bound to the views of others, think for themselves and do not have to depend on anyone, have good judgement, and are independent. This is a good marking if the separation is not too wide.

When the Head Line starts inside the Life Line on the Lower Mount of Mars then crossing the Life Line across the palm of the hand, these people sway one way and then the other, always vascillating. They start many things with enthusiasm and a lively interest. They are always intense in their views and continually changing their minds. Because it is hard for them to stick to one thing, they are rarely successful. When the Head Line starts at the Lower Mount of Mars these people pick quarrels and are frequently in trouble.

When the Head Line starts on the Mount of Jupiter it indicates the capability for leadership, they are self confident, and have a strong mentality. These people are diplomatic and it helps them deal with delicate situations. They are brainy, brilliant and successful.

If the Head Line starts at the Life Line but a branch runs to the Mount of 'upiter. These people are ambitious and desire to be great or famous. They will always try for the better things in life.

When the Head Line runs straight across the palm of the hand. These people have fixed ideas, they are evenly balanced mentally, practical, use common sense and outside influences have very little effect on them. They see the practical side. They are however, too rigid, unimpressionable, and it is very hard for them to adopt.

When the Head Line curves under the base of the Mount of Saturn, this person will love to study and do research.

When the Head Line curves toward the Mount of Apollo. These people love art and beauty. They enjoy pleasure and gayety.

When the Head Line curves toward the Mount of Mercury. These people can be very persuasive, good communicators of their opinion, elegant orators, love public speaking. They have strong minds and would make good physicians, scientific investigators, teachers or lawyers.

When you find a wavy Head Line it indicates a lack of continuous mental ability in any one direction; these people are changeable in their purpose in life, they are not self reliant. It is an unstable line and indicates unstable ideas.

When the Head Line curves upwards toward the Heart Line this indicates the heart is a stronger factor in this persons life than the head, their emotion will rule them and they are very sentimental.

When the Head Line curves downward, it shows a person that is impractical, with a great imagination. They are strongly impressed with the psychic phenomena. This line has been seen on the hands of Spiritualists.

If the whole Head Line is curved either up or down, there is a conflict between this person's desire to be practical and the desire to indulge in impractical and imaginative things. If the line straightens near the end, they can become practical toward the middle or end of their life.

If the Head Line begins deep and well defined and the center of the line becomes thin, with the end of the line chained, this person was born with a healthy vigorous mind, which then becomes weak and finally impaired by an illness or accident. Look at both hands and study the other lines and signs to determine the cause.

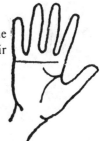

If the Head Line is very short, this person has a weak mentality or the termination of their life will be at an early age by death or the loss of their mind.

If the Head Line is short and runs upward on to the Mount of Saturn, this person will have a health defect which will cause their death at an early age. Because this is the Head Line, the cause of death woud be something effecting the head and the brain, this being a Saturn influence, paralysis could also be the cause of death.

If the Head Line is short and turns upwards toward the Mount of Apollo and the Heart Line, it is an indication that this person is not especially strong. Because the Heart Line runs upwards but not long enough to reach the Mount of Opollo or the Heart Line, they allow their heart or sentiments to rule their reasoning.

When the Head Line runs to the Heart Line and merges with it, this person allows their feelings to overcome their judgement. Palmist have read this marking as an indication that this person has criminal tendencies. It does show that if the emotions, the sentiments, feelings or desires are aroused they will lose self control and often commit a crime.

If the Head Line runs through the Heart Line to the Mount of Apollo to the base of the Apollo finger, it indicates a complication of the heart and a disorder in their mental health. It could cause a sudden loss of sensation, a brain hemorrhage known as apoplexy. At this point you must look at the color of their hands nails and the other lines in their palms.

When the Head Line goes clear up into the Mount of Mercury, it is a strong warning to the health of this person. There is a tendency toward biliousness, a stomach disorder and nervousness which effects the head and causes vertigo. Because this is at the end of their Head Line this person would be about seventy or older and it would be a weakening factor endangering their life.

When the Head Line runs into the Upper Mount of Mars it shows that this person has practical common-sense. They are under control and calm when facing a challenge.

If the Head Line slopes toward the Mount of the Moon it indicates that this person has great amount of imagination and tends to be impractical. If the Head Line is long and strong, they will be a sensible, self contained person that has a good imagination.

If the Head Line drops down low on the Mount of the Moon and ends in broken lines it is an indication of mental disturbance.

If the Head Line starts straight and then slopes downward to the Mount of the Moon this person will begin life with a very practical mind then change toward imaginative ideas when older, the time of the change can be read from the point where the slope in the Head Line begins. A violent change or marking on a line is not always the best, the change would be better if the line curved gracefully.

When the Head Line forms a Fork at the end, it indicates versatility. The person has good reasoning power, both practical and imaginative ideas. They can see things from a double point of view.

If the Head Line forms a large wide Fork at the end it indicates that this person has a strong practical side of them as well as a strong imagination. They can see things from both the practical and fanciful sides. They are never narrow minded because they can see both sides of a point of view.

If the Head Line has a Fork at its end with one of the lines running to the Upper Mars Mount, with this Fork again making an additional Fork running to the Mount of the Moon, this person has a double pointed imagination. Their imagination is so vivid that they may lie when the truth would be better. They possess such an enlarged imagination they magnify everything

If the Head Line has a Fork at its end with one of the lines running to the Upper Mars Mount with this Fork again making an additional Fork running to the Mount of the Moon. This person has a double pointed imagination, their imaginations are so vivid that they lie when the truth would be better. They possess such an enlarged imagination they magnify everything. When the Head Line divides into three Forks - one Fork running toward the Mount of Mercury, one toward the Mount of Mars and the other toward the Mount of the Moon. This is a very good sign to see on the hand, it shows a person with a diversity of intellect, adaptability, versatility, and imagination. They usually are successful and will achieve their goals.

A Head Line that curves around and ends on the Mount of Venus is a sign that is rarely seen it is usually long and clear it indicates a good mentality and by ending on the Mount of Venus this person will have a pleasant, healthy, happy and agreeable personality and are attractive people but their morality will become a problem at times.

When the Head Line is broad and shallow this person does not have physical or mental strength. They will never be robust. This line also indicates a person that is uncertain and lacks self reliance.

When the Head Line is broad and shallow at the start of the line, in the earlier years and then becomes clear and deep. This person was dependent at a young age and then became strong and the line changed to become stronger and deeper as they took charge of their life.

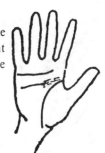

If the Head Line begins thin and then becomes deep along the line and then thin again. This is a dangerous sign. These people alternate between being intense, eager, full of enthusiasm and then into despair.

If the Head Line has many small lines that rise from it, this person wants to improve themselves and hopes to advance in life.

If the Head Line has many fairly large and long lines rising on it. This is not too good a sign. These people will be uncertain, they are influenced by too many things, they have trouble concentrating and their mind tends to waver. If the Head Line slopes toward the Mount of the Moon, they are also a day dreamer.

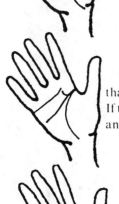

If the Head Line has many lines below it, this indicates that this person is easily discouraged, they have a negative attitude of life. They believe their failures are from bad luck. They seem to enjoy sorrow and disappointment.

If the Head Line has a line rising under the Mount of Jupiter, it indicates that this person is ambitious. They will want to achieve fame and fortune. If the Mount of Jupiter is large and full the person will have great ambition and pride in themselves.

If the Head Line has a line that rises under the Mount of Saturn this person's character will be sober, studious and they will have wisdom.

If the Head Line turns toward the Mount of Mercury this person will have a talent for making money. They would even ruin their health or make any sacrifice to obtain it. They are exacting, love a bargain, go miles to save a few pennies.Their life is measured by money value.

If the Head Line has a line that rises to the Mount of Apollo it indicates this person has a desire for wealth and fame. They are proud people with a love for art and beauty.

When the Head Line has a line rising from it to the Heart Line it indicates a person that is very sentimental and affectionate. Their love life is very important to them . They are unusually sympathetic and humane.

If the Head Line looks broken or ladder-like, this indicates that the person lacks stability; they tend to be fickle and tricky. They have poor health, headaches and see imaginary phantoms. They need help for they can become insane.

Breaks in the Head Line cause lack of concentration, lack of self control or illness. These people tend to be nervous, changable. Look at the other lines and nails for an indication of their problems.

A Head Line that is thin and then becomes very deep then becomes thin again indicates great mental exertion and times when the pressures of work or over-excitement will put too much pressure on the brain and cause a collapse and nervous prostration. This marking will often be found on the hands of active businessmen and professional people. The age of the person must be estimated when the markings are seen and a warning to ease up must be given.

The Medical Stigmata indicates a special aptitude for medicine. The sign is recognized by numerous small vertical lines on the Mount of Mercury. When the Head Line runs to the Heart Line it also indicates a strong desire to make money. These people have a talent for medical studies. These markings will be found in the palms of prominent and successful doctors. The Medical Stigmata also includes the talents and interests of nurses, diagnosticians, general practitioners and also occult scientists.

Another type of Double Lines of the Head is one where the main Head Line seems to separate about the middle of the palm of the hand and where one branch goes across the palm, the other descends towards the Mount of the Moon. This indicates the person has a double mental personality, but one which is more under the control of the will of the subject. The two Distant Double Lines indicate that the two mental personalities seem to act independently, one from the other. The Double Lines in both cases are a wonderful sign to have and will lead to wealth and success.

The Double Lines of the Head are very, very rarely seen. The persons that possess these lines are usually capable of an enormous amount of mental work and can carry out two separate mental lives with great success. The lines are often found with only the Head Line joined to the Life Line and the other starting from the Mount of Jupiter. This formation would indicate that one side of the person's nature is extremely sensitive and cautious. The other side is self-confident. The person with the Double Lines of the Head have a remarkable degree of mentality.

# Signs and Markings on the Head Line

When a Cross is seen at the end of the Head Line it indicates the stopping of the current of life, ending the mentality and causing death.

A Cross at the end of the Head and Life Line is read the same as the Stars. The Crosses stop the current and life cannot continue. You must look at both hands and try to determine the cause.

If the Head Line is short and runs upward on to the Mount of Saturn with a Tassel at the end. This person will suffer from paralysis. The Tassel indicates the gradual dissipation of their mental powers. A Tassel is not a sudden shock as a Star or Dot would be. Although there will be a short life, it will end gradually.

If the Head Line runs through the Heart Line to the Mount of Apollo to the base of the Apollo finger and there is a Star at the point where the two lines cross the danger is serious for an explosion is most likely to happen.

If the Head Line runs through to the Mount of Apollo to the base of the Apollo finger and there is a Star followed by an Island at the point where the two lines cross, the shock will permanently weaken the mind and cause brain fever.

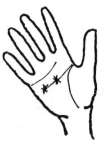

A thin Head Line that has Stars on the line will indicate danger of mental health and shows an explosion or break down will occur unless care is used.

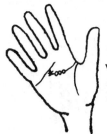

If the Head Line begins as a thin line, then becomes chained as it curves upwards with a Star at the end. This person began life with a weak mind, which was impaired by whatever caused the curve on the Head Line and will end in an explosion, indicated by the Star. This will show either insanity or death. You must look at both hands to determine which.

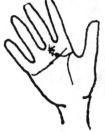

If the Head Line is short and runs upward on to the Mount of Saturn and ends in a Star, a Cross or a Dot the sudden termination of this persons mentality and life is assured. Because the line is on the Mount of Saturn paralysis would be the cause.

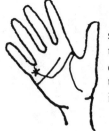

If the Head Line extends up into the Mount of Mercury, it indicates a strong warning regarding the health of this person. The danger is a tendency toward biliousness, a stomach disorder and nervousness which effects the head and causes vertigo; it is a weakening factor and danger to their life. If the Head Line has a Star at the end of the line, sudden death is indicated.

Please note: When seeing a sign of a person that may indicate death, there should NEVER be a prediction of death. No such prophesy should ever be made.

If the Head line droops low on the Mount of the Moon and ends with a Star, it indicates insanity.

When the Head Line droops low on the Mount of the Moon and ends in a Chained Line, it will indicate mental impairment and deterioration.

If the Head Line droops down low on the Mount of the Moon and ends with a Cross, it indicates a check or break to the mentality.

If the Head Line droops down low on the Mount of the Moon and ends with an Island, there is a danger of mental disturbance. The size of the Island will indicate the seriousness of the danger. Be sure to look at both hands for other signs of the trouble.

If the Head Line droops down low on the Mount of the Moon with a Dot at the end it will indicate a danger of mental disturbance. The size of the Dot will indicate how serious the condition will be.

If the Head Line has a Fork at its end with one of the lines running to the Upper Mars Mount with this Fork again making an additional Fork running to the Mount of the Moon and if the Fork on the Mount of the Moon has a Star or Dot at its end, it indicates that this person's enlarged imagination will cause insanity from over imagination and mental disease. When looking for additional signs or markings you will find this person will have Grilled and rayed lines on the Mount of the Moon.

If a Star is seen at the end of a short Head Line it is an indication of a sudden death, the Star is a sign of an explosion.

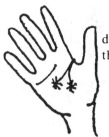

If Stars are seen at the end of the Head and Life Lines of the right hand death is certain, if seen only on the left hand life is threatened. The larger the Stars and the more well formed they are also indicates certain fatality.

A thin Head Line that has Crosses on the line indicates danger of mental health and shows an explosion or break down will occur at the age it appears on the Head Line; this warning must not be ignored.

If the Head Line has cuts or small lines crossing the line, it indicates danger points. If the cuts are small and frequent this person will suffer from headaches.

If the Head Line is thin and the cuts or small lines cutting the Head Line are deep this person will suffer brain fever, nervous prostration or paralysis. You must study both hands at this time. If the Head Line in the left hand is deep and strong and the Head Line in the right hand is thin, the head and brain will be strong but has been weakened and this person must be careful not to exert themselves. If the Head Line is thin in the left hand the person has increased their strength and will be able to overcome the effects of the cuts on their line.

A Chained Head Line is a bad indication. If it is not only broad and shallow but obstructed, this person's mentality will be weak and lacking in powers of concentration. They are timid, sensitive and changeable. They suffer from poor memories, poor judgement, headaches and various mental problems. It is hard for them to work because they do not know how to apply themselves.

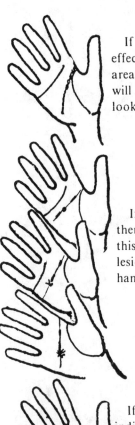

If the Head Line is Chained for a portion of the line, its weakening effects will only effect that part of the persons life at the age the chained area appears. If the line becomes clear and gradually grows stronger this will indicate the progress from their mental illness to a good life. Always look at both hands to make sure of the progress and how it will develop.

If the Head Line begins thin and then becomes deep along the line and then thin again; this is a dangerous sign. f a Star, Cross or Dot appears on this uneven Head Line, it indicates paralysis, a sudden loss of sensation, lesion of the brain that can be caused by a stroke. You must look to both hands and be sure to advise this person to seek medical help.

If the Head Line has a line rising from it to the Mount of Jupiter it indicates that this person is ambitious. They will want to achieve fame and fortune. When the Star appears on the line and the Mount of Jupiter it indicates that success will be their reward for their ambition and their desires.

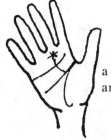

When the Head Line has a line rising from it to the Mount of Saturn with a Star at the end. It is a very good marking. These people will have success and good fortune in their lives.

When the Head Line has a line rising from it to the Mount of Apollo with a Star at its end, it is a very favorable sign. Their chances for success will be almost guaranteed. They will have their fame and fortune.

Cross-bars are lines that cut into a line on the hand. If the Head Line has one or many of these small lines they indicate a brain problem such as a fever, headaches, mental stress. If the Cross-bars are deep it will indicate severe headaches. They are usually found in a very nervous person.

An Island on the Head Line always means a weakness. The size of the Island and the time it appears on the line must always be taken into consideration. The Island can indicate an illness, loss of energy, confusion or a mental breakdown. Both hands must be read so you may understand the problem.

When the Head Line has Dots in the line it indicates acute brain disorder. The size and color of the Dot will show how severe the problem will be. If the Dot is small and white or pink it will not be a grave illness. If the Dot is large and red or purple the brain problem will be severe. The condition of the Head Line following the Dot will indicate if the persons health will improve or be decreased.

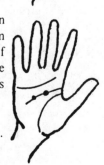

Note: White Dots on a Head Line usually indicate past brain illness. Deep red or purple Dots indicate problems in the future.

When the Head Line has a Dot on it followed by a chained line it indicates that this person will suffer from a brain illness that will impair their mind. Unless the chained line is very short and repaired by a deep, clear Head Line the mind will never fully recover.

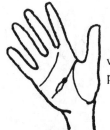

An Island following a Dot on the Head Line indicates great delicacy and weakness of the brain following a severe illness. This is not a good sign, this person will take time to recover.

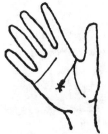

A Star or a Cross following a Dot at the end of the Head Line will mean a fatal termination of an illness. If the Life Line has the same markings it is certain to be fatal.

An Island followed by a Dot and ending with a Star on the Head Line indicates a severe brain illness at the age when the Dot appears on the Head Line, then the illness was followed by a period of delicacy and low energy because of the Island and a fatal ending at the age the Star appears on the Head Line.

An Island on the Head Line followed by a Dot, then a Star and with the line continuing, indicates a severe brain illness at the age the Dot appears. This illness may be followed by a period of delicacy and low energy because of the Island. The Star indicates insanity for the remainder of their life.

Crosses on the Head Line are also dangerous if large and deep; they are as dangerous as a Star.

Stars found on the Head Line are always a danger. It produces an explosion. This may mean a sudden collapse, epilepsy or insanity.

When the Head Line has a line rising from it to the Mount of Mercury it indicates a love of science and scientific study. Look for the Medical Stigmata on the Mount of Mercury. The line on the Mount also indicates a love of the business side of the profession, such as an administrator.

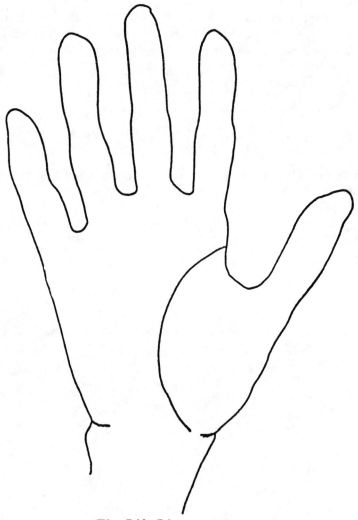

**The Life Line**

# The Life Line

The Life Line or Vital Line is never completely absent.

The line starts about halfway between the index finger (Jupiter) and the thumb, then curves around the thumb and the Mount of Lower Mars and Venus usually ending under the Mount of Venus at the base of the palm near the wrist. The Life Line indicates the vitality, energy and health throughout the life time of your client. The greater the curve, especially when it is unbroken, the better the physical strength. The Life Line can be broken, wavy, or chained. The line may have a companion line running along side of it which is called the Line of Mars. If you interpret the Life Line properly you can help your client. The Life Line also acts as a health line. It describes any unhealthy tendencies which you should discuss with your client. Explain the time it shows the problem so they can take care of their health and hopefully offset the problem.

Clients always ask "How long will I live", it is impossible to tell the length of the Life Line, since the quality of life rather then the length, is or should be more important. You must never make any predictions on the length of life.

# Variations of the Life Line

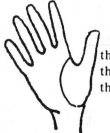

The Life Line is the map of the natural cause of a persons life. It shows the health, physical strength, and vitality. There are a very few cases that the Life Line was not present, there will always be a remnant of it, showing that the line has existed in some form.

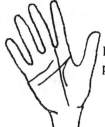

The Life Line may sometimes be difficult to distinguish from the Fate Line, the inside line will be the Life Line. In this case the Fate Line takes up a part of the Life Lines function from the time the Life Line leaves off.

The Life Line may sometimes be difficult to distingush from a strong Line of Influence found inside of the Life Line. This line gives it strength.

In a very rare occasion the Life Line may begin high from the Mount of Jupiter. This indicates that this person is very ambitious, with the desires for wealth, success and fame and they will take every opportunity to become acquainted with important people.

When the Life Line swerves toward the Mount of the Moon on the opposite side of the palm of the hand, it indicates a restless nature which may lead this person to world travel and live in foriegn countries with their death in a foriegn land.

At the beginning of the Life Line on the side of the hand at the base of the Mount of Jupiter. If there is a branch, it indicates there was a near miscarriage or problems before birth.

When the Life Line is narrow and runs close to the thumb and reduces the size of the Mount of Venus, this person can be cold and unsympathetic and may lack sexual drive and attraction for the opposite sex. They can be repelled by advances of the opposite sex.

When the Life Line makes a wide circle into the palm around the Mount of Venus, it increases the mount. This person will be passionate, full of desire and warmth, generous, sympathetic and will attract the opposite sex. Usually marry young with a desire to have children.

If the Life Line is a broad and shallow line it indicates the lack of vitality, poor resistance to disease, weak constitution, no physical vigor, and little or no muscular power. Because of their poor constitutions, they become dependent and tend to lean on friends and family.

A Life Line that looks like a ladder is not a good sign. their health will be very unstable, they are delicate, and suffer repeated illnesses. It has the same effect as the Life Line that is broad and shallow.

When the Life Line consists of several fine lines close together it indicates an intensly nervous person, in delicate disability. These fine lines reduce their strength and they will not be able to lead an active life.

A Chained Life Line shows great obstruction to the energy and life current. This person will be delicate and suffer repeated illnesses. If the chaining runs the entire course of the Life Line the poor physical condition will always be present, but if it covers only part of the line, the delicacy will only extend to the part of the life covered by the chain.

The Life Line in almost every hand is chained the first few years or poorly marked in some way. This indicates the time of life covered by infantile disease. If it continues for a long distance, the child did not pass the danger until later in life. When it runs only a short distance the childish delicacy was soon over, and the line should become deep and strong. If the line should be thin and continue this way to the end, this person did not have a vigorous constitution to start with and was never robust.

When the Life Line is marked with short thin lines at its beginning, it becomes strong for a time , then weaker again. It indicates that this person will have years in their life when they will be ill, then their health will improve for several years, then ill and the end of life will improve again.

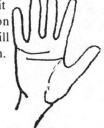

When the Life Line is interrupted or cut continually by little fine lines. These show innumerable worries and this person will become intensely nervous and will be prone to illnesses which can cause depression or ill health.

If a Cross-bar cuts the Life Line and runs to a wavy Line of Health, it indicates a severe bileous fever and jaundice at the time the line cuts the Life Line.

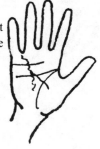

When a Cross-bar cuts the Life Line that began on the Influence Lines on the Mount of Venus. In these cases worry has caused an illness at the time it has cut into the Life Line.

If a Cross-bar that narrows the Quadrangle, is a sign of asthma. The narrowing of the Quadrangle is an indication that shows a tendency toward attacks of asthma.

Breaks in the Life Line are common and they vary in their seriousness according to the line they appear in, how wide the breaks are, if they have been repaired, and how the repair is accomplished. When a break occurs in a deep, strong line it is not as serious than one on a broad and shallow or chained line. All breaks indicate an obstacle or impediment to the health from an illness or accident. Accidents are very hard to diagnose.
If the hand is healthy in every other way, a break in the Life Line should be read as an accident.

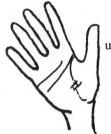

When the Breaks on the Life Line are small and have been repaired. usually by a Square, they are not considered serious.

When the Breaks on the Life Line are wide and unrepaired, they must be considered threatening to the life.

When the Breaks on the Life Line turn back after a break, it is very serious. The wider the separation (if the break is on the ends and the more the ends look back), the more hopeless is the possibitily that any recovery will occur. Be sure to read both hands to see if there is any chance of repair.

When the Life Line is composed of a series of small breaks the effect will be the same as a chained line, this persons health and vitality will be very low and at intervals they will suffer periods of weak constitution. If after each break the Life Line becomes thinner they will become weaker after each attack and lose their resistance to diseases. This broken line is an indicator of constitutional weakness and attacks of diseases. Each break marks the time of the illness.

When the Life Line is composed of a series of small breaks, and after each break the line becomes thinner, the vitality and health of this person will weaken and they will become less able to resist diseases. They will gradually grow very weak until all their vitality is gone. Look at both hands and try to locate the health problem so you may help them to take better care of themselves.

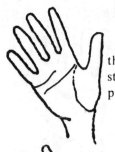

When the Life Line begins with a series of thin weak lines at the start of the Life Line then gradually becomes stronger and joins to become one strong and deep line. It indicates the person will overcome their health problems and enjoy good health for the rest of their life.

When there is Break in the Life Line about the age of 40 years old with the line growing very thin just before the break it indicates the gradual loss of vitality and weakness with little resistance to disease or illness. This person will become ill at the time of the break. If the Life Line continues after the break and gradually becomes deeper, it indicates their strength and health will return. There may also appear an overlapping on the end of the break or a sister line that will repair the break and add strength to the line.

When the Life Line splits and continues as a double line with the two lines running close together, it reduces the strength of the Life Line and this person will experience a decrease in their energy and low vitality. Sometimes the lines will only continue for a short time or they may continue the remainder of the Life Line.

When there is a break on the Life Line when the person is about 40 years old (with the line growing very thin just before the break), it indicates the gradual lose of vitality and weakness with little resistance to disease and an illness will occur at the time of the break. If the Life Line continues after the break and becomes a strong line it will show that the persons strength and good health will return.

When the Life Line has a break it can be repaired by overlapping sister lines. They add strength to the line and complete the remainder of the line.

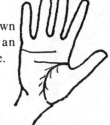

When a strong and deep Life Line has fine hair like lines running down the line, it indicates added strength to the line. This person will have an overflow of energy and vitality as long as these hair like lines continue.

When a Life Line has fine hair like lines rising from the Life Line, which generally appear in the early age of the person this indicates that they are ambitious with the desire to become successful. The time covered by these rising lines on the Life Line are the years of their greatest achievement. It will be the time of the command of their best coordination, abilities and strength. During this time in their lives they should accomplish the most important part of their life's work and ambition.

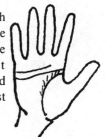

When the Life Line has fine hair like lines that fall downward, the persons enthusiasm, energy and ambition will start to diminish from the time they appear on the Life Line. Sometimes these lines can start after the rising lines on the Life Line.

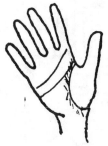

When the Life Line has fine hair like lines that rise from the Life Line at an early age, at the middle of life you will find that the fine hair lines fall downward. This will indicate the turning point in their lives. From this time on they will never be able to achieve the power that they had had before.

When the Life Line has one or more rising lines from the line to the Mount of Jupiter it shows that this person has great ambition which can lead them to a constant struggle to win.

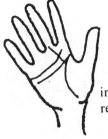

When the Life Line has a rising line that runs to the Mount of Saturn it indicates for this person a great desire to succeed, most likely choosing research or mathematics fields.

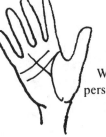

When the Life Line has a rising line that runs to the Mount of Apollo this person has a great desire to succeed in business.

When the Life Line has a rising line that runs to the Mount of Mercury this person will have a great desire to succeed as an Orator, Scientist, Physician or Lawyer.

When the Life Line has a line that runs to the Mount of Upper Mars this person will have a great desire to succeed in the Military or as an Explorer.

When the Life Line has a line that runs to the Mount of the Moon this person will have a great desire to succeed as a Sailor, Sea Captain or Deep Sea Diver.

Comment

All the lines running to the different Mounts are not to be mistaken for Cross-bars or cutting lines.

# Signs and Markings on the Life Line

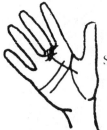

When a Cross-bar cuts the Life Line and ends in a Grille on the Mount of Saturn it indicates an illness at the time the line cuts the Life Line.

When a Cross-bar cuts the Life Line and ends in a Dot in the Heart Line, under the Mount of Apollo, this indicates heart disease at the time the line cuts the Life Line.

When a Cross-bar cuts the Life Line and ends in an Island under the Mount of Apollo, this also indicates heart disease at the time the line cuts the Life Line.

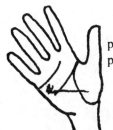

If the Cross-bar runs to a Grille on the Upper Mars, it indicates health problems with the throat, bronchial or a blood disorder. Look to this persons nails to confirm this trouble.

When the Cross-bar runs to a Grille or Cross on the mount of the Moon it indicates problems with the bowel or an intestinal inflammation.

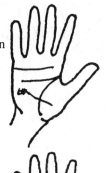

If the Cross-bar runs to a Star or Cross on the lower area of the **Mount of the Moon**, this indicates health problems with the kidneys or bladder.

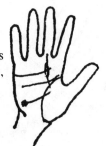

If a line with an Island runs to the Mount of Saturn and a Cross-bar runs to the Mount of the Moon even though there may not be a Grille or Cross, it indicates gout or rheumatic fever.

If a Cross-bar runs to a wavy line to the Mount of Mercury it indicates that this person will suffer an illness such as jaundice or severe billious fever. The time at which the illness occurs can be determined from the point at which the Cross-bar cuts the Life Line.

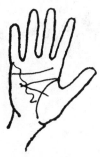

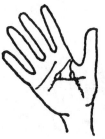

When a Cross-bar cuts through the Life Line and into an Island, Dot, Cross or break in the Head Line and the Life Line has an Island and becomes broad and shallow, the person is not robust, shows a severe attack of the brain which will leave them delicate, from which they may never regain their normal strength or health.

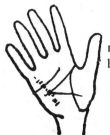

When the Line of Health is formed like a ladder and the Cross-bar line runs to it, it shows that illness will come from stomach trouble for the ladder like Line of Health shows weakness.

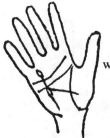

If the Cross-bar runs to an Island on the Line of Health, it indicates there will be problems with the lungs and throat.

When you find Islands on the Life Line they are always an indication of periods of delicacy. The location of the Island will indicate the time of the illness The end of the Island on the line indicates the length of the illness. To find the nature of the illness to the Head, Heart and Health Lines and all other health indications to find out the nature of the illness.

When the Life Line contains a series of Islands and looks like a chained line, it indicates a continuous succession of illnesses. Again you must look to both hands and study all the lines to find where the problem may be located.

When you find an Island on the Life Line and the Head Line has numerous lines cutting it and there are no other health defects on the hand and these cutting bars are fine, this will indicate that severe headaches cause this illness. If the cutting bars are deep there can be brain problems of a serious nature.

If Islands are on the Head Line with an Island on the Life Line, then the head or brain is the cause of an illness.

When Dots are seen on the Head Line with an Island on the Life Line, brain fever will be the cause of illness.

When Dots are seen on the Heart Line with an Island on the Life Line, heart disease will be the cause of illness. This will indicate heart attacks and if there are many Dots these attacks will come frequently causing delicate health which is shown with an Island on the Life Line . Nail color will confirm these problems.

If Islands are seen on the Heart Line a general heart weakness will cause ill health, which is also indicated by an Island on the Life Line. The Islands do not indicate acute heart attacks as indicated by Dots on the Heart Line, but a general structural deficiency.

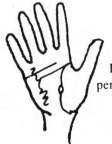

If the Health Line is wavy and there is an Island on the Life Line, this person will suffer biliousness that will cause ill health.

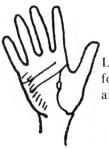

If the Health Line looks like a ladder and there is an Island on the Life Line they will suffer from painfull indigestion, usually chronic and all forms of stomach problems. To locate the cause look for Grilles, Crosses and other markings on the Mounts.

If a Dot is seen before an Island on the Life Line, there will be a period of delicacy. To find the nature of the trouble look to both hands, sometime there will be indications of the trouble on one hand and not on the other.

When there are more than one Island on the Life Line, each will indicate the time there will be a period of delicacy or illness in the persons life.

When two Islands appear on the Life Line. One early in life, and there is an Island or other marking on the Head Line at the corresponding time as the Island on the Life Line it will locate the problem to be nervousness or a break down. If the second Island on the Life Line located later on on the line, and there is an Island on the Heart Line at the approximate time, then heart trouble will be the cause of the illness. The number of Islands seen in the Life Line, indicate the number of times there will be an illness or delicacy in the persons life. The length of these Islands indicate the time it will take to become well again. Each Island may be caused by a different disease which can be traced in the same way by looking for the signs or markings that correspond with the times.

When an Island appears on the Life Line it must be noted, that an Island only indicates health problems on this line. Not financial or any other problems in life.

When there is a Break on the Life Line with an Island located after the break in the line, it indicates the disease which caused the break will have a period when this person will be ill, the length of the illness will be determined by the size of the Island.

When a Life Line has fine hair like lines rising from the Life Line at an early age, it may sometimes be formed around an Island, this indicates an illness at the time the Island appears and decreases the power of the hair like lines which had the Island not appeared would have added great power and strength to the Life Line.

When there is an Island on the Life Line, with a line running to the Mount of Saturn with an Island on it and a third line from the middle of the Mount of the Moon, with a Dot at the end, it indicates this person will suffer with gout or rheumatic fever.

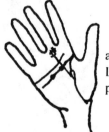

If there is an Island in the Life Line with a Grille on the Mount of Saturn and a line connecting it with the Island, with Dots or Islands on the Head Line under the Mount of Saturn, it will indicate this person will suffer with paralysis. Look also at the finger nails they will be fluted and brittle.

When there is an Island in the Life Line, with a line connecting it with a red or purple Dot on the Mount of Jupiter and a thin Head Line, it indicates a tendency toward epileptic illness. The indication will be stronger if there is a Grille or Cross on the Mount of the Upper Mars. Also notice the color of the hands and lines if they are red, this is another indication.

An Island in the Life Line and a Grille on the Mount of Saturn with a line connecting and a wavy Health Line will indicate extreme biliousness and indigestion health problems. If the skin is yellowish it will also confirm this. If there are Cross-bars cutting the Head Line or small Islands in the line it will indicate the person suffers from bilious headaches.

When an Island appears on a womans hand past forty years of age it usually indicates difficulty with their change of life. The length of the Island will show the time it will last.

A Dot on the Life Line connected by a line to the Mount to the Upper Mars and an Island on the Line of Health shows that the illness will be throat trouble or bronchitis.

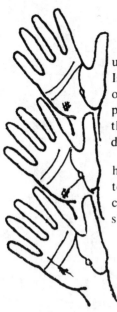

When there is an Island on the Life Line after forty years of age, it usually shows the difficulty women have during the change of life. If the Island is followed by a deep line the effect is only a delicacy during the time of the change. If the line becomes thin, broad and shallow or chained, this person will never recover her full strength and vigor. If there is a Grille on the Mount of the Lower Moon it will cause weakness and add more discomfort.

If you have the opportunity to read this hand before the change of life has occured you should advise them to take precautions. They can avoid too much discomfort by finding medical help. If in addition there is a line connecting to the Grille from the Island or a Star on the Line of Health all show a problem through the change of life.

A Dot on the Life Line is very rare. It is an indication of severe illness or of an accident. These Dots can vary in size from a mere pin point, that are hardly noticeable, to large holes that can destroy the line. They are found in all colors and their importance is judged by their size and color. While Dots are least harmless, red Dots indicate a tendency towards fever. When they are deep crimson and have a purplish hue they indicate grave fevers, such as typhoid and typhus. On the Life Line they are useful in locating the time these incidents can occur, you then look to the hand for Islands, Chains or other markings to locate where the illness is located.

A Dot on the Life Line connected by a line to the Mount of the Upper Moon which has a Grille on it and a line running to the Mount of Jupiter indicates an illnes, such as an inflammation of the bowls.

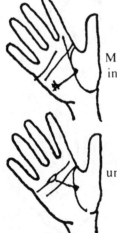

A Dot on the Life Line connected by a line with an Dot, Island or Cross under the Mount of Apollo indicates illness of the heart.

When a Dot is located on the Life line with a line running to the Mount of Saturn with a Cross at its end, it indicates there may be an accident the time the Dot appears on the Life Line.

A Dot on the Life Line connected by a line with a Dot, Cross-bar or a Cross on a wavy Line of Health indicates that this person will suffer from bilious fever.
If there is also a Dot on the Health Line it indicates a bilious attack, the wavy Health Line shows chronic biliousness.

A Dot on the Life Line with Cross-bars, a Grille, a Cross or poorly formed Star on the middle of the Mount of the Moon shows this person suffers from gout. If there is a line running to the Mount of Saturn ending with a Dot, it increases the possibility and makes it more acute.

A Dot on the Life Line that is connected to a line with a Cross, Cross-bar, Grille or poorly formed Star on the Lower Mount of the Moon indicates kidney or bladder problems, and an attack will be acute. You will find the skin yellowish.

When the Life Line is short and there is a Dot, Cross or Cross-bar on a wavy Health Line, a sudden attack of bilious fever will cause the death. A wavy Health Line indicates chronic bilious condition, the sign of the Dot indicates the acute attack.

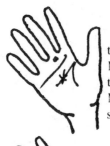

When the Life Line is short and a Dot is seen on a Mount, this indicates the trouble. On the Mount of Jupiter, apoplexy will cause the death, on the Mount of Saturn, paralysis, a Star, Cross or Dot on the Head Line under the Mount of Saturn there is no mistaking the outcome. All the other Mounts must be studied for signs when searching for the reason for the short Life Line. Each Mount indicates its own weakness for a disease.

When the Life Line is short and a deep cut or Cross is located on the end of the Head Line at the corresponding age the Life Line ends, this will indicate the end of life. These signs on the Head Line indicate that some problem relating to the head will be the cause of death.

When the Life Line is short and a Cross, Dot, Star or cut on the end of a short Heart Line is at the corresponding age of the Life Line, it shows a weak or sick heart and the end of life will be due to heart failure.

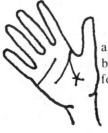

When the Life Line ends in a Cross, the life of this person will end at the age indicated on the Life Line. This is a sudden ending of life and there will be no lingering illness. The cause can be determined by searching the hand for a sign or marking.

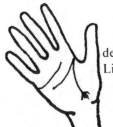

If the Life Line ends in three prongs and the middle Fork is strong and deep it may indicate new vitality and the person may live past the end of the Life Line for several years.

When the Life Line ends with three prongs it scatters the line and the dissipation of this person's vitality is certain.

If the Life Line ends in a Tassel it indicates the entire scattering and dissipation of the person's vitality and the end of life. These Tassels are frequently seen after sixty years of age which indicate a natural end of life. If the Tassel appears early on the Life Line it indicates a premature death of the person at the age the Tassel appears at the end of the Life Line.

When the Life Line runs to a certain age and then crosses the hand to a Mount and if there is no Health Line, the Mount on which the Life Line runs to will show that the Mount qualities will have a great influence in the life of this person. If there is a Grille, Cross, Dot or Cross-bar on the Mount, it indicates the disease that the Mount will have a weakness for, and will effect this person at the age the line starts to reach for the Mount, such as on the Mount of Jupiter, epilepsy, the Mount of Saturn, paralysis, the Mount of the Moon, gout or rheumatism.

When the Life Line is short and ends in a Fork it shows that the strength of the line has been divided and going in two directions, and there is only half a chance for the life to continue. If both branches of the Fork are deep, strong lines there is a better chance that life may be prolonged, but if the Forks are thin, vitality wanes and the division made by the Fork weakens the Life Line. If the Forks are close together it is better for the strength of the line than if the lines are wide apart.

If a Life Line begins deep and strong then begins to taper gradually growing thinner until it fades away, it indicates that the vitality grows less, the person becomes weak and feeble. These people will not die of a sudden death but from exhaustion. They may develop a chronic disease as the Life Line becomes thinner.

If a Cross-bar cuts the end of the Life Line it indicates a sudden death, be sure to look at both hands before making a judgement.

If at the beginning of the Life Line on the side of the hand at the base of the Mount of Jupiter, there is a Dot there was a concussion at or shortly after birth from the doctor using instruments at delivery or by being dropped.

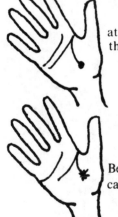

If there is a Dot on the end of the Life Line this person will die of an acute attack. To determine the cause of the attack look for signs and markings on the hands. Be sure to look at both hands.

If the Life Line ends with a Star at its end. This person will die suddenly. Be sure to read both hands and look for signs and marking to determine the cause.

Crosses on the Life Line cause obstacles, defects and hinders the line. Generally there will be Crosses on the Fate Line or Success Line at the same age the sign appears on the Life Line. The Cross can mean an accident or illness.

Stars on the Life Line are a menace and threaten the life of the person. They have been verified many times as an indication of sudden death.

When a fine line that leaves the Life Line and ends with a Star, is a very dangerous sign. it indicates sudden death the Star representing an explosion in the Life Line.

To determine the end of life on the the Life Line it is absolutely necessary to examine both hands. If the Life Line is strong in one hand and weak in the other you must inform them so that they may start to take care of their health and strengthen the weaker line. Try to locate the health problem by looking for any signs or markings, and then inform them where their weakness may lie. Be sure not to indicate the age of death at any time. The Life Line can be strengthened by other lines.

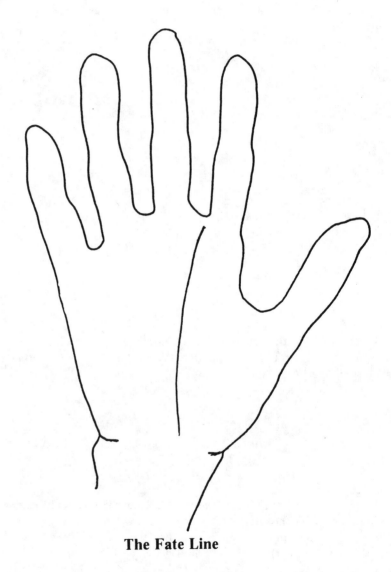

**The Fate Line**

# The Fate Line

The Fate Line has been given several names, such as, the Line of Saturn, the Line of Destiny and the Career Line. When reading for a client I use the Fate Line or Line of Destiny.

The Fate Line runs in a vertical line from the base of the palm toward the Saturn finger. There is no particular starting point of the line, it can start and end in many places. When reading the Fate Line you start at the base of the palm reading upwards.

The Line of Destiny does not foretell a person's future. We all have the right to choose and create our own destiny. You must also always remember to read the lines in both hands. In most cases the times will not be the same. This in itself will give your client choices they must make.

The Fate Line can suggest a person's career, their place in life and success; it is their choice as to the path they will take. The shape of the hand, the fingers and the other lines and markings on the hand will indicate what they are best suited for. The Head Line is one of the most important influences to the Fate Line. When the Head Line is strong it gives wisdom, soberness, energy, common sense in handling money, good instinct for business and the ability to think things out. It is a wonderful line to have; it is usually accurate and important. Palmists generally take a good clear Fate Line as a sign that life will run smoothly with luck in their favor. It gives the gift to see life from the serious side. If the Fate Line extends high on the Mount of Saturn nearly touching the Saturn finger it brings success through old age as well. This line also shows the most productive time of one's life by the depth of the line.

The Fate Line can be seen on new born and young baby's hands. As a Palmist I have read the hands of my own children, as well as my grandchildren and the children of my friends and of our family. It made me happy to find the Fate Line clearly on their hands and have been able to observe them through the years.

The Fate Line does not show health difficulties or the person's general make up or their constitution.

If the Fate Line is absent it will be difficult for the person to establish a career. The Fate Line indicates material success. With no Fate Line it can indicate whether they will have a hard time or with a Fate Line things will become easier for them. Palmists have given a hand without the Fate Line a negative existence. In my study of Palmistry I have found many people without the Fate Line who are successful. The "self made man or woman". There are people who have begun life under hardships and with their energy and will have made their way in the world. I also believe if they can understand the need to find the right partner in life, some one with a good Fate or Success Line and the energy to match, together they can go far. "The woman behind the man."

The Fate Line, like many other lines are not in every hand but this does not mean the absence of these lines that a person can not lead a useful and good life. There is nothing wrong with a quiet life, having a good job and being able to spend more time with family and friends.

People with a strong clear Fate Line could be called an "A" type personality.

When the line starts high in the palm of the hand it will mean that you will have to judge the approximate age when their career will have a good beginning.

When the line starts low in the palm of the hand it shows that the person has set goals early in life and may have had an early career.

# Variations of the Fate Line

When the Fate Line starts inside the Life Line and runs to the Mount of Saturn, it indicates that this person will have material success in life and that near relatives have helped them.

When the Fate Line starts from the center of the palm and runs into the Mount of Saturn it indicates that this person will achieve success in life by their own efforts.

When the Fate Line starts from the Mount of the Moon and runs on to the Mount of Saturn, this person will achieve success in life by help and assistance from the opposite sex. Either from advise or financial help.

When the Fate Line starts high on the Plain of Mars, it indicates that this person will not achieve much in early life, but at the point where the Fate Line begins, they will start to accomplish their goals. Look at the Fate Line in both hands, you will find that sometimes the other hand has a Fate Line that starts near the base of the palm. This person will have a choice, they can be an early achiever or go with the lazier hand and start later in life.

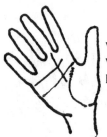

If the Fate Line starts high on the Plain of Mars, the Life Line may be weak at the beginning of life. As the Life Line becomes strong the Fate Line will start at the same age and this person can have a very successful and productive life in their middle and older years.

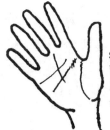

If the Fate Line starts late, there may be a defective Head Line at the start of the line and the person was impaired at the beginning of life by brain weakness. As the Head Line becomes strong and is repaired the Fate Line will begin at that period of their life and they can achieve success in the middle and older years.

When the Fate Line is broad and shallow it indicates a condition that is little better than if there were no line at all. Their will be a continual struggle in life to succeed.

When the Fate Line is long and deep it is very favorable and success will last through their entire life.

If the Fate Line is short and deep starting early in life. The most successful time would be during their childhood. This can be unfortunate, for they are seldom able to take advantage of their opportunities.

The deep Fate Line is always the best line to possess. A thin Fate Line is also a good sign on the hand .It indicates they have success in their favor however, they will have to work harder to achieve their goals.

If the Fate Line is chained the entire length of the line, this person will have continuous obstructions and their life will not be an easy one; it will be full of disappointments. You must remember that people with a Fate Line will always have the desire to be successful. It is hard to see a bad line but they will have to work harder to achieve their goals.

When a Fate Line is defective at the beginning and then grows deep and strong this person has overcome their problems and success will start at the age the line becomes strong.

Cross-bars cutting the Fate Line are obstructions to a career. Each one of the Cross-bars is a separate obstruction and by judging the depth of each one you can tell how serious it can become. If only a faint line that does not cut through the Fate Line indicate continual annoying interferences. If the Cross-bars cut the Fate Line in two they are serious setbacks that can destroy success at that point. The age of each interference must be read on the Fate Line as well as the seriousness so you can warn your client so they can be prepared and have time to stop the problems. Look at both hands and all the other lines you may be able to locate the problem.

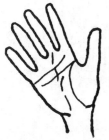

When there are breaks in the Fate Line it is very serious. At the time the breaks occur some problem has been strong enough to check the career of this person entirely, and if the line takes a new character, starts in a new direction, or does not start at all, these breaks indicate an entire change in the cause of this persons life work. Each break indicates a different change in the course of this person's life.

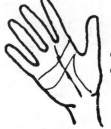

If the Fate Line is uneven alternating from a deep line to a thin line. The career of this person is continually changing from good to bad. Their career will be unreliable and varied.

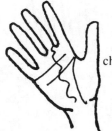

If the Fate Line is wavy, it indicates this person will constantly be changing careers.

If the Fate Line begins deep at the start and runs to the Head Line and stops. The career of this person was favorable to this point in their life. Then errors in judgement will interfere. Their period of greatest production has passed.

Note: Today the Fate Line stopping at the Head Line usually means that this person has decided to retire and of course their period of greatest production has passed. It also indicates no second career will begin.

When the Fate Line has many little fine lines rising from them or falling in a downward direction. The lines rising from the Fate Line indicate the upward tendency of the persons life and these lines add strength to the Fate Line at the time they appear and give hope and ambition. This will be the most successful periods. When the downward lines appear life will become harder, there will be discouragements and progress will be slower. The health of this person should be noted. When the little line branch upwards the physical strength will be good. When the little downward lines appear their health should be watched carefully.

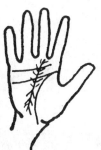

When the Fate Line has little upward lines and if Worry Lines from the Mount of Venus cut the Life Line through the upward lines on the Fate Line there will be constant interference to upset the effect of the Fate Line. These will not only be an annoyance to their career but will also effect this persons material gains.

The Fate Line always runs to the Mount of Saturn, with only one exception. It may run to the Mount of Jupiter. If the Fate Line runs through its usual course in the center of the palm and ends on the Mount of Jupiter, the success of this person will be the result of a great ambition.

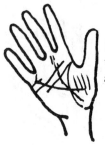

If a Fate Line has a Worry Line from the Mount of Venus cutting the Life Line, and crossing the palm of the hand and also cuts a Forked Line of the Marriage Line, an unhappy marriage has injured this person and it has affected their career.

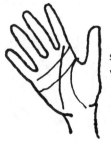

If the Fate Line starts on the Mount of the Moon and runs deep and strong to the Mount of Jupiter, the influence of the opposite sex together with a great ambition will give them their fortune and success.

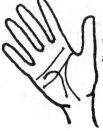

If the Fate Line ends on the Upper Mars Mount, this person will achieve their success from their leadership, power of resistance and because they are not easily discouraged.

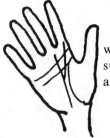

If the Fate Line runs to the Mount of Saturn, which is its usual course, with a branch line running from it to the Mount of Jupiter, this persons success will be due to their ambition and the ability to be in command of any situation and obtain peoples support, such as a politician.

If the Fate Line runs to the Mount of Saturn, which is its usual course, with a branch line running to the Mount of Apollo, this person will have success in business, as an actor or in the field of art.

If the Fate Line runs to the Mount of Saturn, which is its usual course, and has two branch lines running from it, one branch to the Mount of Jupiter and the other to the Mount of Apollo, this person will have an assured future of fame and fortune. They will excel in busineses as well as the arts.

If the Fate Line runs to the Mount of Saturn and has a branch line running to the Head Line but does not cut the line, this person will have a good head for business which will help them succeed in their career.

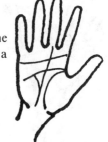

If the Fate Line runs to the Mount of Saturn and has a branch line running to the Mount of Mercury, this person will be shrewd, have good business ability, express themselves well, with a scientific mind and will have success in their life.

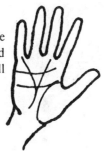

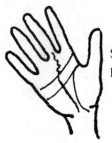

If the Fate Line runs strong and deep for only part way to the Mount of Saturn and ends with a wavy line, the career of this person will become a problem when they are older.

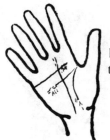

If the Fate Line becomes broken on the Mount of Saturn and the Life, Head and Heart Lines are defective at the same age, it indicates ill health in their old age will interfere with their career.

If the Fate Line is deep and strong and starts from inside the Life Line ending on the Mount of Jupiter. The influence of relatives and their great ambition unite to make the career a success.

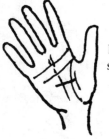

If the Fate Line is cut by a line running from a Line of Influence on the Mount of Venus and the Fate Line becomes a broken line, this will cause a serious problem and they will never be able to recover from their reverses.

If there is a break in the Fate Line it can be repaired by a Square. The person will have serious setbacks at the age indicated on the line, but will be able to get through it as the Fate Line continues.

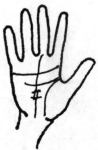

If the Fate Line starts inside the Life Line and runs deep and strong for a while but then becomes weak and defective, the assistance of their relatives and all the ambition may help for a while, but does not bring continued success.

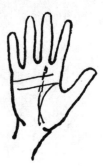

# Signs and Markings on the Fate Line

    If the Fate Line starts high on the hand, and the Line of Influence on the Mount of Venus ends in a Star early on the Line, it indicates a death of a parent and this could prevent a good start in the persons' life which could have effected the late start of the Fate Line.

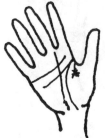

    If there is a short Line of Influence on the Mount of Venus that ends with a Star, and the Fate Line is Chained at its beginning, the death of a parent has effected the early career of this person. The age of the parents' death can be read from the location of the Star on the Life Line.

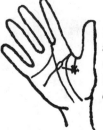

    If a short Line of Influence ends in a Star and a Worry Line runs from it and cuts the Life Line and ends with an Island on the Head Line, the death of a parent has caused this person mental problems and the length of the Island will determine when they will regain their strength and begin their career again.

    If a line with a Star on the Mount of Jupiter cuts into the Fate Line, this person will suffer severe loss from too much ambition. They always try to know distinguished people which lead them to take foolish chances that will injure their business prospects.

If the Fate Line is covered with Crosses between the Head and Heart Line, this person will have repeated reverses in their career, which they withstand if the Fate Line continues, but if the line stops they will be overcome.

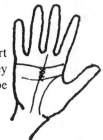

If the Fate Line is cut by many Cross-bars the person will meet with obstacles in their career. If the Fate Line cuts through these bars and severs them they will overcome the difficulties, but if these Cross-bars cut the Fate Line they will be in great difficulty.

If a Line of Influence on the Mount of Venus ends in a Star, and a Worry Line from it cuts the Fate Line between the Head and Life Line. The death of a relative will obstruct the career at this period in their life.

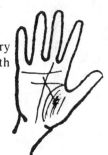

If a line with a Star on the Mount of Jupiter cuts into an Island on the Fate Line. This persons ambition will cause them to be too extravagant and they will have financial difficulties.

If the Fate Line ends on the Mount of Saturn with an Island and the Life Line has downward branches with a long tassle at its end of the line, it indicates financial difficulties due to ill health near the end of life.

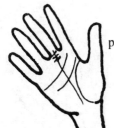

If the Fate Line has Cross-bars which cut into the Mount of Saturn, this person will suffer losses and trials in their old age.

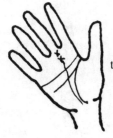

If the Fate Line has Crosses on the Mount of Saturn it indicates serious trials and misfortunes will harass these people in their old age.

When there are Islands on the Fate Line it indicates a setback in the persons career. Usually financial difficulty which last the length of the Island.

When there is an Island at the beginning of the Fate Line and Worry Lines are running from the Lines of Influence on the Mount of Venus to the Island. It indicates financial problems that are caused by their parents.

If the Head Line is chained early on the line and an Island at the beginning of the Fate Line poor mental health will cause problems in the start of this persons career. Their career will improve as the lines grow clear and stronger.

If there is an Island at the beginning of the Fate Line and the Life Line begins with either a chained line, broad and shallow lines or broken lines and continues until 20 or 25 years it indicates illness and weakness at that time and will cause difficulty in their life. After the line becomes deep and strong they will enjoy success in the future.

When the Fate Line has an Island at the beginning and Worry Lines on the Mount of Venus to the Island, it causes constant annoyances early in their career that causes financial setbacks.

If the Fate Line is broken in many places it can be repaired by a Square or Sister Line. Each time the break is repaired it will be a continuous fight and will require will power and strength to carry on. You must look at both hands to see the strength of the Fate Lines, and then to the other lines and signs so that they may help you to understand the problems.

When the Fate Line has little downward branches and there is an Island on the Life Line, then the set back of their career will be caused by ill health shown on the Life Line.

If the Fate Line has little downward branches and there is an Island in the Head Line at the same age as the other lines, the difficulty with their career will be brain and mental problems.

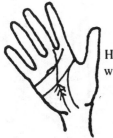

If the Fate Line has little downward lines and there is an Island on the Heart Line at the same age as the other lines on the Fate Line the difficulty with their career will be caused by heart disease.

A Circle at the end of the Fate Line on the Mount of Saturn can indicate a loss or ruin. If the Fate Line is very strong it can offset the problem and this person will have the strength to overcome their problems and save their career and fortune.

A Circle on the end of the Fate Line that ends on the Mount of Apollo indicates success owing to this person's recognition in their career. When the Fate Line has ended on the Mount of Apollo it is a great contrast to the Fate Line that ends on the Mount of Saturn.

If the Fate Line ends with a Trident on the Mount of Saturn it indicates that this person will have success and personal recognition in their chosen career.

A Triangle attached to the side of the Fate Line on the Life Line side of the palm, has a very curious significance. If found on the hand of a person in the military it indicates a successful military career, otherwise this marking indicates that this person will have to fight for their success but will succeed.

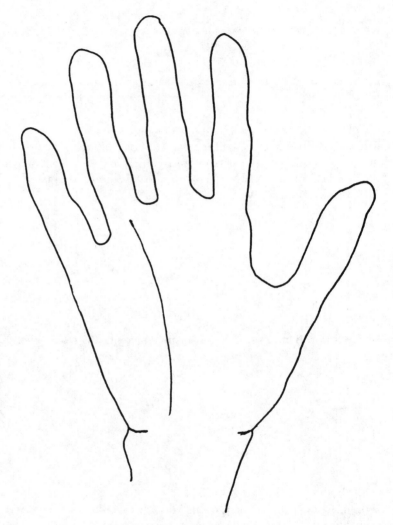

**The Line of Success**

# The Line of Success

The Line of Success is known by several names such as The Line of Apollo, The Line of Sun, The Line of Brilliancy and The Line of Fame. I choose to call this line the Line of Success for this writing.

The Line of Success is not present in every hand in fact it is extremely rare.

The Success Line can start in various areas of the palm of the hand. The closer to the base of the palm, the stronger the line is. The Line of Success always runs upwards towards the Mount of Apollo.

I have listed the Line of Success under Major lines because it is one of the most important lines on the palm of the hand even though it is rarely seen. When giving a reading you must be careful not to mistake it for the Fate Line. Some Palmists look at the Success Line as a sister line to the Fate Line. I read them as two separate lines. Although when the Success Line is in a hand that also has a Fate Line, I believe it gives strength to both lines.

This vertical line indicates the potential for great achievements in life, such as, honors, success, money, creative talents, careers in the arts, the theater, television, advertising and music. Writers have a strong Line of Success. It also means the enjoyment and love of music, art and beautiful things.

People with a good Line of Success are blessed with a sunny, confident nature and charm. Lady luck seems to shower them with all kinds of wonderful favors.

The Line of Success or Line of the Sun is the companion line to the Fate Line, it is said that when the Line of the Sun appears in the palm of the hand, it is to the hand what the sun is to the earth. It gives golden promise of success, good luck, financial gains and rewards, honoring their name and reputation.

The Line of Success promises wealth and success in art, literature or business according to the tendencies of the hand. It must be backed by a good Fate Line to produce the best results.

The clearer and less crossed the line, the better the success will be for the person. A single line is the best of all because then the attention is concentrated.

Although the Success Line is known for its blessing to the arts, it can give brillance to all walks of life. Those who posses this line in any field of endeavor will be successful.

# Variations of the Success Line

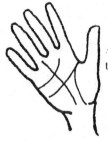

The Line of Success, when long and strong and ends on the Mount of Apollo, gives the person with a good hand, brilliance, a gift of great artistic talents, fortune and fame.

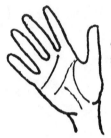

If the Line of Success begins low on the palm and only runs a short distance, this person has talents, but will not have good results if they reach success early in life. It will only last a short time.

If the Line of Success starts between the Head and Heart Lines, the special talent of these people will only be successful for that period in their life.

In many cases when the Line of Success and the Fate Line run side-by-side, one will be strong at one time while the other is weak. When this appears, they operate with each other as sister lines and one repairs the damage to the other.

If the Success Line starts, then breaks and disappears and then begins again, the talent of this person during the disappearance of the line becomes dormant for that period of time until the line begins again.

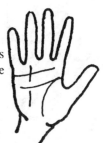

If the Success Line starts, then breaks and disappears and then begins again, the talent of this person during the disappearance of the Line becomes dormant for the period of time until the Line begins again. To find the cause of why the Success Line has vanished, look for the problem on the other Lines of the hands. In this case the Life Line has islands and downward branches that correspond with the time of the break on the Success Line.

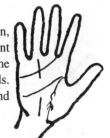

If the Success Line starts, then breaks and disappears, then begins again and the Head Line is defective, the mental powers of this person will be weakened and they will not be able to give the attention needed to make themselves successful.

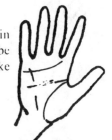

A Line of Success that starts from the Life Line and ends on the Mount of Apollo can be mistaken for many other Lines for it is not in the location where it normally begins. Because this line ends on the Mount of Apollo, you can assume that it has all the good qualities of the Success Line.

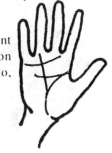

If the Line of Success has a Branch Line that ends on the Mount of Apollo, it adds greatly to the success and career of this person. Please Note: I also interpret this Branch Line or the line that runs parallel to either the Line of Success or the Fate Line to mean that the person with a good hand will have success in more than one career for the length of time the two lines run parallel to each other.

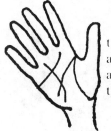

When the Success Line starts on the top of the Mount of the Moon near the percussion side of the hand, it indicates a person with an imagination and the power of language and this person will achieve success as an author. The shape of the fingers and size of the Mounts will determine the type of subject they will be interested in writing about.

If the Success Line starts from a good Upper Mount of Mars, these people will be calm and will never allow themselves to become discouraged. They know they will eventually achieve success and a good reputation in their chosen career.

The character of the Success Line is very important. It indicates the intensity and power the line represents. The best type of line is a deep, straight and well cut line. This will give the most beneficial qualities to these people. It indicates success, a good reputation in their chosen career and creative powers. These people can become distinguished in their field and may even become very famous.

When the Success Line is thin, it will decrease the power of the line. This person will not have the great creative powers of the deeper line. They will be achievers, but will have to work harder and make less money than those with the stronger Success Lines.

If the Success Line is broad and shallow, it indicates this person loves pretty things, is fond of art, but not interested in producing any art. They may enjoy showy things.

If the Success Line is chained, it indicates a lack of artistic talent, although they think they are knowledgeable about art and are usually incorrect. These people do not realize their lack of knowledge, but love to talk about art anyway.

When the Success Line alternates between deep and thin, this person will have a series of successes and failures. If the Success Line is strong and deep at the Mount of Apollo, they will finally achieve success during the remainder of their life.

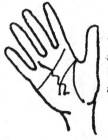

If the Success Line is wavy, it indicates that this person will not know whether to choose a career. They are always undecided. They are brilliant and talented, but have trouble going forward in one direction. If the line becomes strong when it reaches the Mount of Apollo, they may be able to accomplish a career as they become older.

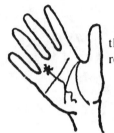

If the Success Line has a Star at the end, even though the line is wavy, these people will end life brilliantly and will have achieved a wonderful reputation in their career.

When the Success Line has two parallel sister lines on each side of it on the Mount of Apollo, the lines give added strength to an already good Line of Success. When the Success Line is supported on both sides by strong sister lines, this person will have great success.

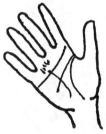

If the Success Line stops at the beginning of the Mount of Apollo and there are many vertical lines on the Mount, this person has a little talent in many directions, but because of all the diversity, can only accomplish a little.

When the Line of Success has one line that branches to the Mount of Saturn and one that branches to the Mount of Mercury, it is a good sign. It indicates that this person will have the combined wisdom of Saturn, the brilliancy of Apollo, and the shrewdness of Mercury. With this wonderful combination they will have wealth and fame.

When the Success Line has fine lines that run upward on its line these lines increase the strength of the Success Line and will make success for this person certain. They will be able to rise over any obstacle.

If the Success Line has fine lines falling downward on its line, it indicates that they will need greater and more constant effort to achieve their success. They will not be able to overcome obstacles easily and will have an uphill pull.

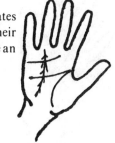

When a Branch Line from the Line of Success runs to the Head Line, it indicates that this person will have good mental powers and their brain will give them good judgment and self control which will help them achieve success.

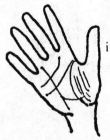

When a Branch Line from the Line of Success runs to the Heart Line, it indicates this person is warm, sympathetic, very affectionate and kind.

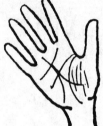

When Influence Lines from the Mount of Venus run along side the Line of Success, it indicates these people have had assistance from their relatives to gain success. It also can be read as an inheritance or relatives who have been a great help with their sympathy and support.

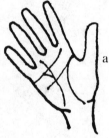

When a Branch Line from the Heart Line cuts the Line of Success, love and emotion will stand in the way of the person's success.

# Signs and Markings on the Success Line

Islands on the Success Line indicate serious problems. If the Islands are deep, it indicates a time of loss of reputation and money. This sign on any hand, no matter how good, should be considered a threat.

Cutting-bars interfere with the persons success when found on the Success Line. These Cutting-bars are caused by various problems. Look at other lines for signs and markings that correspond to the Cutting-bars to understand the problem. If the bars are little fine lines, they are only annoying interferences that will cause worry. If the Cutting-bars are deep, it will affect one's career and cause a setback.

Dots on the Success Line are always a threat and a menace to a reputation. If the Dot is small, the threat may not affect one's career, but if the Dot is deep and large, it indicates this person will lose their good name.

A Dot at the end of the Success Line is a bad sign. This person will have a successful life, but lose their reputation at the end of their life. A warning would be well advised so that they may be able to straighten out their affairs. This does not have to happen to them.

287

If the Line of Success has two Stars, this person will be brilliant and become very famous. The first Star will indicate the age at which they will first achieve their great success. The Star at the end of the Success indicates that their prosperity and renown will continue to the end of their life.

If a Success Line ends in a Star, it is an excellent sign; it indicates a brilliant success. A Star on the Mount of Opollo is like an electric light intensifying the brightness of the line. This person will have great fame in the arts. If the person is of the business world, they will have good fortune and an outstanding reputation.

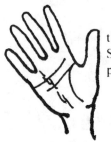

Breaks on the Success Line indicate that the person will have setbacks. If they are business people, they will only be moderately successful. The Success Line indicates a love of art, however, Breaks in the line indicate the person is not a creator but a patron of the arts.

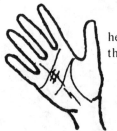

If there is a Break in the Line of Success look for repair lines which will help to overcome the obstacles and bring about better conditions. One of the best repair signs is the Square.

If the Success Line starts deep and strong and gradually becomes thin and fades away, the best time for success and ambition will be the time when the line is deep. The balance of their career will be ordinary unless there is a strong Fate Line that will continue their career.

If the Success Line begins with a Star and ends with a Star it is a wonderful sign. It indicates that this person will have a brilliant and successful life from birth and throughout their entire life.

If the Line of Success ends with a deep Cross-bar, this person will meet with obstructions near the end of their life that they will be incapable of overcoming. Look for signs and markings on the other lines so that you may be able to find out what has caused the problem.

If the Success Line with a deep Cross-bar, this person will meet an obstruction near the end of life that they will be incapable of overcoming. If there is a Tassel, Fork, Island or other defect on the end of the Life Line, this will indicate that ill health and weakness from which they will not recover, has caused an obstruction in their career.

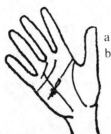

If the Success Line ends with a deep Cross-bar and there is an Island and a Star on the Head Line, this person at the age of about fifty years, will fail because of mental illness, for they will be too ill to carry on.

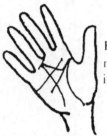

If the Success Line ends with a deep Cross-bar and a line splits on the Head Line and runs to a Bar on the Mount of Apollo, it is a bad sign. Their mistakes will cause failure; they may have made bad mistakes in their investments, from which they will never be able to recover.

A Square at the end of the Success Line is a good sign. This sign gives protection from damage, harm or misfortune; it is a lucky sign. It will have a strong influence not only at the end of a career, but during the whole life of this person.

When there is a Cross at the end of the Success Line, it is not a good sign. It indicates poor judgement. These people will make mistakes that will cause them to have a very bad reputation.

When the Success Line ends with an Island, it is a bad sign. No matter how strong the Success Line may be, during the last days of this person's life they will have a loss of their money and reputation.

A Fork at the end of the Success Line weakens the line. This person has more than one talent which may cause them to accomplish less than if they would have concentrated on just one of their talents.

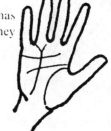

If the Success Line has a well-marked Trident on the end, it is a good sign. It indicates that this person will be successful and famous, and become wealthy through their mental powers.

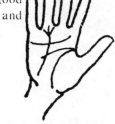

When the Success Line ends with a Tassel, it is not a good sign. This person will scatter their efforts in so many directions that they will accomplish very little.

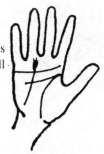

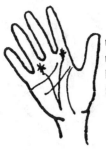

If there is a Star at the end of the Success Line and a branch line runs to the Mount of Jupiter with a Star, it is a wonderful sign to have. It indicates that this person has strong ambition, great talent and the power of leadership. With this combination they are sure to achieve great fame and fortune.

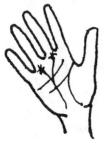

If there is a Star at the end of the Success Line and a branch line runs to the Line of Saturn, with a Star on the Mount, the success of this person is certain. If they are in the business world, they will gain wealth as well as fame. Look at both hands and other signs and markings so that you can see the degree of their success.

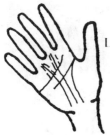

If there are Sister Lines on either side of the Success Line or the Fate Line, this will bring great success to this person.

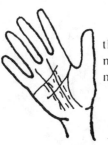

If the Line of Success and the Fate Line have many vertical lines around them before they reach the Mount of Apollo and the Mount of Saturn, it is not a good sign. This person will not reach success because they have too many interests and are unable to concentrate on only one talent.

If there is a Star at the end of the Success Line on the Mount of Apollo, and a branch line runs to the Mount of Mercury with a Star, it is a very good sign. This person will gain success.

If there is a Star at the end of the Success Line and a branch line runs to the Mount of Mars, this will bring this person success. Because of the Mars influence, they will be very self reliant, and be able to defend themselves. They are not easily discouraged and if necessary, through forcefulness, will gain success and become famous.

If there is a Star at the end of the Success Line on the Mount of Apollo and a branch line runs to the Mount of the Moon, this person will have a great imagination, the ability to speak well and express themselves. They will make successful writers.

If there is a Star at the end of the Success Line and on the Mount of Apollo and a branch line runs to the Mount of Venus, this person will be very fond of music. If their fingertips are smooth and pointed, they will be very musical and enjoy expressing themselves through their music. The Star will bring them great success and they will achieve distinction as a musician. I must add, square or spatulate fingertips are also excellent for a musician.

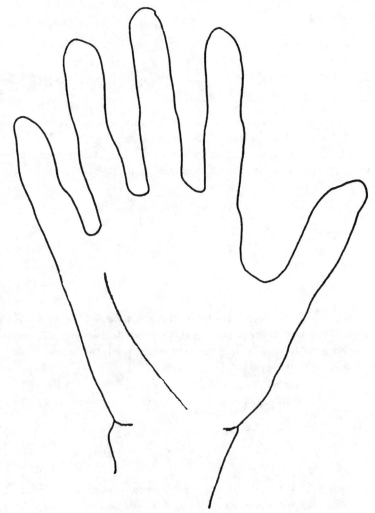

**The Health Line**

# THE MINOR LINES

## The Health Line

The Health Line, Liver Line, Line of Mercury and The Hepatica.

You will find all these names for this line. I will refer to the line as the Health Line.

If there are many vertical lines on the palm of the hand it may be difficult to recognize and seperate them. The Health Line should start at the Mount of the Moon and run upwards on the percussion side of the palm towards the Mount of Mercury and end under the little finger.

During our long and slow development in the study of Palmistry, the Line of Health has remained an indicator of the general state of health. Because of the direction the line takes to the Mount of Mercury it also relates to intuition, business and temperament. Because the line ends under the finger of Mercury it takes on its qualities as well, such as intelligence, readiness, intuition and organizing ability.

There are some lines and signs we are pleased to have on the palm of the hand, others that are better if they are missing. One of these lines is the Line of Health. The absence of the Line of Health indicates a sound robust constitution, strength, health and temperament that will be free of nervous strain and stress. People who exercise and lead physical out door lives, that have no genetic problems rarely have a Health Line. Those who are of an easy going nature and take life as it comes and do not worry over little things. People who have a cheerful disposition rarely have a Health Line.

The Health Line is a valuable barometer to the condition of health. It can give Palmists a wide scope in reading and diagnosing diseases and tendencies toward disease. The state of the digestive system and the operation of the liver. When poor conditions are seen in other lines of the hand you can refer to the Health Line for an explanation. Some of the most accurate readings in the range of palmisty have been done with the aid of the Health Line. It can also indicate the approximate time that illness can take place. The Health Line can be one of the most changeable lines and if the line is studied and read and a forwarning given of the health problem, then the problem can be avoided. Thus the line can change.

A clear Line of Health is very rare. When it does appear it is a fortunate sign, it indicates a perfect balance between intellectual and physical abilities, this balance gives equal intellectual culture and in business. A good memory, energetic, unselfish and a healthy life.

# Variations on the Health Line

The Health Line usually starts on the Mount of the Moon and runs upwards to the percussion side of the palm to the Mount or Mercury. This Line is an indicator of the condition of the digestive system and the liver, and indicates various illnesses connected to the digestive system.

Although the Health Line should start from the Mount of the Moon it rarely does. The Health Line can also be found starting near the Line of Success, the Fate Line or the Life Line. The Health Line can be seen starting from the center or base of the palm and often from the Plain of Mars.

One of the best locations for the Health Line to start is between the percussion side of the palm and the Success Line.

The Health Line starting from the Life Line is one of the most unfavorable signs. A Health line that touches the Life Line is always a bad marking indicating health problems.

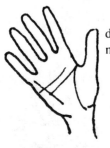

When a Health Line is deep and in its normal location it indicates good digestion, a healthy liver, good vitality, a strong constitution with a clear mind and good memory.

If the Life Line is thin and the Health Line is deep and strong the line will have the same favorable aspects as a strong Mars Line, and will help repair and strengthen whatever weakness the Life Line may have.

If the Life Line is chained and the Health Line is deep and strong, the line again will help repair and strengthen the weakness of the Life Line, as it has the same effect on the Life Line as the Mars Line. The Health Line often replaces the functions of the Life Line and will account for the improvement of the health of a person who has a defective Life Line.

When the Health Line is defective and stops at the Head Line, it can effect and disturb the head both emotionally and physically.

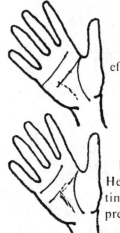

If the Head Line is defective and a defective Health Line stops on the Head Line, you must inform your client of this weakness by judging the time of the problem so that they may take care of their health or be prepared for any emotional problems.

If the Health Line is defective and reaches a defective Heart Line, it indicates a chronic heart disease that may be caused by stomach problems, which is a disturbing function of the heart. This person should be advised to seek medical help so that the heart disease can be diverted.

If the Heart Line is defective and the nails of the person also indicate a heart problem, a deep, strong Health line will often indicate a good digestive system and liver function and the effects of the weak heart may never become serious.

When a hand has a strong Heart, Head amd Life Line, with a good Line of Mars and a deep, strong Health line, it indicates that this person will virtually never have a sick day in their life.

If the Health Line is long and strong and runs to the Mount of Mercury, its good influence will be felt during the person's entire life and they will have good health and success.

If the Health Line is thin it does not lessen its influence, but still shows good support because the liver is in good operating condition, although not to the degree it would have been with a stronger Health Line.

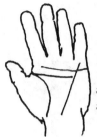

If the hand shape is elementary and has a strong Life, Heart and Head Line with a good Line of Mars and a deep, strong Health Line, it indicates intense good health and strength, but with vitality that increases their passions. They have excessive appetites and are often prone to becoming rapists and drunkards or dependent upon drugs. If reading a young client, advise them to choose an occupation that is always out of doors in the fresh air and to get lots of exercise to work off their excess vitality.

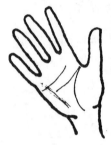

When the Health Line is broad and shallow, it indicates that the person will have low vitality, and any severe tax on their stomach will cause disturbance to their system. The liver will become unsteady and not function properly, which can cause headaches, heartburn, sour stomach, painful digestion, and also depression and gloominess. With a broad and shallow Health Line, this person should be constantly aware of their diet and hygene so that they can be healthy and have sufficient vitality to achieve their ambitions.

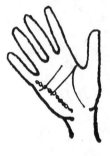

If the Health Line is chained it indicates that the liver and stomach are diseased, which may be the cause of inflammation of the gall duct, gallstones and cirrhosis of the liver, which is always serious and can be fatal. The Chained Line is a bad sign and the person that has this sign suffers not only from conditions of their diseased liver but also mental depression. They are pessimistic, suspicious, intensely nervous and cross. Life becomes a burden to them. It is very difficult for them to think clearly or be in command of themselves. They will have very low vitality and this will interfere with their business success. The old Palmists read the Chained Line as "poor success in business." With poor health we can understand this very well and they are correct.

If the Health Line starts deep and strong and then becomes chained this person will become ill with a serious liver condition and stomach problems which will impair their health and success.

If the Health Line starts deep and strong and then becomes chained and the Life Line is defective at the same period of time on their palms, it becomes very serious and will endanger their life.

If the Health Line starts deep, then grows thin and then grows deep again and if this person takes good care of their health, they can overcome this period of ill health and become strong again.

If the Health Line is long but defective, it will indicate ill health and a struggle in the person's business their entire life.

When a Health Line is long and only defective in one or two places on the line, you will be able to judge when this person must be careful and take of their health. It will also indicate the best time for them to enjoy their strength and have their most productive periods in their career.

If the Health Line runs to the Head Line then stops between the Head and Heart Lines and continues again on the Mount of Mercury, this person will loose the strength of the Health Line at the most critical period in his or her life. When the line continues they may be able to gain strength to continue.

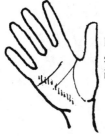

If the Health Line is composed of little broken lines that resemble a ladder, it indicates the worst form of stomach problem. This person will suffer chronic illness such as gastric fever, inflamation of the bowl, intestines and stomach which will cause accute attacks.

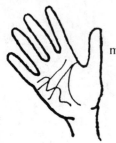

If the Health Line is wavy, the business or career of this person will have many changes.

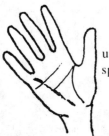

If the Health line is strong and then becomes weak and continues in this uneven manner, it indicates that this person will have irregular and spasmodic problems with their liver and stomach.

When the Health Line is broken in only one or two places, the breaks indicate a weakness in the person's health at the age of the breaks. If the Health Line is continuously broken it indicates that this person will be extremely sick bacause of their digestive system and liver, the same as a laddered Health Line.

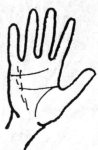

If the Health Line is broken, a Sister Line can repair the breaks and this will avert the danger of illness.

If the Health Line is strong and deep and there are branches rising from it, this person will enjoy excellent health and great success in their career.

If the Health Line is deep and has branches that droop downward, this person will have success but will have to work hard to accomplish their goals.

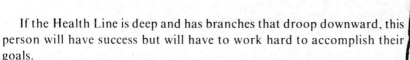
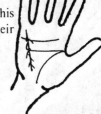

When the Health Line is deep and a branch from the line reaches upwards to the Mount of Jupiter, this person will be successful and will have the added advantage of ambition and the ability to be a leader.

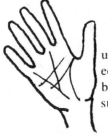

If the Health Line is deep and strong and a branch from this line runs upward to the Mount of Saturn, this person will have wisdom, exercise economy and will be careful in their goals. They have the ability to look at both sides of a problem and understand what must be done to be successful.

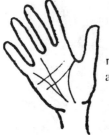

When the Health Line is deep and strong and a branch from this line runs upwards to the Mount of Apollo, this person will have shrewedness and business ability; they are brilliant and have an agreeable personality.

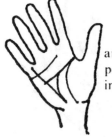

If the Health Line is deep and strong and a branch from this line runs to and merges into a strong deep Head Line, it will indicate success due to this person's mental powers. This combination of lines forms a triangle, which in this position will always indicate mental brilliance.

## Signs and Markings on the Health Line

If the Health Line begins strong and becomes chained at the Head Line and the Head Line has an Island on it, liver trouble will affect the mental strength of this person. This can cause a sudden attack of temporary insanity or a nervous breakdown.

If the Health Line begins strong and then becomes chained at the Head Line, and if the Head Line has a Star on it or near it, then the liver trouble will be very serious and will cause mental problems, pain and a nervous breakdown.

When the Health Line is deep and a branch from the line reaches upward to the Mount of Jupiter, this person will be successful and have the added advantage of ambition and the ability to be a leader. If a Star is on the Mount of Jupiter, **they** will have influential friends who will be of great help to them.

If the Health is composed of little broken lines that resemble a ladder, it indicates the worst form of stomach problems. These people will suffer from chronic illness. If this Health Line has a Dot, a severe stomach attack will occur at the age indicated on the line.

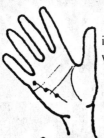

Dots on the Health Line, wherever seen on any kind of Health Line will indicate an acute attack of biliousness or stomach problems at the age at which they are seen on the line.

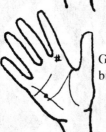

If the Health Line has a Dot and the Mount of Jupiter has a Cross or Grille on it, this indicates that this person will have an acute attack of biliousness at the age indicated on the Health Line.

If the Health Line has a Dot and the Mount of Saturn has a Cross or Grille on it with a defective Health Line, it will indicate that this person will have an acute attack of biliousness with the added health problems of gout and rheumatism.

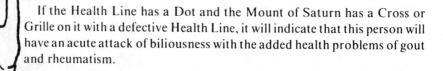

If there is a Dot on the Health Line and the Heart Line has a defective marking such as an Island, Grille or Dot under the Mount of Apollo, it indicates a severe heart attack brought on by the digestive organs. The age that this may occur can be told by the position of the Dot on the Health Line.

If there is a Grille on the Mount of Apollo, this sign will intensify the problem and indicate that the health problems will be chronic.

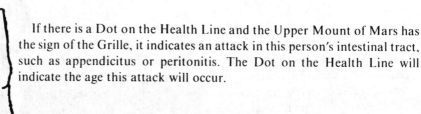

If there is a Dot on the Health Line and the Upper Mount of Mars has the sign of the Grille, it indicates an attack in this person's intestinal tract, such as appendicitus or peritonitis. The Dot on the Health Line will indicate the age this attack will occur.

A Dot on the Health Line and a Grille on the Mount of the Moon indicates that this person may suffer from rheumatic fever or gout which can occur at the time the Dot appears on the Health Line.

If there is a Dot on the Health Line and the Health Line becomes defective on the Mount of Mercury, it indicates a severe attack of biliuosness or gastritus will occur at the age indicated by the Dot on the Health Line.

When there are Cross-bars cutting the Health line, these Cross-bars can be very fine lines or deep bars. The extent at which they cut the Health Line indicates the severity of the effect on the person's health problems. The age the Cross-bars cut the Health Line will indicate when these health problems will occur.

When the Health Line and the Head Line have fine Cross-bars, it indicates that this person suffers from nervousness, billiousness and sick headaches which are all caused by the condition of the digestive system and the liver.

If there is an Island on the Health Line, it indicates a weakness at the age that it appears on the line, which may be caused by the liver or stomach. It may also indicate an inflamation of the appendix. The presence of an Island on the Health Line does not always indicate that this person's health problems will relate only to the stomach or liver. The Island on the Health Line only states that this person will be ill and weak at the age that it appears on the line.

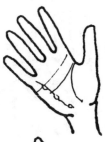

If the Health Line has many Islands, it will be an indication of weakness of the throat and lungs.

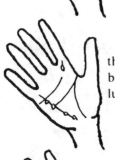

If the Health Line has many Islands on it and also an Island located on the Mount of Jupiter, this person will have a weakness towards consumption, bronchitis, pneumonia and all other types of diseases of the throat and lungs.

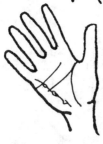

Some old references state that Islands on the Health Line indicate bankruptcy. They arrived at this statement because the health of the person would impair their ability to be successful in business. While the old references do have a good foundation, you will find Islands on the Health Line of persons that are no means bankrupt, but they are bankrupt in their health.

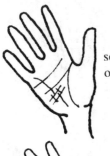

When the Health Line is broken, it can be repaired by Squares. If a serious break on the Health Line is repaired by a Square, then the danger of illness has been averted.

If the Health Line runs to the Head Line and then stops between the Head Line and the Heart Line and then continues to the Mount of Mercury, this person will loose the strength of the Health Line.

If there is a Cross-bar, Cross, Dot or Island near or at the end of the Health Line it will indicate that this person will not recover.

If the Health Line ends in a Cross-bar or a Cross, the career of this person will be hampered.

If the Health Line ends with a Grille, it is a very bad sign, for this person will have serious problems which may be the result of poor health or a bad reputation.

If the Health Line ends with a Star, this is one of the best markings that a palm can have. This person will be successful in whatever career that they may choose.

If the Health Line ends with a Fork this person will divide their energies between several talents and will not be able to achieve the great success that they could have, if they had concentrated on just one career.

If the Health Line ends in a Tassel, the efforts for success will be too scattered and no great success can be achieved.

If the Health Line has a Star at the point where it crosses the Head Line, it indicates serious brain trouble, a nervous breakdown and even insanity.

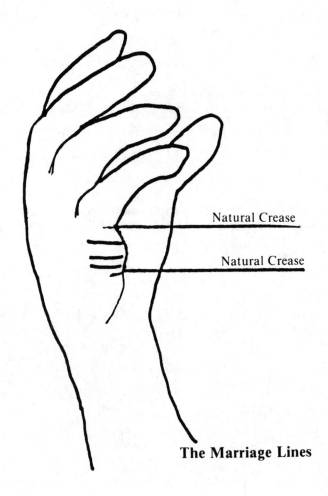

Natural Crease

Natural Crease

**The Marriage Lines**

# The Marriage Lines

Marriage Lines are probably the most difficult to read for Palmists, even the most experienced. In the past Marriage Lines were supposed to indicate marriage, however, in today's modern relationships it is difficult to distinguish between Marriage Lines and Lines of Affection. Although these lines are considered minor lines we are asked to read these lines most often. It is the curiosity of the very young to the old who want to know "When will I marry?" "Will I marry?" "Tell me about my love life".

Marriage Lines are no longer quite the right terminology to describe these lines. Today this sign has many meanings. It would be more logical to use any of these terms instead, such as, cohabitation, affection, union, attachment, relationship, significant other, living together, common-law-marriage, Pal-A-Mony and commitment. One reference work used the term Line of Sex Influence.

I use the terms Commitment or Affection Lines when giving a reading. To use the word Marriage Line is misleading for there is no way that these lines indicate a legal marriage contract. The hand does not recognize the fact of a ceremony whether civil or religious, it only can register the influence of the emotions of the person involved. They are seen when the person has loved as though they had been joined in wedlock. In such cases the Marriage Line appears the same as though the ceremony had been performed. The fainter lines represent romantic involvements. The fact that these lines are marked many years in advance they are part of our destiny, however, we do have choice.

Marriage Lines are horizontal lines located on the percussion side of the hand between the natural crease of the Heart Line and the natural crease at the base of the little finger on the edge of the Mount of Mercury. These lines do not show the number of marriages, however, what they do show is the number of love attractions. The depth and consistancy of the lines indicate how deeply felt and stable are the relationships. These lines do not indicate the love of the person's family, blood relations do not show in this area.

In the older reference books the Marriage Lines related only to the opposite sex, man and woman. The union between the same sex does not leave its sign. To-day in reading a hand of a Homosexual you will find the Marriage Lines very visible for emotions; love, affection and commitment.

To judge age on the Marriage Line, the line close to the Heart Line crease can be estimated to be about 18 years for a woman and 21 for a man. A person whose Marriage Line is located at the center of the two natural creases should be judged to be about 42 years and close to the crease of the little finger approximately 70 years. To be more accurate try to obtain the age of the first Marriage Line and the length of the relationship.

# Variations of the Marriage Lines

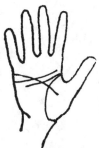

A Marriage Line that slopes down past the Heart Line and cuts through the Life Line into the Mount of Venus indicates that there has been a separation. If this line appears in both hands the divorce has taken place.

When there are many Lines of Affection, this person is sensitive, emotional, and easily influenced and will be susceptible to love affairs. The seriousness of these affairs will depend on the strength and length of the lines. The longer, deeper ones most likely will consumate into marriage.

If there is only one long and deep Line of Marriage on the hand, it indicates a deep affection for one person. You must read both hands before making any statement for they may differ.

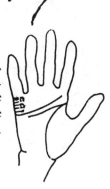

When judging the age or time on the Marriage or Affection Lines, determine the age or time of the first line located nearest the Heart Line. Marriage Lines are read from the Heart Line crease up the side of the Mount of Mercury to the natural crease of the little finger. Locate the center of the area, then you can determine the time of the lines on the hand. using 42 years for the center of the area.

Today with the average hand having more than one line and each line a different length or depth, it is difficult to determine the length of a Marriage Line. The reading of any Line of Affection is very difficult and can only be a judgement.

When you find two Lines of Affection that run alongside of each other and are of equal length and depth this person has been or is in love with two people at the same time.

When the Marriage Line starts deep then gradually becomes thin this person is gradually losing their affection for the loved one.

When the Marriage Line starts thinly and then gradually becomes a strong line the union will grow strong and their attachment will become deeper.

If a Worry Line runs from the Mount of Venus and cuts thru the Line of Marriage, it indicates that a relative is interfering with this marriage.

A Marriage Line that is straight, long and deep and does not wander, indicates that from the start of this marriage there will be a real understanding between the husband and wife, and this will be a long and happy union.

When the Marriage Line begins as a double line, then becomes a single line and then proceeds straight, this can be regarded as an open Island, and indicates that this relationship is in danger and a separation on the grounds of incompatibility is probable.

A Marriage Line that runs upward toward the base of the little finger, indicates an obstacle to this marriage coming from the person. They will have trouble facing responsibilities and making a commitment. A Marriage Line of this kind usually indicates a fragile relationship.

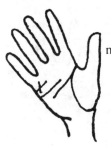

A Marriage Line with a short line that crosses it indicates obstacles that may come from the family or because of economic reasons.

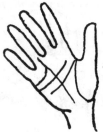

When a Marriage Line or an upward branch from the line, extends to the Line of Success but does not cut through it, this indicates a lucky sign for a brilliant marriage. This person will marry someone who is very well known and wealthy.

A branch that extends upward from a Marriage Line on the Mount of Apollo indicates a brilliant marriage.

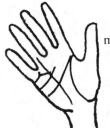

A branch that extends downward cutting the Line of Success indicates a marriage to someone of inferior position.

When a Line of Influence from the Mount of Venus cuts the Lines of Life, Head, Heart and Marriage, it indicates troubles connected in the marriage, generally due to interference of relatives.

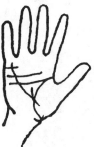

A Line of Influence from the Mount of Venus cutting a small upward branch of the Life Line and merging into or cutting a Marriage Line, indicating a legal separation.

When a Marriage Line or a branch from this line extends to the Line of Success and cuts through the line it indicates a marriage to some one of inferior position, or misalliance.

# Signs and Markings on the Lines of Marriage

If an Island appears on the Marriage Line, there will be some unhappiness during the marriage.

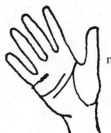

If there is more than one Island on an Affection Line, this person will never marry during this time, even though they may be in love.

If there is a Cross on the Line of Affection there will be a serious impediment that will make it impossible to marry.

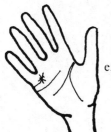

When the Marriage Line ends with a Star, the marriage will end in an explosion.

If a Line of Marriage is cut by a line that has an Island, a Cross-Bar or a Dot in the Head Line, there will be interference with the marriage due to some form of brain trouble.

If there are branches on the underside of the Marriage Line the married life will be full of sorrow and disappointments.

When there are branches on the Marriage Line that rise up from its line, this person will have affection and the union will be an uplifting one.

If the Marriage Line is broken, it will indicate that love and affection has been interfered with or broken in some way. Look at both hands, if the break in the line is enclosed with a Square then this will repair the union.

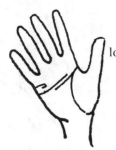

If the Line of Marriage makes a Hook under the line, this person will lose their loved one who will not return.

When a Dot is seen on the Line of Marriage, it indicates an obstacle or an impediment to the marriage.

If the Line of Marriage has a Dot and the end of this line has a Fork, Trident or a Tassel, the marriage will be wasted and dissipated.

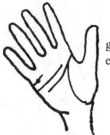

When the Marriage Line has a Dot on it and the line continues but gradually grows weaker and disappears, love and affection comes to an end.

When the Marriage Line sends a branch into the Mount of Apollo with a Star at the end, this person will have a marriage with someone brilliant and famous.

If the Marriage Line has a Fork at the end, the affection and love will separate and become less strong. This sign has been used by the older Palmists as an indication of divorce. However, there may be an interference in the married life but not always a divorce. One must look at both hands before making any statement. Also determine the width of the Fork, are the branches wide or narrow? If narrow, it will not be serious.

If the Marriage Line ends with a Trident or a Tassel, it indicates complete dissipation and the scattering of the affections.

A Fork at the beginning of a Marriage Line indicates that there will be a delay and some frustration before the marriage date can be arranged, and there will be a time of loneliness for this person because of a separation from their loved one.

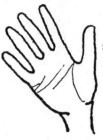

When the Line of Marriage begins with a Fork, it indicates unusual strength to this union. When the two lines of the Fork unite to form one line it gives a double strength to the line.

A Fork at the beginning of the Marriage Line on the percussion side of the palm indicates a separation by the fault of this person not by the other party.

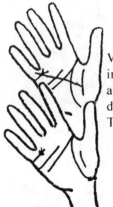

When a Worry Line starts from a Line of Influence on the Mount of Venus and runs through a Marriage Line with a Fork at the end this indicates this marriage will be interfered with by a close relative. The Fork at the end of the Marriage Line shows the loss of enjoyment of the marriage due to the interference of the relations. If the Marriage Line has a Tassel or Trident at the end the interference is intensified.

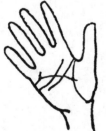

When a Marriage Line has a Fork at the end and the Fork extnds to the Life Line, there will be a legal separation with complications, a struggle over custody of the children and division of property.

The Line of Marriage ending with a Fork on a branch that drops toward the Heart Line indicates a divorce in favor of this person.

When a Line of Influence from inside the Triangle cuts the Lines of the Fate, Head and Heart and it terminates after cutting a forked Marriage Line, it indicates divorce.

Comment-

In my research for this reference book there are **several interpretations** of a Fork on the Marriage Line, as well as other Signs and Markings. To interpret all their meanings we must read both hands and all the other Signs and Markings before making any statement as to which will be the correct interpretation of the Fork on any line. Of course this will hold true to all our readings on any given Sign or Marking.

When the Marriage Line is full of little Islands or downward branches it indicates this person will not marry. It also indicates excessive indulgence and the pursuing of pleasure to the point of excess causing impotency.

An Island at the end of the Marriage Line with another Island on the second phalanx of the thumb indicates a marriage of near relatives.

# Sign of Widow or Widowhood

When a death of a marriage partner brings deep sadness and sorrow, the Marriage Line will descend down towards the Heart Line, and on to the Head Line with a deep Dot.

When the death of a marriage partner does not cause deep sorrow, the Marriage Line ends with the line running toward the Heart Line but it does not touch the line.

A black Dot on the Marriage Line indicates widowhood.

A break in the Marriage Line indicates the sudden death of the partner.

When a Marriage Line is cut at its termination by another line it indicates that the marriage will end with the death of the partner.

When the Marriage Line terminates in a Star on the Mount of Mercury it indicates the death of the partner.

To determine the time these events may occur, look to the Life, Heart or Fate Line and examine them for an indication of change or shock at the age corresponding with that of the sign on the Marriage Line.

# Homosexuality

The same-sex orientation or Homosexual as described in the older reference books on Palmistry refers to the homosexual as a male and we know that we must include the female as well. It is very difficult if not impossible to determine sexual preference from the hand. People who prefer their own sex for partners are found in every walk of life and with all ranges of characteristics, values and activites with a wide range of personalities and emotions. The union between the same sex does not leave its sign. When reading the hand of a homosexual you will find they have the same emotions, desires, ambitions, affections, commitments and troubles. Some are extremly creative and some are very strong, and when in the services; very brave. They can be very intelligent as well as very unwise.

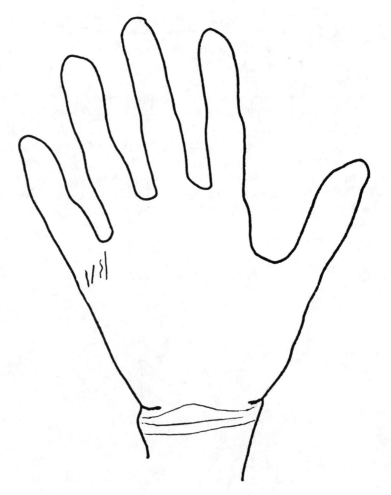

**The Lines of Children**

# The Children Lines

Again, I must disagree with the older traditional Palmists and live up to the name of this book,

To see the number of children on the palm is almost impossible to read with reliable accuracy.

There are Children Lines on the Palm, located at the base of the little finger, on the Mount of Mercury on the Precussion side of the hand.

Perhaps in places like Latin America where contraception and abortion are still uncommon, you would be able to indicate the number of children on the hand fairly accurately by the lines under the little finger. Here in the United States, Europe or Great Britain and other industrialized countries, being able to read the number of children is very difficult if not impossible. Abortions and miscarraiges can be recorded as possible children. Now with advanced knowledge and artificial contraception done by doctors, we have choices in the number of children we choose to have or not have. The modern woman makes her own decisions in these matters.

I am often asked, "Will I have children?" I look to the Bracelet Lines for this information. I believe the first wrist line is a better indicator than the Children Lines. The line shows fertility in both men and women. If the first line of the Bracelet is clear and encircles the wrist in good condition it will indicate the ability to conceive and bear children without complications.and in a man the line will indicate fertility or a problem with sterility. Cheiro states that a person with a poor development of the Mount of Venus is not likely at any time to have children. The Mount must be full and large.

For Children Lines look for upright lines above the Marriage Lines and under the little finger. Deeply marked lines stand for male children and faint lines stand for females. You are more likely to see these lines in a mothers' hand rather than in the hand of the father who may not be as attached to the children.

Clear Children Lines denote strong, healthy children, irregular lines, sickly children. Because these lines are difficult to locate, a magnifying glass would help greatly. To count the lines start on the precussion side of the hand reading inward toward the palm. There are Palmists who believe that Children Lines are sometimes found on people who are childless, who have become very attached to children belonging to someone else.

327

# Variations of Children Lines

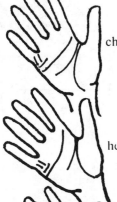

If the Children Lines are long and run into the finger of Mercury, the children will be successful.

If the Children Lines are straight and deeply marked it indicates a healthy male child.

If the Children Lines are slanting this indicates a healthy female child.

If the Children Lines are wavy or irregular, it indicates poor health of he child.

If the Children Lines are short the children may be separated from their parents at an early age.

When one of the Children Lines is longer than one of the others it indicates that the child is the favorite of the family.

The theory that the Bracelets indicate fertility is one I share. If the first Bracelet on the wrist arcs upward to form an arch or bow in the center of the wrist, it indicates a problem in childbearing and the reproductive system. It does not mean that there will not be children, only a problem in conceiving or delivering a child.

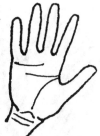

A clear, unbroken line under the first Bracelet, crossing two-thirds of the wrist, indicates a living child.

If an unbroken line under the first Bracelet ends halfway across the wrist, then the child may have died in infancy.

The number of children does not always show on one wrist, but can be read as composite on both wrists.

# Signs and Markings on the Children Lines

If the Children Lines have a Star or Cross they indicate danger of an accident, the same as they would be on any other line.

If a line under the first Bracelet travels the length of the wrist but becomes shallow or has an Island, it indicates a child will suffer poor health.

Twins are shown by double parallel lines. These lines are close to each other and sometimes touch.

Twins can also be shown by a single line that ends in a Fork under the first Bracelet.

If a line travels toward the first Bracelet with Islands on it, it would indicate a miscarriage or abortion.

If the lines under the first Bracelet have Dots on them it indicates one or more abortions.

330

## The Bracelet Lines

The Bracelet Lines can also be referred to as Rascettes or Wrist Lines. These lines run parallel across and below the base of the hand. There may be one, two or three Wrist Lines sometimes crossing and running into each other. There are pros and cons about the influence of the Bracelets. In the old tradition of Palmistry, Wrist Lines when deep and clear would add **longevity, each line** adding twenty-five to thirty years. But today's Palmists believe this to be obsolete, some even feel that except for the first Wrist Line all other lines are unimportant. Today's Palmists believe the presence of all three lines in a clear, good condition can add robust health, great fortune and happiness. With all this good fortune, then why not longevity. The Magic Bracelets.

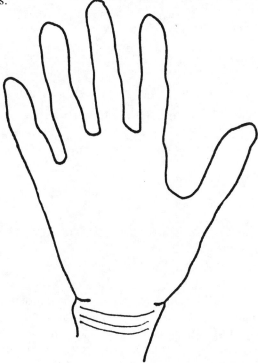

**The Bracelet Lines**

# Variations of the Bracelet Lines

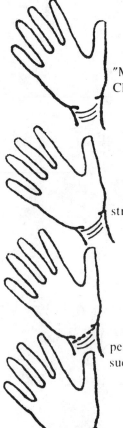

When all Wrist Lines are well formed it is usually referred to as the "Magic Bracelet". It signifies great fortune, happiness and ripe old age; "a Charm Bracelet".

If the first Wrist Line of the Bracelet is clear and deep, it indicates a strong constitution, fit and healthy, and good prospects in the owner's life.

If the first Wrist Line of the Bracelet is Chained or has an Island in it, this person will have a life of care, anxieties, hard work, and will not achieve success until later in life.

If the first Wrist Line in the Bracelet is poorly formed, it indicates this person may tend to be extravagant and lack caution, which can contribute to their own misfortune.

When the first Wrist Line curves upwards like a bow it is an indication of internal trouble, and is most often seen on female hands. Its owner will have trouble conceiving children and delivering a child. It can even be the sign of sterility, but you must search both hands carefully before making any statement. You may find the bow in only one hand.

If the first line of the Bracelet is clear and encircles the wrist in good condition it will indicate the ability to conceive and bear children without complications. In a man the line will indicate fertility or a problem with sterility.

A Bracelet Line that is wavy or traced indicates an extravagant nature, this person will experience bad luck and their life will be shortened by dissipation.

# Signs and Markings on the Bracelet Lines

A Star in the middle of the top Bracelet forcasts a legacy. An Angle Line in this same area indicates that this person can look forward to inheriting money and position late in life.

A Cross at the beginning of the top Bracelet indicates that this person will have personal difficulties but in their middle age will be secure.

A Bracelet Line that is Chained indicates a life of struggle, hard work and worries.

A Bracelet Line that has Islands indicates worry, weakness and stress.

## The Travel Lines

You will find Travel Lines in many Palmistry books. There is no denying that the Travel Lines do exist, but only in few hands. They are more likely to be seen on the hands of a person who has traveled very little, to these people traveling would be important and very exciting, therefore it would be recorded on their hands. For to-day especially with our universal trend for the young, middle age and Senior Citizens to vacataion all over the world, or a commercial pilot, the traveling salesman, business men, and world travelers, would all have Travel Lines covering their hands.

The following information on Travel Lines and diagrams will be as complete as possible, so you may make your own judgement regarding these lines.

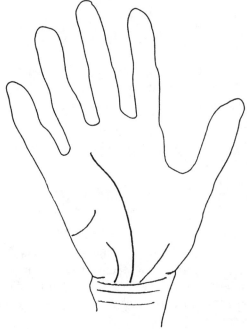

**The Travel Lines**

# Travel Lines starting at the Top Bracelet

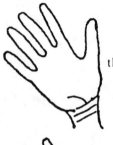

When the Travel Line starts at the top Bracelet and ends in the area of the Mount of the Moon it indicates a trip by land, sea or air.

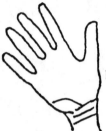

When a Travel Line starts at the top Bracelet and goes across to the Mount of the Moon it indicates an importnat trip to a far off land.

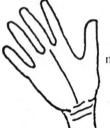

When a Travel Line starts at the top Bracelet and runs upwards to the middle finger onto the Mount of Saturn, it indicates a hazardous journey.

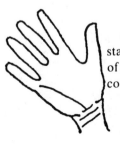

A Travel Line starting from the top Bracelet and running upwards and starting towards the Mount of Mercury below the little finger is a good sign of sudden wealth. Its owner will gain fortune either during their travel or in connection with a distant journey.

A Travel Line starting at the top Bracelet running upwards by the Line of Success and ending on the Mount of Apollo indicates a journey to a country with a hot climate. This Travel Line can also be interpreted as benefits coming to this person through valuable contacts made while traveling.

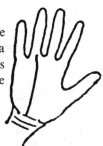

A Travel Line starting from the top Bracelet and traveling upwards ending at the Mount of Jupiter indicates a long journey that will give this person a great advantage in life, indicating wealth coming through a very successful journey.

A Travel Line starting from the top Bracelet and ending on the Life Line indicates the possibility of death on a journey.

When a Travel Line starting at the top Bracelet crosses another Travel Line, it indicates the journey will be repeated for some important reason.

# Travel Lines starting on the Mount of the Moon

The Mount of the Moon is associated with Travel Lines, whether the lines are horizontal or vertical it indicates travel across water.

Starting on the Mount of the Moon a horizontal Travel Line that is deep, straight and long will indicate a enjoyable journey.

Starting on the Mount of the Moon a Travel Line that curves upwards indicates a succesful business trip.

Starting on the Mount of the Moon, a Travel Line that curves down toward the wrist indicates an unsuccessful trip.

A horizontal Travel Line starting on the Mount of the Moon, across the palm, and reaching the Fate Line, indicates that the journey will be longer and more important but does not mean leaving the country.

## Signs or Markings on Travel Lines

If there is an Island at the end of the Travel Line, no matter how small, the journey will result in a loss.

When a Travel Line ends with a Cross, the journey will end in disappointment.

When the Travel Line ends with a Square there will be danger during the journey, but the owner will be protected.

An Island on the Travel Line starting on the Mount of the Moon will indicate danger from water, if found in both hands, it becomes very dangerous.

A Travel Line that runs to the Head Line and ends in a Spot, Islands or Break, indicates some danger to the head when on a journey.

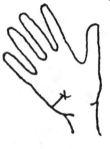

A Cross on a Travel Line starting on the Mount of the Moon will indicate the possibility that an accident may occur. If the sign appears in one hand it can be avoided. Judge the time at which the line appears and advise the client to cancel the trip.

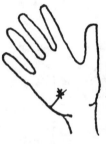

A Star at the end of the Travel Line has a traditional meaning. The sign indicates death by drowning. Again judge the time of the line and advise your client to avoid traveling on or near water.

# The Ring of Solomon

The Ring of Solomon Line starts between the fingers of Jupiter (the index finger) and Saturn finger, running downward and encircling the Mount of Jupiter finger and ending near the beginning of the Life Line.

This semi-circle sign is a very interesting because like all the other minor lines, it can either modify or add to the reading of the major lines. This sign has a "sixth sense" attribute. These people can be adept and skillful in the Psychic Practices. You will seldom see this line; very few people have this sign.

The Ring of Solomon signifies wisdom, common sense, intuition, objectivity and the ability to adapt to life. Often they are able to use these qualities to an advantage in choosing a lifestyle suited to their potential. They need solitude so that they can study and improve their spiritual self through meditation.

The Ring of Solomon has always been an inborn, inherited and genetic sign giving natural ability for the occult. For those who have this sign, choosing to study hand analysis or any branch of the psychic sciences, would be very successful.

The Ring of Solomon may also form one side of a Square on the Mount of Jupiter. When this Square is present it is known as a "Teachers Square" and adds wisdom to knowledge and a sense of security.

**The Ring of Solomon**

# Variations on the Ring of Solomon

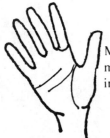

A Ring of Solomon that encircles the base of the Jupiter finger on the Mount of Jupiter indicates the love for occult studies. It is an inherited mark. The person with a clear, strong Ring of Solomon is intuitive and has inherited good common sense.

A true. clear Ring of Solomon is rare. Most common is a broken line which, although not having the strength of a clear Ring of Solomon, still carries the desire and interest of the occult, but not as a serious study.

An incomplete Ring of Solomon with a second incomplete Ring of Solomon below it reenforces the ring, bringing it added strenth. It is important to look at both palms in order to understand the degree of strength it adds to this person's interest and abilities for the occult.

A Ring of Solomon is usually found on the hand that has a Croix Mystique located at the quadrangle. These people have a great aptitude for occult studies and psychology.

A Ring of Solomon with a Croix Mystique at the quadrangle and a much lined or rayed hand indicates great aptitude for the study of the occult and psychology. They have a great impressionability of the mind and senses and they are always interested in new things.

The Ring of Solomon is most often seen in a much lined hand and generally a Croix Mystique or Mystical Cross is found in the center of the Quadrangle, between the Head and Heart Lines.

The Ring of Solomon may also form one side of a Square on the Mount of Jupiter. When this Square is present it is known as a "Teachers Square" and it adds wisdom to knowledge and a sense of security.

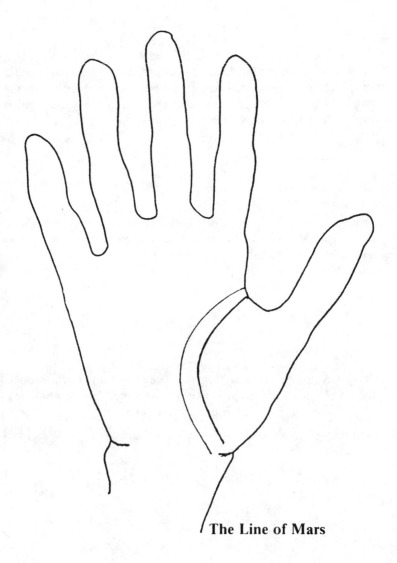

**The Line of Mars**

# The Line of Mars

The Line of Mars starts on the lower Mount of Mars, from which the line receives its name, it encircles the Mount of Venus inside the Life Line. The Line of Mars is also referred to as the inner Life Line or Sister Line to the Life Line.

The Line of Mars also runs parallel inside the Life Line and is a sister line to the Line of Influence. The Lines of Influence are associated with the effects from relatives, children or lovers. The Mars Line relates to the health of the person and always for the best in sustaining the Life Line and strengthening it.

In order for the Mars Line to give its full strength to the Life Line it must run as close to the Life Line as possible. Because the Lines of Influence also occupy the Mount of Venus you must be careful not to confuse the "Lines" of Influence with a "Line" of Mars.

The Mars Line is a very fortunate line to have, what ever strength the line has it is added to the Line of Life.

The Line of Mars is not always present on the palm of the hand, but when it does appear it is never alone, for if it was, it would be regarded as a Life Line. When the Mars Line covers a short area along the side of the Life Line its strengthening influence is limited to the period of time it follows the Life Line.

When this line is clear and strong it is like a second Life Line and acts as a reinforcement to the Life Line. It adds great vitality, power to resistance to illness and disease because of this influence it is an excellent line to have.

If there are any breaks bad signs or markings on the Life Line they will be reduced and minimized, almost help in healing by the pressure of the Mars Line.

The only fault with the Line of Mars is when it is too strong, and with a deep Life Line, it may add too much activity to the Life Line. These people never seem to do thing in halves. They have vitality to spare. This could cause strain and physical exertion. They may work off this surplus energy with too much work, drinking or over eating and even getting into fights.

# Variations of the Mars Line

When the Line of Mars is deep and strong and the Life Line is deep and strong, the Line of Mars adds vitality, endurance and aggression. This vital force may endanger the person, for they tend to overdo; they are constantly wanting action and never do anything halfway. They have vitality to spare and are constantly looking for an outlet for their energy.

If the Line of Mars runs only part of the way along the side of the Life Line, its strengthening power will only be present to the time or age at which it appears beside the Life Line.

If the Life Line has any defects and a Line of Mars runs past the area of the defects, the delicacy or danger of the Life Line will not be fatal because of the underlying vitality and strength of the Mars Line beside it.

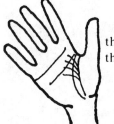

If the Line of Mars has lines rising from it and they cross the Life Line, this indicates a constant tendency of this person to rise in life, because of the strengthening of the constitution by the presence of the Line of Mars.

If a line or lines rise from the Line of Mars and merge into the Head Line, this person will have increased mental strength because of the energy and vitality flowing to the Head Line.

When a line from the Line of Mars rises and merges into the Fate Line, it increases the value of the Fate Line, making it more certain that this person's career will be successful because of the strong vitality of the Mars Line.

If the Mars Line has lines rising to the Head Line and cutting the line, this is not a good sign. The strong vitality of the Mars Line will be too strong for the brain and will injure it by the constant straining. These people will not know that they are overtaxing the brain. This condition can cause a breakdown.

If this person has a strong Girdle of Venus with a large Mount of Venus, a strong Life Line and Line of Mars, they have an excessive sexual appetite. These are very healthy people so their sexual powers can be great and they will not stop to consider the morality of their acts.

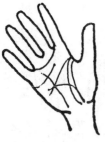

If the person has a strong Girdle of Venus with a strong Mars Line and Life Line; if a line rises from the Mars Line and cuts the Success or Fate Line, their sexual indulgences and desires will cause a decided setback of their career at the time or age the Mars Line cuts either of these lines. Look at both hands before making any statement.

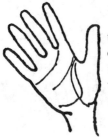

If the Line of Mars sweeps down across the palm of the hand and ends on the Mount of the Moon, it indicates a great amount of vitality. This also can be a marking of a person that can become an alcoholic with a restless nature. They are great travelers and expend a great deal of energy in this way. The rest of their energy will be spent on "wine, women and song."

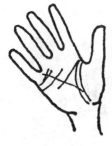

If the person has a strong Girdle of Venus with a strong Life and Mars Lines, with a line rising from the Mars Line and cutting the Line of Affection that ends with a Fork, the unfaithfulness of the person will ruin the happiness of their married life, with the Fork on the end of the Line of Affection intensifying the problem.

# Signs and Markings on the Line of Mars

If the person has a strong Girdle of Venus with a strong Life and Mars Line and the Mars Line cuts the Line of Success which has either a Dot, Cross or Cross-bar at the end of the line, the reputation of this person will be lost.

If the Line of Mars sweeps down across the palm of the hand and ends on the Mount of the Moon; if this line ends with a Cross, Star, Dot or Cross-bar and the Life Line ends in a Cross or Star, this will intensify the seriousness of this person's condition and they will die of excessive alcohol or abusive substance.

If the Line of Mars sweeps down across the palm of the hand and ends on the Mount of the Moon with a Cross, Star, Cross-bar or Dot at the end and the Head Line is defective about halfway, it indicates that the drug abuse or alcoholism has become too rapid and the brain is being exhausted.

If the Line of Mars sweeps down across the palm of the hand and ends on the Mount of the Moon, and this line ends with a Cross, Dot, Star or Cross-bar, this person will die very suddenly after great excess of alcohol or drug addiction.

If the Line of Mars sweeps down across the palm of the hand and ends on the Mount of the Moon with a Dot, Star, Cross or Crossbar at the end, and the Head Line ends in a Star, this person will become insane at the time or age the Star appears on the Head Line.

349

# The Line of Influence

The Line of Influence or Family Lines are located on the Mount of Venus running parallel with the Life Line. they also radiate from the Mount of Venus and run through the Life Line to the major lines. These lines are also called Rays of Influence. These Lines of Influence signify disturbances in the personal mode of living, the persons sensitivity, their reaction to their environment and the nervousness caused by them.

The Line of Mars also runs parallel inside the Life Line and is a sister line to the Line of Influence. The Lines of Influence are associated with the affects from relatives, children or lovers. The Mars Line relates to the health of the person and always for the best in sustaining the Life Line and strengthening it.

The Line of Influence are caused by the nervous reaction from others such as the family, loved ones, best friends. Marriage of course is included in the family influence. The lines that run closest to the Life Line have the most effect and are usually associated with a mother, father, brother or sister. Faint lines show lesser influence of other people, deep lines indicate many influences. If only a few deep lines are present the person has had only a few close relationships. The Mount of Venus with many fine lines indicates the person has many friends and acquaintances. If all the lines are contained within the Life Line without crossing the line then their relationships have not changed their life. Influence Lines also can tell the need of affection, attention and friends.

**The Line of Influence**

## Variations on the Lines of Influence

When the Lines of Influence are thin, shallow, chained, uneven or broken then their influence is not strong.

When a Line of Influence begins deep and then becomes thin, until it gradually fades away, the influence was strong in the beginning, but has gradually grown weaker until it loses its effect.

If a Line of Influence starts deep then becomes thin, reviving itself, gradually growing stronger, the influence will return into the life of the person and this person will grow in strength.

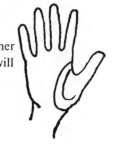

If the Line of Influence draws away from the Life Line and grows thinner at the same time the influence of the situation will go away and will disappear

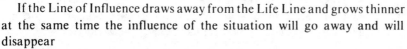

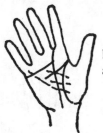

If the Line of Influence breaks following the point of crossing any major line, it will weaken the line at the time it reaches it. Examine the other hand and lines and their condition before advising your client.

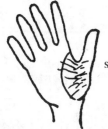

Multiple Lines of Influence indicates a person with many relationships, some who have greatly changed the outcome of this persons life.

The formation of strong, deep lines circling the inside of the Life Line indicates resistance of other people, with a dislike to being told what to do by friends or their relatives. These lines of resistance also apply to their own health, they seem to have a built in immunity from many deseases.

When Lines of Influence begin thin and grow stronger and then break and are replaced by another line and then another line, it shows that one after another different relatives have replaced each other as an influences to this person.

When the Lines of Influence run parallel to the vertical lines such as the Fate Line and Success Line strengthens the line. It repairs a split or strengthens the section of the line that may have an Island or is Chained.

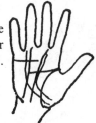

Lines of Influence starting from the Mount of Venus and move across the palm, generally indicates obstacles, traumas and nervous times.

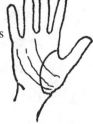

A long deep Line of Influence starting high on the Mount of Venus to the Mount of Mercury under the little finger denotes a strong, deep and long lasting relationship which will have a great influence in the persons life.

Deep long Lines of Influence that are contained in the circle of the Life Line indicate a person who has many friends and affections but does not allow them to change their life style or personal environment. It may also indicate a gregarious person who enjoys the company of others and who is affectionate and secure enough to gather many friends and lovers.

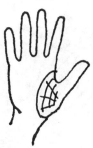

If the Life Line is very defective, thin, chained, broad, shallow or broken, and a Line of Influence is strong, it indicates that this person is subject to delicate health; a relative has been their mainstay in life. This line has the same effect as the Line of Mars and the influence may be constant nurturing to keep them alive.

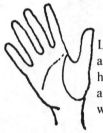

If the Head Line is poor early in life and gradually grows stronger, and a Line of Influence is strong deep in the beginning and then becomes thinner as it continues, the weak mental condition of the person in early life will be helped by the strong Line of Influence by someone giving the help needed, and as the head grows stronger, the influence will no longer be needed and will fade away.

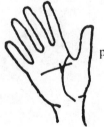

A rising branch from the Life Line indicates an upward tendency in this persons life, but Worry Lines are effecting it.

If Worry Lines are seen in the same area of the Lines of Influence, their presence when crossing a Line of Influence may indicate legal difficulty. When reading their lines, examine both hands. Some of our older Palmists saw their markings as an indicator of divorce

When the Worry Line runs from the Life Line across the hand and cuts the Marriage Line that is forked then this will indicate a divorce.

When the Line of Influence is broken, starting at about twenty or thirty years and has another line beside it beginning at the same time and this line is strong and deep, it indicates a relationship that may be stormy; however, the strong Line of Influence strengthens it by the support of parents. The stronger line can sometimes help a poor marriage.

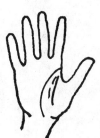

If a Line of Influence begins away from the Life Line and gradually comes toward it and grows stronger it indicates that the influence of a distant relative is gradually coming into the persons life and will become important. This line may cut through other Lines of Influence which also indicates its strength.

If a Line of Influence breaks and after a short space starts again and repeats itself it indicates that the influence of a person in their life will come and go.

Light horizontal lines on the Mount of Venus indicate persons and events which have crossed our lives and that have hindered and impaired us and put obstacles in our way.

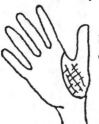

Light parallel lines are not obstacles and though they may be weak or broken, they are not a hostile influence. When the lines are crossed it adds obstacles to our lives and this indicates worry and nervous reaction.

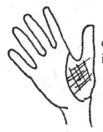

When a number of Lines of Influence run parallel to the Life Line and cut by numerous lines, the family life of this person has suffered constant interruptions and is an unhappy situation.

# Signs or Markings on the Lines of Influence

If an Island is at the end of the Line of Influence where the line reaches, such as the Head Line or Success Line would effect the line it touches. It indicates illness or an accident. Examine both hands, their lines and their condition before advising your client.

If the Lines of Influence cross a line, either the Life Line or the Head Line and a red Dot is formed, a major illness or accident is possible. Judge the time on both hands before advising your client. This mark will affect the line it touches

A Star at the end of a Line of Influence indicates the end of that influence.

If a Line of Influence, beginning early by the Life Line and ends in a Star and has an Influence Line beside it that is longer and strong, it indicates that their mother or father has died at an early age which can be judged by the end of the Star to the Life Line and that a distant relative has come into their life and taken care of them.

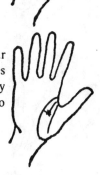

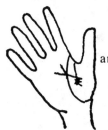

When a Worry Line starts from a Star on the end of a Line of Influence and cuts past the Life Line it indicates a death of a relative.

An Island on the Line of Influence that ends with a Star, Cross, Dot or Cross - bar indicates a poor relationship which will die or end at the time indicated by its location of the sign on the Life Line.

When a Line of Influence is cut by a strong cross - line which has an Island and a Star at the end, some disaster has happened to the influence which has brought an illness that has ended in death. If the cutting line is deep and starts early in life it could be a parent.

When a cross - line on the Line of Influence has an Island in it there will be something unpleasant connected to this persons' life owing to their own fault.

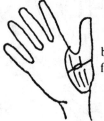

When an Island on the Line of Influence has numerous small lines running to the Life Line, the illness of a relative will be a constant worry.

When a Line of Influence ends in a Star and is connected by a Worry Line with an Island on the Head Line the illness and death of a relative produces a weakened mental condition in this client.

When an Island on the Life Line and an Island on the Line of Influence with numerous small lines cutting into the Life Line, the concern over a relative's health will cause worry which will seriously affect the health of this person.

When a Line of Influence is deep at the beginning and gradually grows thinner with a Star at the end and with a Worry Line running across the Life Line which is thin and has a Dot on it, it increases the illness of the person. If there is a Dot at the end of the Life Line, the illness will cause their death.

When the Line of Influence ends in a Star, and Worry Line connects with a Dot on the Head Line, the death of a relative will bring a severe illness to the brain of this person.

# The Worry Lines

Worry Lines are located on the Mount of Venus inside the circle of the Life Line. Worry Lines run across the Mount of Venus and often leave the circle touching or cutting other lines. When a Worry Line does leave the circle of the Life Line and touches or cuts another line it indicates what the person is concerned about. They will actually begin to worry at the point or time where the line has cut out of the Life Line. Many Worry Lines on the Mount of Venus are also called Ray Lines, these lines indicate a person who is a worrier and frets over their troubles. The time at which their troubles occur is judged by the place at which the lines start or cross the Life Line.

A well defined sister line known as the Line of Mars protects against the troubles that may mark the Life Line.

Worry Lines are also caused by stress, either business or personal problems.

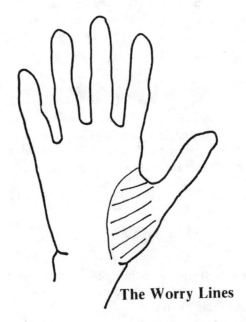

**The Worry Lines**

# Variations of the Worry Lines

A Worry Line that runs to the Fate Line and crosses it, means worry about money.

A Worry Line that crosses the Success Line indicates its owner will be concerned about their reputation.

Worry Lines which are thin and puny are only caused by annoyances.

Worry Lines that cross the Life Line that are deep and red indicate, obstacles, disabilities and must be regarded as serious according to their depth and length. When deep they indicate illness.

Worry Lines that are continuous and rayed on the Mount of Venus indicate a worrier. This person worries over everything. If the lines are short there will only be temporary annoyances.

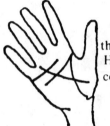

A Worry Line that runs to the Heart Line and crosses it, indicates that there will be trouble either in a love affair or there can be trouble with the Heart. Study the Heart Lines in both hands to make sure of their condition.

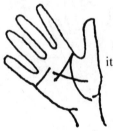

A Worry Line that cuts the Head Line will be disturbed by foolish acts of its owner.

# Signs and Markings on the Worry Lines

An Island on the Worry Line that starts on the Mount of Venus to the Heart Line indicates an unhappy love affair and the consequences are serious and even shameful.

A Fork at the end of the Worry Line that crosses the Heart Line indicates an unhappy marraige or a divorce.

A Worry Line from a Star on the Mount of Venus indicates quarrels with relatives ending in ruin if the line runs up to the Mount of Apollo.

# The Via Lascivia Line

Also called the Milky Way and The Cepholic Line.

The Via Lascivia Line also know as the Sister Line to the Health Line is seldom seen but when present it is a short line, often well defined running parallel to the Health Line. When this happens it strengthens the Health Line. The Via Lascivia Line starts near the Health Line, farther over on the Mount of the Moon towards the percussion side of the palm of the hand and ends on the lower part of the Upper Mount of the Moon. People with a strong and clear Health Line usually have the Via Lascivia Line. When this does occur it denotes a strong leaning towards sensuality as well an intense love of money.

The Via Lascivia Line probably received its name from the fact that a strong Line of Health and the Via Lascivia Line could largely increase the intensity of passion, giving added force to ardor and energy in all pursuits of life and good health.

This line does have a negative side. It can reveal a strong and intense sensitivity to drugs, alcohol, tobacco and other addictive substances with the loss of sensuality.

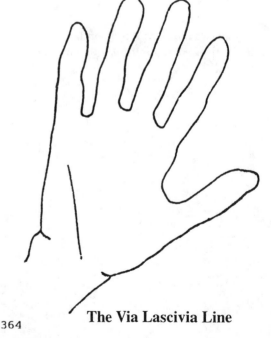

**The Via Lascivia Line**

# Variations of the Via Lascivia Line

The Via Lascivia Line is seldom seen, but should run as a sister line to the Health Line. It is a slanting line starting from the inside of the base of the Mount of the Moon and ending on the lower area of the Upper Mount of Mars near the percussion side of the hand.

If the Via Lascivia Line is deep and cuts a Line of Affection which ends in a Fork, the lustful and sensual desires of this person will ruin their marriage.

If a rising branch line from the Via Lascivia cuts the Line of Success, lustful and sensual desires will ruin the chance for success for this person.

If a rising branch line from the Via Lascivia cuts the Health line, the lascivious, sensual desires will injure the health and success of this person.

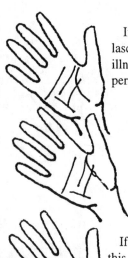

If a rising branch of the Via Lascivia crosses the Life Line, their lascivious and sensual desires will injure this person's health and cause illness. If after cutting the Life Line it will become defective and will cause permanent damage to their health.

If a Line of Mars runs to the Mount of the Moon to the Via Lascivia Line, this person will have a heavy drinking or drug problem.

If the hand has the Via Lascivia Line and the Line of Health is wavy the Via Lascivia line will act as a Sister Line and reinforce it, preventing a serous attack from biliousness that would have occurred without it.

A broken Health Line with the Via Lascivia Line and the Sister Line will help overcome serious stomach problems.

If the Via Lascivia Line runs beside the Health Line that runs to the Mount of Mercury, it is a good sign and this person will enjoy good health and success.

# Signs And Markings On The Via Lascivia Line

If a branch line from the Via Lascivia end with a Dot on the Life Line, the lustful and sensual desires will cause severe illness at the age or time where the Dot is located.

If there are many branches from the Via Lascivia Line running across the Head Line, the excesses of lustful and sensual desires will weaken and impair the brain and this person will have many headaches. If a Dot, Cross or Cross-bars occur in the Head Line after these branch lines, this person will have an attack of brain fever. If any of these signs appear and are seen on the Head Line, this person may become insane.

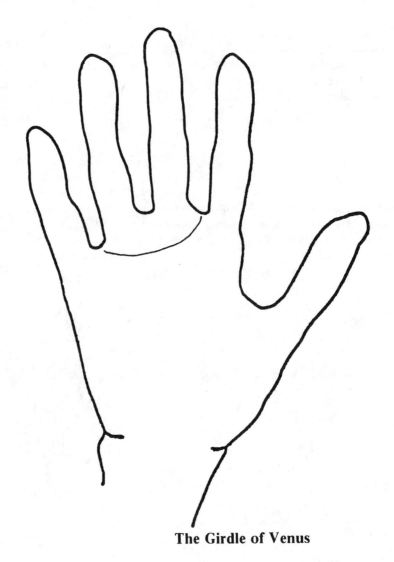

**The Girdle of Venus**

# The Girdle of Venus

The Girdle of Venus is a semi-circular line, starting from or near the base of the first finger, on the Mount of Jupiter continuing on a loop connecting the Mount of Saturn, and Mount of Apollo. It can touch the Mount of Mercury or even at times extending to the Percussion area.

Although the Girdle of Venus is called a sister line to the Heart Line and in some cases when the Heart Line is absent, the Girdle of Venus can take its place, it does not mean this in the physical sense but in reference to affections and for this reason the line was named Girdle of Venus meaning the (Girdle of love and passion).

This line is a subject of much misunderstanding, and has been wrongly accused. Many Palmists have had a mistaken notion that this line represents promiscuous and indiscriminate behavior. Today we realize that in most cases this is not true

Some of the older Palmists have gone as far as to refer to the Girdle of Venus as a line of prostitution. Prostitutes either male or female do not perform this act of passion or sexuality, but simply for money or gains of some kind. Not all the old traditional interpretations given to the Girdle of Venus can be denied. The line does indicate nervous energy which can be expanded into sexuality and a passionate flirtatious nature. They enjoy the opposite sex and can be tempted to physical passion. They also enjoy thinking, dreaming, reading and fantasize about sex. They appreciate all that is beautiful, mainly in the human form.

The Girdle of Venus is considered an abnormal line, by the virtue of its location. It is believed that the line is found more often in the hands of women. The line nearly always indicates an intense state of nervousness and in a large majority of cases a great tendency toward abnormal emotions and hysteria. In a large percentage of hands, the palm will be crossed with innumerable lines running in every direction. This alone indicates the intensely nervous person, but with the addition of the Girdle of Venus there is an increased degree of nervousness.

The presence of the Girdle of Venus is by no means an uncommon sign, it can be seen frequently in all types of hands.

# Variations of the Girdle of Venus

When the Girdle of Venus is made up of broken lines, it increases the nervousness of the person, with the danger of abnormal excitement and habits. The sign of Venus is love and passion.

If the Girdle of Venus is made up of double or triple lines, which is very common, it indicates that this person will have the strong bad qualities of the sign.

If the Girdle of Venus is made up of a number of broken lines and this person is nervous and sensitive, the danger of hysteria is very great and the nervous symptoms are increased.

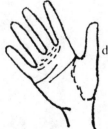

If the Girdle of Venus is made up of numerous broken lines, with a defective Life Line, it indicates ill health and unhappiness.

# Signs and Markings on the Girdle of Venus

If the Girdle of Venus is made up of numerous broken lines and there is a defective Fate Line with a Star or Cross on the line the Girdle of Venus may be the cause of the problem.

If the Girdle of Venus is made up of numerous broken lines and the Head Line has a Dot on it, there can be danger of insanity. A Cross or Star on the Head Line will also indicate a weak brain and a tendency toward insanity.

If the Girdle of Venus is made up of numerous broken lines and the Line of Success is defective with a Cross or Star on it, the Girdle of Venus may be the cause of this person's hysteria and nervous excitement.

When the Girdle of Venus is made up of numerous lines and the Mount of Venus has many nervous lines or rays on it; if the Head Line slopes low into the Mount of the Moon and ends with a Star this indicates a danger of insanity.

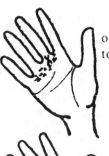

When the Girdle of Venus is made up of broken lines and there is a Cross on the Mount of Saturn, this person can become erratic, cranky and hard to get along with.

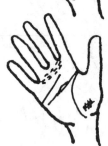

When the Girdle of Venus is made up of broken lines and there are Dots or Islands on the Head Line under the Mount of Saturn, a Grille on the Mount of the Moon and the nails are fluted or brittle, this person is in danger of having paralysis.

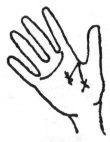

When the Girdle of Venus is deep and the hand has a thick base and the fingers are thick and the other lines on the hand are deep and red with the Head and Life Lines short and ending with a Star or Cross, this person will die suddenly at the age at which the Life Line ends, in pursuit of excessive pleasure and self indulgence.

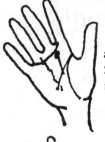

When the Girdle of Venus is deep and cuts a weak, scattered Fate Line, and there is a Dot on the Mount of Apollo or on the end of the Line of Success, this indicates that the pursuit of pleasure and self-indulgence will ruin this person's career and reputation.

If a deep Girdle of Venus cuts a Line of Affection and if the Heart Line has descending Lines drooping from it, the Head Line becomes defective. If this line ends with a Star and the Fate Line has a Cross-bar that stops it, this person will ruin their marriage and career, ending their life with impairment of their mental facilities and insanity.

# The Psychic Hand

A hand that bears the Ring of Solomon, the Bow of Intuition, the Mystical Cross or Croix Mystique, an X on the Mount of the Moon, a High Mount of Neptune and Pluto, this persons life, consciously or unconsciously, will be influenced by the psychic senses. They will enjoy being involved in the occult and the spiritual world. To have all these signs or markings in one hand would be very rare, but you will see palms with these markings and signs.

The Ring of Solomon is located on the Mount of Jupiter; it forms a semicircular line that almost completely surrounds the base of the index finger. It is the sign of wisdom, common sense, intuition.

The Bow or Crescent of Intuition is a semicircular line starting on the Mount of the Moon and ending on Upper Mars. It gives exceptional intuition and is usually found on those involved in ESP.

The Croix Mystique lies in the center of the Quadrangle between the Head and Heart Lines. It always shows the influence of psychic power.

An X on the Mount of the Moon shows an interest in the occult sciences.

The Mount of Neptune is located at the base of the palm between the Mount of the Moon and the Mount of Venus; it indicates the dividing line between the conscious and the unconscious zones of the palm. With a high Neptune Mount, it brings instinct and enchantment and mystery with the power to mesmerize an audience.

The Mount of Pluto located at the bottom of the Mount of the Moon, is in the unconscious and passive zone of the palm: life, death and regeneration. A high Mount of Pluto gives the power of imagination and the occult.

**The Psychic Hand**

373

# Variations of the Psychic Hand

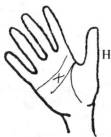

The Croix Mystique lies in the center of the Quadrangle between the Head and Heart Lines. It always shows the influence of psychic power.

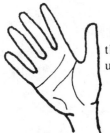

The Crescent of Intuition is a semi circular line starting on the Mount of the Moon and ending on Upper Mars. It gives exceptional intuition and is usually found on those involved in E.S.P.

The hand that has the Ring of Soloman, Bow of Intuition and the Mystical Cross or Croix Mystique life consciously or unconsciously will be influenced by the psychic senses. They will enjoy being involved in the occult and the spiritual world.

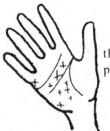

Many Crosses scattered over the palm are Psychic or "Witches" Crosses, the hand of an old soul. These people are in tune with the future and have psychic ability.

The shape of the Psychic Hand. The palm is long and narrow and the fingers are long and usually tapered at the ends. These people are very sensitive and spiritual.

A Triangle on the Mount of Saturn indicates talent for the occult and intuitive.

The Psychic Hand will often have a palm with many fine spidery lines that crisscross the palm in all directions.

The Mount of the Moon that is greatly developed toward the wrist indicates intuitive and occult powers.

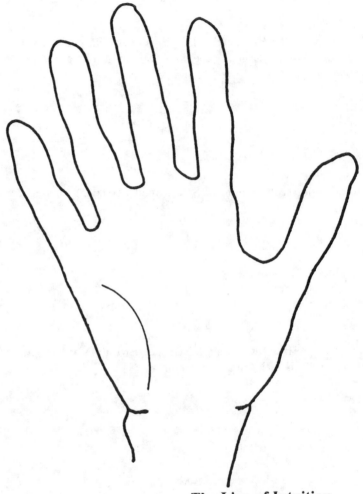

**The Line of Intuition**

# The Line of Intuition

The Line of Intuition is also referred to as the Line of Luna and the Line of the Moon. This line lies on the palm near the Percussion side of the hand. It starts on the lower area of the Mount of the Moon, and runs upwards in a curved line toward the Plain of Mars and ends on Upper Mars or near the Mount of Mercury under the little finger. The Line of Intuition can be mistaken for the Health or Mercury Line, however, you will be able to recognize it by its crescent or arc shape.

The Line of Intuition is a very favorable line to have, it adds greatly to one's intuitve powers. People with this line receive impressions which they cannot account for, a sort of sixth sense and an interest not reasoned by the mind but by instinct. People who possess this sixth sense are often unaware of it themselves; when questioned they are unable to explain; they have a sensitivity and understanding of other people. Those who do not understand this gift just go along following their feelings and instincts.

Most people wilth a Line of Intuition will be interested in or working in the Psychic Sciences. This line is usually accompanied by the Ring of Solomon and the Croix Mystique or Mystic Cross on the palm, however, it is more often found on the Philosophic, Conic and Psychic hand than on any of the other seven types of hands.

The Line of Intuition is one of the most unusual lines that a hand can have. Its presence is significant with regards to psychic gifts or powers, intuition and prophecy.   Those with this line have abilities above and beyond the range of the normal senses. Some one who is psychic, clairvoyant or mediumistic can use practically anything as a focus for concentration to bring their gifts into play. While concentrating on a line of the palm they may suddenly get a "flash" of information which could not possibly have been gained by normal means. The "flash" may relate to the person's present, past or something that may happen in the future.

Scientists believe some day all human beings will be able to receive impressions which are in no sense mysterious but merely are too delicate to be registered. We will someday find that there does exist waves or particles which are functioning outside of ordinary time that would tell us of the past or future and we may some day understand them, just as we have found light waves which the eye does not register but which can make their impressions on sensitive instruments.

When you see the Line of Intuition in the right hand you can assume that the person is aware of and has consciously developed these gifts. If the line is on the left hand, but not on the right hand, then this is an inherited or inborn power and they are operating on a subconscious level.

Some people with this line do not try to develop their gifts, however, they do use their sixth sense unconciously; they may be a little scared to use this power or do not know how to develop it. Others are simply too busy and do not recognize that they are using it instinctively; they assume that their insight is just coincidence.

# Variations on the Line of Intuition

The Line of Intuition is located at the percussion side of the palm. It starts on the Mount of the Moon and curves toward the Plain of Mars, and ends on or near the Mount of Mercury.

When the Line of Intuition starts on the Mount of the Moon and curves toward the Plain of Mars and ends on the Mount of Mercury these people have true, strong intuition impressions. Whatever intuition is, it operates to give mental impressions from one person to another and those who have the Line of Intuition in their hands seem to be endowed in the highest degree with this faculty of receiving these impressions.

If the fingers are long and the tips of the fingers are pointed; if the Mount of the Moon is full and the Head Line slopes down; if the tips of the thumbs are pointed and a strong Line of Intuition is in the palms, this person will have good psychic powers.

If the Head Line slopes low to the Mount of the Moon and the Line of Intuition cuts it, the mental forces will be injured by allowing too much imagination.

If a branch line runs from the Line of Intuition and runs to the Mount of Jupiter, this person will be ambitious to accomplish their intuitive powers. These people make successful occultists.

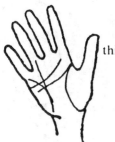

If a branch line from the Line of Intuition runs to the Mount of Apollo, this person will achieve renown through their intuitive powers.

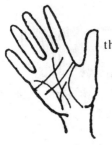

If a branch line from the Line of Intuition cuts the Fate Line, it indicates that this person's intuitive powers will bring trouble to their career.

## Signs and Markings on the Line of Intuition

An Island in the Line of Intuition will indicate that their intuitive nature will bring them poor success.

If an Island is at the beginning of the Line of Intuition, it indicates a tendency toward sleepwalking or somnambulism.

If the Line of Intuition ends in a Star this person will have great success from their intuitive powers. If the Mount of Mercury is well developed, this person will make money from their intuitive powers.

If the Line of Intuition merges into the Fate Line, the intuitive powers will assist the career of this person with good common sense. This combination of lines is a help to any hand.

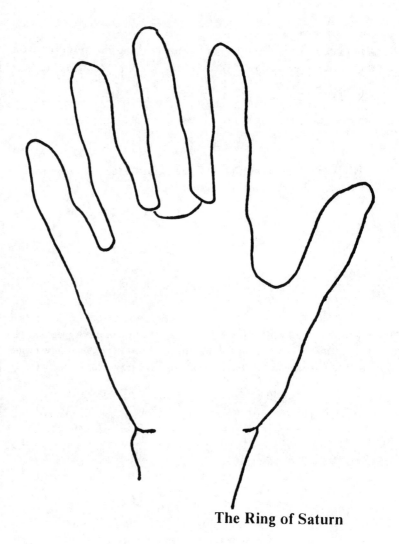

**The Ring of Saturn**

# The Ring of Saturn

The Ring of Saturn starts between the fingers of Jupiter and Saturn, forming a half circle and terminating between the fingers of Saturn and Apollo, forming a ring like mark. In some cases it can be composed of two lines which cross each other on the Mount of Saturn. This is also the natural point of termination for the Fate Line. It is considered by Palmist that any sign or line that interupts the course of a major line will disrupt its influence and hinder its funtion. If this happens and the current of the Fate Line is interrupted the material security in old age will be hampered.

The Ring of Saturn is considerably rare and can appear after some emotional upheaval has occurred. It is an unfavorable line. When the line is seen on the palm of the hand you must make your client aware of it and give warning for they are in grave danger. Because of its meaning, it is your responsibility to warn them and then search the hand for all positive indication which will help them overcome the negative aspects of the line. A strong phalanx to the thumb with a good and strong Head Line will help greatly.

The Ring of Saturn has been found on the hands of those who have committed suicide. Because this crescent shaped ring cuts completely across the Mount of Saturn it makes the Mount defective and shuts out its wisdom, seriousness and its balancing qualities and turns them into defects. The Ring of Saturn is an ill omen. It shows a tendency toward despondency and is considered a mark of misfortune. Its owner, as a rule, seems unable to achieve success or happiness. They lack a definite purpose, often changing moods as well as occupations. It effects the function of the mind and hampers any success in life. They have the attitude of failure and self doubt and seem to approach every thing they do with the thought that they will always fail. "What's the use".

# Variations of the Ring of Saturn

The Ring of Saturn encircles the base of the finger of Saturn on the Mount of Saturn.

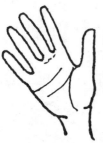

If the Ring of Saturn encircles the finger of Saturn and the ring is clear and complete, it is not a good mark to have. The presence of this line indicates a person will jump, from one job to another and never stay in any one job long enough to experience any success. The Ring of Saturn is often seen on persons in prison who have been imprisoned for serious crimes. It is also found on hands who have committed suicide.

If the Ring of Saturn does not completely encircle the base of the Saturn finger and is broken, it is not as unfavorable as a solid ring, and the Mount of Saturn will not become so defective. However, even with an imperfect ring there is a degree of defect present; this person will have a tendency to be flighty, restless, changeable and unsuccessful.

Note: Whenever the Ring of Saturn is seen on the hand, you must warn your client of its danger and they must understand its meaning so that they can avoid or overcome this negative tendency and seek professional help.

# Signs and Markings on the Ring of Saturn

When there is a Ring of Saturn on the hand and the Fate Line has a defect such as a Cross, Dot or Star, it will indicate that the career of this person has been ruined because of their lack of concentration of their purpose in life.

When there is a Ring of Saturn on the hand and the Line of Success has a defect such as a Cross, Dot or Star, it will indicate that this person's career has been ruined because of their lack of concentration on their career.

Ring of Saturn will often furnish an explanation for the cause of disaster or physical defect, such as a Head Line which has an Island or broken line that intensifies the changeable personality and character of this person.

If a person with a Ring of Saturn has a Head Line that slopes low on the Mount of the Moon which is large and Grilled, it indicates extreme imagination. These people are flighty, restless, changeable and unsuccessful.

When the Ring of Saturn is composed of two lines that form a Cross on the Mount of Saturn, this line must be read in the same manner as a large Cross. This is not a good sign; it indicates that this person has suicidal tendencies.

# The Great Triangle

The Great Triangle is formed by the Head, Life and Health Lines. When the Great Triangle is large and well formed by good clear lines it is an excellent sign. The Life Line when clear indicates good health; the Head Line adds intelligence and the power to reason and the Health Line, when not touching the Life Line adds active intuition and mental awareness. Those with this type of Great Triangle will have great dignity, good morals and high values; they will be daring and bold and have a generous and kind disposition. They always aim high in their goals and have the energy to achieve success.

A poorly formed Great Triangle, ill-shaped by irregular and poorly traced lines, indicates that this person will tend to be lacking in balanced character and unlikely to achieve any high caliber in their profession.

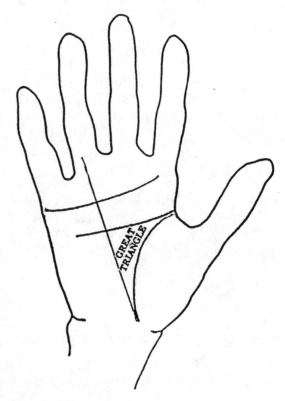

When a blunt angle of the Great Traingle is formed by the Life and Head Lines being separated, this indicates a high-spirited person who is independent, bold, daring and shows no fear.

If the angle of the Great Triangle is too wide and the lines are well separated, it indicates a reckless disposition. These people can be foolhardy and do impulsive and risky deeds.

When the lines of the Great Triangle are formed in such a way that make the triangle narrow, it is a sign of pettiness. This person tends to be mean, greedy, grasping and even miserly. They will be fearful and rather cowardly.

The Angles of the Great Triangle need special examination. This angle is called the First or Supreme Angle by the connection of the Life Line and Head Line. When this junction is sharply pointed and clearly defined, it indicates a good mind, common sense and a refined nature.

## The First Angle

If the Life Line is joined to the Head Line deep into the palm and the angle seems to be more blunt than it should be, this person will tend to be of a fearful nature and materially insecure. They are anxious and fear poverty. They become so concerned with their material well being that they are unaware of other people's feelings. They lack self-confidence and courage

387

If the angle is blunt and formed by a short Head Line, it indicates a lack of intellect, a slow, dull mind and a tendency to be crude and unrefined.

## The Second Angle

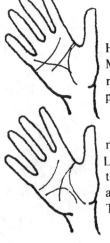

The Second or Inner Angle is formed by the connection of the Head and Health Lines. When the junction is sharp and well defined, it indicates a potential for longevity and good intellect. These people have active and brilliant minds.

When the Second Angle of the Great Triangle is very sharp and the Health Line starts at the Life Line making a sharp angle to the Mount of Mercury, this is not a good sign. It could indicate poor health and a nervous disposition depending upon the condition of the Life Line. These people can be erratic and not have good control of their reactions.

When the Second Angle of the Great Triangle is obtuse or greater than a right angle due to the downward curve of the Head Line and the Health Linewhich starts on the Mount of the Moon close to the percussion side of the palm, these people will have an extremely nervous disposition. They are without self discipline and are given to very quick changes in their lives. They can be very abrupt in their reactions and highly inflammable.

## The Third Angle

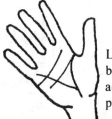

The Third Angle of the Great Triangle is formed by the connection of the Life Line and Health Line close to the wrist. When this junction happens to be sharp and well defined, it indicates a tendency toward neuralgia an acute pain along a nerve and fainting spells. It also indicates heart problems.

If the Third Angle of the Great Triangle is very obtuse, or greater than a right angle, leaving a large space between the Life Line and the Health Line it indicates a strong tendency toward deceit and faithlessness. These people cannot be trusted and are inclined to cheat, be disloyal and will take advantage of others.

When the Life Line and Health Line come close to one another and do not join it indicates a good potential for an active life and good health.

# Signs and Markings in the Great Triangle

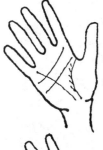

Upward branch lines on the Life Line terminating inside the Great Triangle indicates that riches and honors will come to this client after many struggles.

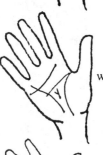

If there is a short, forked line inside the Triangle, it indicates a general weakening of the system.

A Cross in the center of the Triangle indicates trouble from others brought on by a quarrelsome disposition in this person.

A Star in the center of the Great Triangle indicates great riches and success.

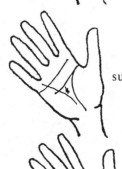

A Grille in the center of the Great Triangle indicates hidden enemies.

A Star very near or on the Health Line is not a good sign; it indicates blindness.

A Circle in the Triangle indicates problems from a person of the opposite sex.

A Square in the center of the Triangle indicates a very serious warning of danger.

A Triangle between the Life Line and the Fate Line indicates a military career.

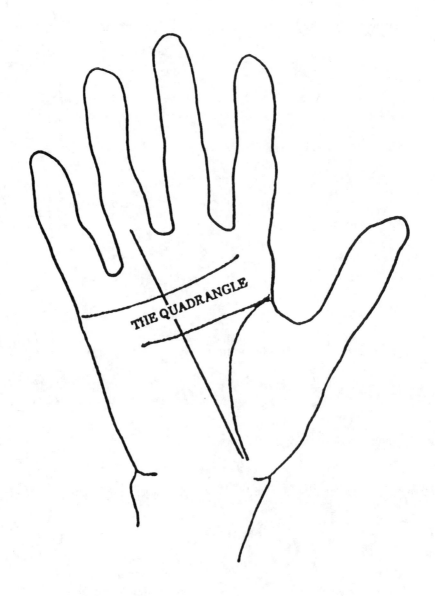

THE QUADRANGLE

# The Quadrangle

The Quadrangle, also known as the Table of the Hand, is located between the Head Line and Heart Line, but excluding the Mount of Jupiter and the Upper Mount of Mars. The Quadrangle is the area of activity where the mental processes come up against the emotional desires because of its location between the Head and the Heart Lines. It is important that there are no unusual markings or criss-cross lines in this area as they will disturb the Quadrangle.

The best type of Quadrangle to have is a well balanced or regular shape with the Head and Heart Lines about the same width apart with only a slight narrowing at the center. This narrowing at the center is important with the Head and Heart Lines well placed and clear.

This Quadrangle indicates a person with an even temper, honest and with a sense of humor. They must set goals for themselves in order to become an achiever because they are so easy going, however, they can become successful in a calm and steadfast way.

## Variations of the Quadrangle

If the Quadrangle is narrower on the percussion side of the palm it indicates that this person is hesitant about expressing their feelings. Their emotions will be well balanced. If the Head Line is straight, it will indicate stubbornness.

If the Quadrangle is higher toward the percussion side of the hand, it indicates that these people will be frank, reasonable, sensitive and straightforward.

When the Quadrangle is very narrow and the Heart Line and the Head Line are too close leaving a narrow space between them, this is an irregular Quadrangle and indicates a narrow minded person who would also have a tendency to be mean and very self-centered. The health of this person can be impaired; they could have breathing and respiratory problems.

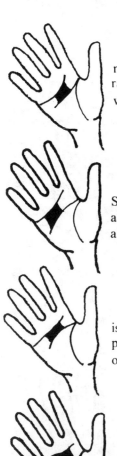

If the Heart Line bends toward the Head Line making the Quadrangle narrow at the center it indicates a person who will be ruled by their head rather than by their emotions. This is also a sign of a poor lover; they would rather choose wealth than love.

If the space is wider under the Mount of Apollo than below the Mount of Saturn, it indicates that this person will be sensitive about their reputation and public opinion. They are very careful of their public image and want to always give a good impression of themselves.

If the Head Line bends toward the Heart Line, it indicates a person who is ruled by their emotions rather than good reason. This person's personality and character is too easy going, giving too much influence to others instead of being able to make their own decisions.

The width of the Quadrangle under the Mounts Saturn and Apollo are important. When the Quadrangle is wider under the Mount of Saturn than the Mount of Apollo, it indicates that this person is careless of public opinion and what others say and may think about them, and not at all concerned about their reputation.

The total absence of the Quadrangle which is usually due to the Heart Line either joining the Head Line or not existing at all indicates a cold, hard nature.

# Signs and Markings in the Quadrangle Area

It must be noted here that other major lines can enter the Quadrangle area, such as the Fate Line, Success Line, Health Line and Psychic Cross.

When a clear independent Psychic Cross is not touching either line, this person will have clear vision, psychic powers, an aptitude for the occult studies and metaphysical interest. However, if the Psychic Cross is poorly formed, it is not a good sign; it indicates that these people can become easily excitable, overly sensitive, hasty and unwise in their reactions. They often cannot be trusted because of their impulsiveness; they seem to make a mess of their lives.

If there are thin criss-cross lines or other defective signs in the area of the Quadrangle, this will disturb the area and cause restlessness, irritability and hypersensitiveness to the character and personality, also worrying and impulsiveness, except in the case of the Star or Triangle.

A Star is usually an indication of some outstanding success. When the Star is located under the Mount of Saturn in the Quadranlge area, it indicates a brilliant career.

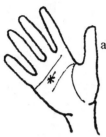

A Star found under the Mount of Apollo indicates great fame in the arts and literature. They will achieve wealth and success.

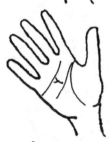

A Star located under the Mount of Mercury is also a wonderful sign. These people will achieve great success as a scientist or engineer and will reach great heights in their profession.

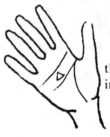

A Fork in the Quadrangle area indicates an unbalanced mind.

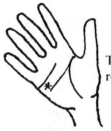

A well shaped Triangle located in the Quadrangle is an indication that this person will have an aptitude for research and scientific study. They are interested in unveiling secrets and problems of everlasting values.

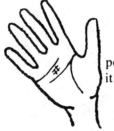

A Square in the Quadrangle indicates an extremely quick tempered person. These people should take good care of their eyes and take no risks; it would be dangerous for their eyes.

Three Circles joined together under the Mount of Saturn indicates epilepsy.

A Grille located in the Quadrangle can indicate mental problems, especially if the space is wide and the Mount of Mars is exaggerated.

# Defective Lines and Repair Lines — Signs and Markings

The Uneven Line is a defective line and can be seen on any line. The Uneven Line can be deep then become thin and continue that way the length of the line. Sometimes the Uneven Line is broad and shallow, then fading away entirely. The Uneven Line must be examined to determine the age when the line is deep and when it becomes thin, this will indicate the times when health or success will become strong or weak. The age of the person is important. You must look at other lines to be able to determine what the cause may be. On the Life Line this line indicates lack of vitality, weak constitution, no resistance to diseases. On the Head Line, lack of brain power, headaches and deterioration of the brain. On the Heart Line it indicates poor circulation, unreliable, weak, inconsistant and changeable. On the Fate Line it indicates prosperity then loss, unreliable and unstable affairs with a continual struggle. On all Uneven Lines indicates problems to the life of the person on the line that it effects.

The Broad and Shallow Line indicates a person that is uncertain, with poor self control and undetermined, one who vascillates and has little concentration and has trouble remembering.

Capillary Lines are finely traced lines that run together until uniting into one line. They are delicate ethereal lines that weaken the strength and line they appear on. When a Mount has many Capillary Lines the power of the Mount is lessened. On the Mount of the Moon the Capillary Lines develop an extreme sensitiveness and occult or intuitive powers.

 Wavy Lines show uncertainty, lack of decisions and force.

The Tassel is composed of many lines extending from the end of a line. The Tassel is always a defect and generally marks the end of the usefulness of a line. If the Tassel is located early in a line and not its end, you may find a single thin line continuing after the Tassel. A Square can protect the line on which the Tassel appears.

If a Tassel is on the end of the Life Line it will indicate loss of all nervous energy. Tassels can be found on the end of a short Life, Head or Heart Line which indicates dissipation of energy, diffusion of strength, distraction of the mind and an end of usefulness. Instead of the line continuing, it scatters, diffuses and spreads itself like a Tassel or fan, dissipating its force and ending the qualities indicated by the line.

Broken Lines or breaks in a line are seen very frequently and always indicate of a defective condition. The kind of break will make a great difference in the outcome of the defect. Each break is a defect and some repair must be made or the health or success of the person will be effected. A small break and a continuing line will only effect the person for a short time. When there is a large break it is a serious danger but can be repaired. A broken line can be repaired when the broken ends overlap above each other or by a small line uniting the ends of the two lines, by Sister Lines running alongside the line and the break, or, by a Square between the breaks of the line. The breaks are always a danger and must be regarded seriously. The size and the repair signs will give an estimate of the outcome. Be sure to look at both hands before making any decisions.

The Broken Hook or Turned Back Line are lines that turn back after a break. Lines that start to run back toward the main line and lines that form a little hook at the end are all dangerous and of the worst form of line. They can produce disaster. These lines can be repaired by lines joining the turned back end of the line, by Sister Lines, by a Square or by Overlapping Lines. Every turned back line is very serious; they check or stop the persons life, health or career, depending upon the line that they are found. If they have not been repaired it can be fatal.

The Chained Line is formed by lines joining together forming small link-like uneven lines which weaken the line. A Chained Line is always a serious defect; they are one of the hardest defects to repair unless the chain only covers a very short area. The repairing qualities of a Square could not be large enough to repair a long Chained Line. The line may also be repaired by Sister Lines.

If the Chained Line is seen on a Head Line it indicates headaches, lack of self-control and brain diseases. If the Chained Line is only part of a line the weak and poor health or condition of a person will last only during the period of time the Chained Line continues to exist. The Chained Line causes a labored, strained and weak condition, with a lack of force and purpose.

Sister Lines are repair lines. If a major or minor line is weak, broken or defective in any way, Sister Lines are very valuable, they increase or double the power of any line whether weak or strong. The Sister Lines run alongside a line adding strength and repairs the qualities of the line.

Overlapping Lines are breaks in a line that may be repaired when the ends of a broken line overlap each other or if there is a small cross line that unites or overlaps the two broken lines. Breaks in a line can also be repaired by a Square or Sister Lines running alongside.

A Dot or Spot is a sign of a temporary check of the qualities of a line or mount on which it may appear. A Dot or Spot on the line weakens it and checks its growth. These signs may vary in size and depth, and are always a defect either on a line or mount. A Dot or Spot on a line forms an obstruction. If they are large it indicates destruction of the line, however, very small Dots are not as serious. Dots may be red, blue, white or yellow. A Square can help repair the time the Dot appears.

The Triangle is formed by the splitting of a line or as a sign by itself. It can be found over a line or by the crossing of Main Lines which have different qualities. A Triangle never applies to health but adds brilliancy to the mental side of the location where it is found, it has good mental attributes.

If the Triangle is formed by crossing lines it is not as powerful as a single sign by itself. The strongest Triangle is a single sign and is always favorable.

The Circle is a rare sign, although, it is usually not a perfect circle, sometimes their edges do not close or they overlap each other, they may be one continuous line or made up of little short lines. The sign is not a good one. Circles can indicate problems on the lines or mounts where they appear and exaggerate their weaknesses.

The Trident can be found at the upper end of a line or as a single sign. When at the upper end of a line it is a good sign and adds strength to the line. On a mount it increases the good side of the mounts' qualities.

The Split Line is a defective line that has small thin lines that resemble splinters covering it which produce defects on any line they are seen on. The Split Line reduces the clearness and strength of a line and impairs the line. A Split Line indicates a weakness of the line during the period of time they cover the line. The split Line only runs a short distance and stops, and when the line continues deep and strong the strength of the line will be regained.

The Grille is composed of vertical and horizontal lines crossing each other to form a network or block to obstruct the line. A Grille with lines not running exactly vertical and horizontal are not as bad as those that are composed of the vertical and horizontal lines running at right angles.

A Grille in any hand is a serious problem and it causes a defect and a menace. A Grille on a mount is a bad sign. The Grille can be repaired by a Square if it is able to box it in entirely.

The Square is a repair sign. It is the best of all repair signs. It can protect impending danger. The Square is always a good sign where ever it appears no matter what line the break appears on or what menace a sign may be. A Square surrounding it will help repair and check the danger. If a Square is found on a Mount where it does not surround a defect of a line, it indicates that the defects on the Mount will not affect or control the person. A Square is called the Mark of Preservation. It indicates escape from danger at the point where danger may appear. The Square is always a protection from danger.

An Island is always a defect where ever it appears on the hand. It indicates weakness or failure on a Line or Mount, a warning to look for something to happen, and must never be disregarded. An Island divides the strength and force of the line or area in which it is seen. The Islands can be in all sizes from very small to large ones indicating the length of time the illness or problem will last and how severve the condition will be. It indicates impending trouble, weakness and impairment. An Island is always a menace to the person on the hand in which it is seen.

Cross-bars are small horizontal lines closely grouped together. They are a bad sign for they entirely block or stop a line and bring out the bad qualities of a mount.

A Fork is a split of a line that occurs in the end of a line. Generally, the Fork is a good sign. It increases the quality of the line. When found at the end of a Head Line, the Fork gives dual mentality and versatility.

When a Fork is found at the end of a short Life, Head, or Heart Line, it is not a good sign. It indicates its desperation. It scatters and diffuses the strength of the line and its usefulness.

The Star is an important and valuable sign; they can be found in all locations of the hand. The Star can be a good sign as well as a bad sign depending upon where it is located. The best location for a Star is on a mount. If a Star is on a line it is usually a bad sign. A Star on a mount brings out the best qualities on the mount upon which it appears. A Star should be well formed with each line having the same length and starting from its center. If the Star is imperfect it has less power. A Star can either light up the hand and make things wonderful or it can explode and destroy. The Star on the line is a bad sign, except when it appears on the Fate Line or Success Line where it brings success and fame.

Ascending Lines, when present, are nearly always found at the beginning or ending of a line. These lines always add power to the line they rise from They increase the effort and energy of the line and indicate riches, warmth, good luck, intelligence, and abundance to the qualities pertaining to the line.

Descending Lines, when present, are nearly always found at the beginning or ending of a line. These lines always indicate loss of power, energy and effort to the line they descend from and accentuate the lines bad qualities.

The Cross on the palm of the hand is a common sign. It is not always a good sign. Generally, a Cross on a line is an indication of an obstacle or a defect and brings out the bad qualities of the line, health problems or a change in the course of a persons life.

A Cross on the Mount of Jupiter is a good sign, it indicates a fortunate love which will come into a persons life. A Cross on the Mount of the Moon shows an interest in the Occult Sciences.

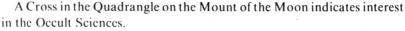

A Cross in the Quadrangle on the Mount of the Moon indicates interest in the Occult Sciences.

The Mystic Cross is always found between the Head and Heart Line, indicating great psychic power. The occult will always be of interest.

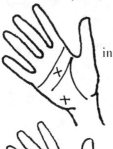

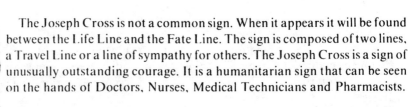

The Joseph Cross is not a common sign. When it appears it will be found between the Life Line and the Fate Line. The sign is composed of two lines, a Travel Line or a line of sympathy for others. The Joseph Cross is a sign of unusually outstanding courage. It is a humanitarian sign that can be seen on the hands of Doctors, Nurses, Medical Technicians and Pharmacists.

In a book written in 1986, by Pam Pormehala, she has written a chapter called "Letters in the Palm." This is a very new concept, one not found in any earlier research done before, and will not be included in this book but noted here only as a reference. The chapter theorizes that every hand has at least two letters beside the letters H and X. The letters given in the chapter are K, A, N, Y, V, E, M, F, L, T, W and B. These letters are formed by the lines in the palm. Each letter on a line adds one meaning to the line. The chapter also theorizes the letters come and go, informing of the time they will be an influence.

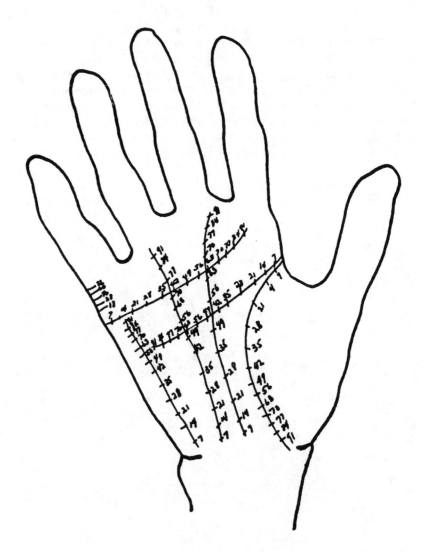

**Judging Time on the Hand**

# Judging Time on the Hand

When reading palms and trying to judge time on the lines of the palms, I use the system of seven which I first read about in Cheiro's book on palmistry. I have found it to be very accurate. I recommend this system to you. Nature seems to use the system of seven. From the medical and scientific standpoint, the number seven is the most important point of calculation. Our entire system undergoes a complete change every seven years. There are seven stages prior to birth, and the brain takes seven forms before it takes on the unique 'one of a kind character' of your human brain. We have also discovered that the number seven has played a very important part in history. There are seven human races, seven wonders of the world, seven days in a week, seven colors, seven minerals plus the three parts of our body each containing seven sections. The most important point to us in judging time on the lines of our palms is that our entire system undergoes a complete change every seven years. By using the seven year cycle on the lines of the hand, you can divide the lines into sections giving dates as accurately as possible. When judging time or age on the Life Line, Fate Line and all other vertical lines, I use the base or the second phalanx of the thumb and draw an imaginary line across the palm of the hand which is about the center of the hand, and use the imaginary line as approximately 42 years. All measurements of time or age in terms of years can only be approximate as we do not know the time of death. When judging time on the lines, in all instances the measurements are spaced wider at the beginning of the lines and narrower towards the end.

# Judging Time on the Heart Line

The Heart Line is read from the percussion side of the hand under the Mount of Mercury, it forms a natural crease in the palm and runs horizontally across the palm toward the Mount of Jupiter under the index finger. To estimate time on the Heart Line I use the rule of seven. Divide the Heart Line in half using the age of 42 years as the center of the line starting on the percussion side of the hand, under the Mount of Mercury. The center of the palm can also be used if the Heart Line is short. When judging periods of time on the Heart Line look to the Life Line to see whether any markings or signs correlate with the Heart Line.

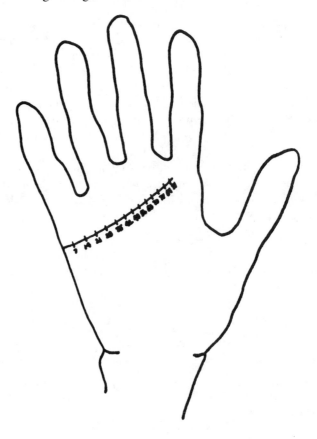

## Judging Time on the Life Line

The Life Line begins under the index finger circling the Mount of the Lower Mars and the Mount of Venus and in most cases ends under the Mount of Venus. When judging time on the Life Line use the base of the second phalanx of the thumb and draw an imaginary line across the palm which is about the center of the hand which indicates approximately 42 years. When judging periods of time on the Life Line the measurements are placed wider at the beginning of the line and narrower towards the end.

Never, make any predictions of time of death. First of all the chances are you will be wrong. I've seen people in their seventies with short Life Lines, others with a long Life Line. I've known persons with long Life Lines die before their sixties. You must never even think of saying anything negative about the length of life. You must always give a positive reading. If they question a short Life Line show them the other good lines that will strengthen the Life Line. Also that lines can be improved on by their health habits and attitudes towards life.

# Judging Time on the Head Line

The Head Line starts either above the crease of the Life Line or attached to the beginning of the line, below the Mount of Jupiter and usually runs horizontally across the palm to the percussion side of the hand. When judging the periods of time on the Head Line it can be useful to look at the Life Line to see whether any marks or signs correlate with the Head Line. To estimate time on the Head Line I use the same rule of seven. Divide the Head Line using the age of 42 years as the center of the line. If the Head Line is unusually short the center of the palm will indicate the weakness of the line.

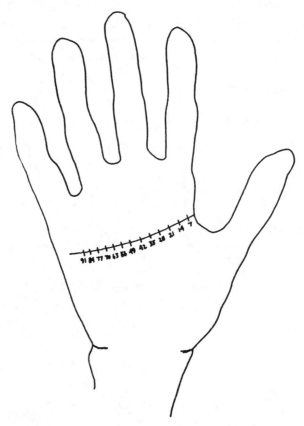

# Judging Time on the Health Line

The Health Line can start from the Mount of the
Moon and run upward on the percussion side of the
hand towards the Mount of Mercury (the little
finger). It can also find it's beginning by the Life
Line. Time on the Health Line is read from it's
beginning upwards. It is often important to read age
on this line because it is such a valuable line in
connection with the Life Line.

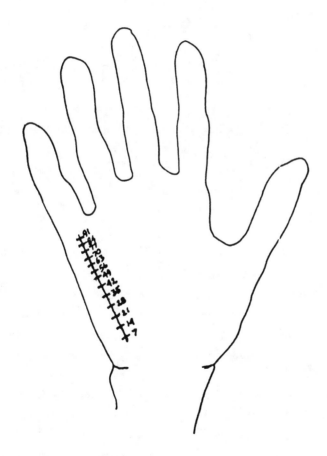

# Judging Time on the Fate Line

Age on the Fate Line is read from the base of the palm above the Bracelets upwards vertically toward the Mount of Saturn through the center of the palm. When judging time on the Fate Line use the base of the second phalanx of the thumb and draw an imaginary line across the center of the hand and use this as 42 years and then use the rule of seven.

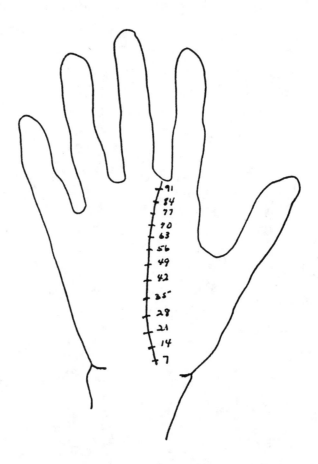

## Judging Time on the Success Line

    The Line of Success is a vertical line starting, if long, from the upper area of the Mount of the Moon. If the line is short it will start higher on the hand and run upwards toward the Mount of Apollo. When judging age on the Success Line I use the base of the second phalanx of the thumb, and draw an imaginary line across the palm which is about the center of the hand and use this as 42 years and then use the rule of seven.

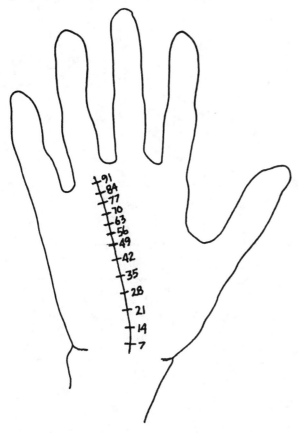

# Judging the Length of a Marriage Line

The Marriage Line is read from the percussion side of the hand towards the palm. To determine the length of time a relationship will last is very difficult to judge because the life span of each individual is very different. If there is more than one Line of Affection try to obtain information about the existing relationship which will enable you to judge the other lines. If it is a very young person use your best judgement.

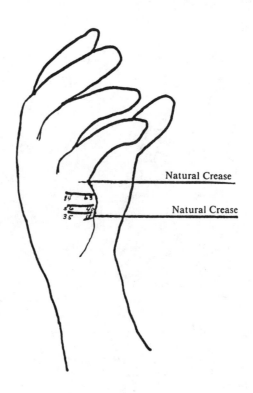

## Judging Time on the Marriage Line

To judge the age or time on a Marriage Line, have the person show you the percussion side of their hand between their little finger and the natural crease of the Heart Line. Have them bend their hand slightly so lines will relax and become more visable. Starting from the crease of the Heart Line and reading upwards toward the natural crease of the base of the little finger you will find the first Marriage Line. If close to the crease it indicates a marriage at about 18 years of age for a woman and 21 years for a man. A Marriage Line in the center of the two natural creases should be judged at about 42 years and close to the natural crease under the little finger approximately 70 years. To be as accurate as possible try to obtain the age of the first marriage and the time the couple had been together.

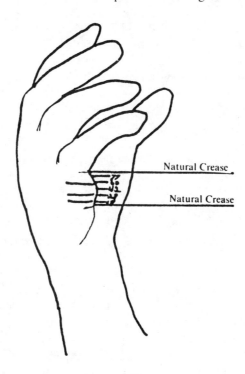

Natural Crease

Natural Crease

# Infants' and Children's Hands

Reading an infant or very young baby's hands is a wonderful experience. However, it can be quite difficult for they keep their little fists clinched tightly with great determination. I use my thumb and index finger of my left hand to gently open their little hands and fingers, hopefully with the help of their mothers.

The newborn baby's hands are often very spiritual for they are between the spiritual world and new life. Have you ever watched a sleeping infant and noticed their eye movements, their lips moving and smiling? My mother used to say, "they are talking to the angels."

Right from birth the principal lines and fingerprints are quite clearly formed, which will be the fundamental traits of their personalities and character.

A Simian Line which can be seen in the palms of an infant can pose complex problems in a healthy, normal infant, as well as medical problems in a sick infant.

There are no medical explanations for the formation of the lines in the palm of the hand. These lines are not caused by the position of the hands prior to birth. It is, however, true that there are similarities between the hands of individual families and their children; inherited personality traits genetically from our forebears.

Today's infant girls' hands are especially interesting and exciting when comparing them with hands of women born fifty years ago, when there were so few choices for our daughters, compared to the wonderful opportunities the newborn girl child will have in today's future, and it shows in their hands.

Years ago parents did not worry about advanced education for their girl child; she could always work at a menial job until she got married. Girls were rarely given the opportunity to have a good college education, even when they showed promise. Today young girls are encouraged not only to get a good education, but to branch out in all fields, even those so-called masculine studies and sports.

A child's hand becomes easier to read when they are about four years old. The chubbiness thins down and the hand takes on its own shape and style. By examining the child's hand, you will be able to tell what they are like, how to gain their cooperation and how to bring out the best in them.

From the minute you have analyzed their hands, palms and fingertips, you can understand and help them better than any doctor who has written a book on how to bring up children. Their hands will reveal how well they react to instruction, what type of persuasion to use, or if they may have a problem with criticism and how they will behave under pressure.

My favorite readings have always been children's and young adults' hands; they can be fascinating to study.

No aspect of palmistry is more rewarding or useful, or holds greater promise than the study of the hands of normal children. It gives insight to their personality, character, aptitude and abilities. It can be a guide to helping their emotional needs and to understand their stress points, to encourage them to develop their unique talents and how to increase their self-esteem. It is a very great resonsibility. You must be very careful to always give a positive reading. Children are very impressionable and vulnerable. I'm sure you remember your first reading; it has stayed with you all your life.

I always take a print of my young client's hands and when reading, explain and show them the areas I am reading. I treat them as I would any client, with respect.

# Dermatoglyphics

The study of Dermatoglyphics and its analysis can easily be a field of its own. As palmists we can only touch on its importance.

The meaning of the term "Dermatoglyphics" is "skin carvings" and it refers to the patterns of the skin. These skin patterns never change; they are formed in the fourth month of our prenatal life. Hospitals use the hand, fingertips and footprints as a means of identification of a newborn child, together with the mother's hand and fingerprints.

Fingerprints have a long history; some fifteen hundred years ago the Chinese used thumbprints as a signature. In 1856 a Englishman conceived the idea of obtaining fingerprints in order to identify Indian notables when they received their pension so they could not be cheated out of their money by others claiming to be them. However, the fingerprint identification technique was not put into use until 1892 when another Englishman, a scientist, Sir Francis Galton, invented a workable system that is still used for identification, especially for the identification of criminals by criminologists throughout the world. Law enforcers now use fingerprints not only for identification, but for psychological characteristics as well. Scientists have developed a scanner which in conjunction with computers, is capable of scanning the patterns of the palm when placed on a scanner plate, then feeding the information of the patterns of the palm and fingertips into a computer memory bank, which will accurately identify the owner of the skin patterns without any errors.

We know that fingertips and handprints are not only used to identify an individual, but these prints can identify an individual's personal traits as well. This is the focus of the field of Dermatoglyphics. Scientists are deciphering these patterns in order to be able to identify personality and physical traits that are inborn and to use the information in their diagnosis.

It should be noted that Dermatoglyphics deals only with skin patterns, and not the study of the lines of the hand, such as the Heart, Head or Life Line.

Recently it has been discovered that the skin of the palms has the same type pattern, and is just as individual in type, number and style as are those of the fingertips.

It is not unusual to find the palm of the hand to have a large whorl pattern near the outside edge or percussion side of the hand. This sign is believed to be genetic or inherited, and intensifies the characteristic of the area in which it is located.

The skin of our palm is not smooth, but covered with very tiny ridges. The medical practitioners call them epidermal ridges. Many of the same markings palmists have been using for centuries are now being used in the medical field, but with different meanings and with different names. In Dermato-glyphics, the fine skin patterns are called dermal ridges. The lines in the palm of the hand are called flexion creases, except for the Semian Line.

There are a number of identifiable skin patterns found in the palm of the hand. The location of these skin patterns reflects the characteristics associated with the different skin ridges. They are the papillary ridges, the Loops, double Loops, Triads, Whorls, Arches and Tented Arches.

Papillary ridges are any small nipple-like connections of the skin. These ridges are hair-like lines that look like they are sweeping across the palm of the hand in groups of three, which can combine to form these papillary ridges. They can be very fine or very large, depending on the shape and texture of the skin of the hand. The finer the lines, the more sensitive the person. Large papillary ridges indicate an active, physical type person, with a high tolerance for pain, both emotionally and physically. They are good athletes and enjoy physical type work.

Skin ridge patterns never change throughout a lifetime. The fingerprints of a person do not change even after death, only when the skin has decomposed. Archaeologists have found fingerprint patterns on many of the Egyptian mummies still remained legible. Although skin ridge patterns are retained on the fingertips and thumbs, the size of the patterns are usually larger from infancy to maturity, and begin to shrink in old age.

Fingertips are the only indelible signature of man. We can fake and forge a written name or, due to the changes in our personality, our hand-writing can change. As we grow old, or if we become ill, our hand-writing can change. People can change their names and take on new identification, but our fingerprints can never be altered.

It is almost impossible to read and interpret fingerprints with the naked eye. A strong magnifying glass is essential, and even then it is difficult. The best method is to take the hand prints. Then you will be able to see in detail the skin ridge patterns. You may still have need for the strong magnifying glass and good light in order to see the skin patterns clearly and to be accurate. I use a magnifying glass fluorescent lamp.

No two sets of fingerprints are identical, even in the case of identical twins. Criminologists all over the world use fingerprints for identification purposes. Palmists use fingerprints to identify the qualities and characteristics of their clients' personalities.

There is no one type of fingerprint pattern which belongs to any particular shape hand or finger. The fingerprints on a hand may be all the same type or mixed in all sorts of different patterns. Each fingertip, hand shape and fingernail is extremely individual. This is what makes us all so different from each other.

There has been a new development for the use of thumbprints. In an article on September 7, 1989, the State of California businesses will require thumbprints on the checks of their customers when making a purchase or cashing their payroll or government checks. It is called "Operation Check Print." It will protect the merchants, as well as the customers, from other persons cashing their checks. It will provide positive identification against anyone trying to forge or pass a bad check. An inkless fingerprint pad will be used. If a check is returned or reported missing, investigators can run the thumbprint through their statewide computer system to identify the person. This method may be used in other states.

# The Unchanging Fingerprint Patterns

Loop

Composite

There are five basic fingerprint patterns and each has its own individual meaning. There are also several subdivisions and many fingerprint combinations.

Tented Arch

Each of the five types of fingerprint patterns indicate the basic characteristics or tendencies which can either modify, weaken or intensify, not just the characteristic of a person from their finger and thumb prints, but it also gives us an insight to the shape, lines and markings of the hand, for the fingerprints are the unchangeable quality of a person's personality.

Whorl

The position of the fingerprint patterns will vary. Some skin ridge patterns will be centered on the phalanx of the fingertips, some will be off center, to the right or the left of the fingertip. The theory is when the core of the pattern, or the twin core of the composite fingertip patterns, leans toward the percussion side of the hand (towards the little finger) this person tends to be an extrovert. If the core of the fingerprint leans inwards toward the thumb, these people tend to be introvertive. When the core of the fingerprint is verticle and in a line with the fingers, these people have a balanced outlook in life.

Arch

421

# The Loops

The Loop skin patterns are made up of skin ridges that form narrow graceful loops, sometimes symbolized as a reed, and have several variations. The core or apex of the loop can be centered on the top phalanx, or placed low or high on the phalanx of the fingertip.

There are two other types of Loop patterns, the Ulna Loop pattern, which slopes toward the percussion side of the hand (toward the little finger) and the Radial Loop patterns, which slope toward the thumb.

The Loop patterns indicate a quick, flexible, lively mind and quick emotional responses. These people adjust easily to any circumstances and are usually very versatile. They have good working relationships with their loved ones, as well as others.

The Loop pattern influences the characteristics of the fingertips where they are found. If they are found on all the fingertips and thumb of the hand, this person will be very broad-minded. They are interested in many things and will always be open to new suggestions and be very easy to get along with.

If the Loop skin patterns are found on a Philosophic shaped hand, it indicates these people love a change and challenge in their life.

If the Loop skin patterns are found on a Square-shaped hand, it adds a searching intellect.

Loop skin patterns are found nearly ninety percent of the time on the Mercury (little) fingertips and are the ideal skin pattern for that fingertip. These people will prefer to get along with others, especially in relationships and in a marriage. They are flexible in their relationships and prefer their partner to be flexible also. They are broad-minded and enjoy any opportunity to grow and learn new things.

Loop patterns on the Apollo (ring) finger indicate a tolerance for the weaknesses and faults of their friends and for society. They enjoy the theater, music and all forms of art. The Loop pattern on the Apollo fingertips is also nearly always the Ulna type. If the core or center of the loop is low on the first phalanx, it increases their interest in the art of furnishing and decorating their home as well as others. The love of flowers and fashion will also increase. If the core or center of the loop is high on the first phalanx, it greatly increases their interest in art and becoming an artist.

Loop patterns on the Saturn (middle) fingertip indicates these people will be interested in the study of religion. They will have an open mind towards metaphysical subjects and enjoy talking about these various subjects. The Loop pattern on the Saturn fingertips is nearly always the Ulna Loop. If the Loop pattern is low on the core or center of the phalanx, it indicates an interest in forestry, law enforcement and all the down-to-earth aspects of life. If the Loop pattern is high on the first phalanx, these people would be interested in working with research teams.

Loop patterns on the Jupiter (index) fingertip adds flexibility and openness to suggestions and change. These people can improvise and act in many capacities. They believe that the greatest success and achievement comes through cooperation. They are always looking for ways to improve themselves.

Loop patterns on the thumbs indicate a willingness to cooperate and learn from others in order to achieve their goals in life. Because Loop patterns add flexibility and the desire for harmonious relationships and conditions, these people will find it easier to go along with others who may be stronger willed.

A Loop pattern on one thumb can be helpful, but if both thumbs have loops, these people become too accommodating.

## The Ulna Loop

The Ulna Loop slopes toward the percussion side of the hand (toward the little finger). These people have the ability to take the best ideas and assets of others and make them their own. They are adaptable and capable of interaction with a group of people. They are able to give up their personal aims when the goals of others are more important.

Because they are so perceptive, they can recognize the talents or imperfections of others, but they do not see their own. Their quick mind can find loopholes in any situation, even in legal matters. Their insight and quick responses make them impatient with others who may be slow to grasp an idea. They simply cannot understand why everyone is not quick-witted.

They make excellent friends and companions, for they always want to be helpful. They are skillful and competent, but they have the tendency to have too many interests with a short attention span.

The Ulna Loop pattern fingerprints will always add strength and support to all shaped hands.

This type of fingerprint pattern is found more on the Square and Philosophic shaped hand.

The Ulna Loops on the Jupiter (index) fingertip indicates these people are inclined to act on the suggestions that other people may present them. Others always play a role in their good fortune.

Loops on the Saturn fingertip are nearly always Ulna. The study of religious theories and metaphysical subjects are of great interest to these people.

Loops on the Apollo (ring) finger are usually always the Ulna type and indicate the appreciation of new ideas in fashions and everything these people believe in is beautiful, especially in the arts.

## The Radial Loop

The Radial Loop slopes toward the thumb and the inside of the hand. Radial Loops are found more frequently on the Jupiter finger and sometimes on the thumbs, but are rarely seen on other fingers.

The Radial Loop indicates good judgment, insight and perceptiveness. There is often something unusual about the way these people interpret things. They have a different style or flair of their own. They never seem to reach to the same conclusions others do. They have the ability to retain things in their mind for years and can easily recall them.

There is an important difference in the behavior of a person between the Radial and Ulna loops on the Jupiter (index) fingertips.

The Radial Loop indicates adaptability. As long as they have their own interest, they still must do their own choosing. It also gives the person good judgment and individual ability, while the Ulna Loop indicates that these people are more inclined to take suggestions from others and allow them to lead them.

The Radial Loop on the Apollo (ring) fingertip is not considered a good sign and is thought to have a genetic influence.

The Radial Loop on the Mercury (little) finger is extremely rare and I have no information on what effect it would have.

The Radial Loop on a Square and Conic shaped hand adds good judgment, intuition and insight.

The Radial Loop on the Psychic and Philosophic shaped hand increases their intuition and insight.

# Composite or Entwined Loop

A Composite or Entwined Loop has two tri-radius (three straight lines from the center or core of the pattern) and is indexed as a "Whorl," but the mental action or attitude is directly the opposite. In the same way, the "Tented Arch" has nothing in common with the reliable, practical arches.

These Composite patterns can be found on the thumbs, Jupiter fingers and, less often, on the Apollo fingertips. It is rare to find the Composite pattern on the Saturn fingertip.

A Composite pattern may take the form of a neat little S-bend kernel to another pattern or a large easily recognized pair of entwined loops. If traced with an ink line, they may leave the fingertip on opposite sides. No matter on which fingertip this pattern is located, it is a warning of divided thoughts about the finger it is located on and the mount area at its base. The dual character and mental thought creates confusion. The only advantage to this pattern is in the ability to see both sides on any problem or situation. Its weakness is in the difficulty of an inner conflict and self-mistrust.

On the Jupiter (index) fingertip, the Composite patterns are very useful, especially on the hands of a lawyer or an administrator, anyone who has to see both sides of a problem. These people, as children, often would have trouble at school, for they were too quick to see the opposite side of any statement a teacher may make and were accused of being argumentative.

Although it is very rare to find the Composite pattern on the Saturn (middle) fingertip, when found, it indicates a conflict between the spiritual world and material values. Because the Saturn finger is so closely associated with the ethical aspects of religion, the Composite pattern would be suitable there.

When found on the Apollo (ring) fingertip, the Composite pattern adds independence of opinion and great care and thought before making any decisions. These people will weigh things very slowly and carefully before making any statements.

The Composite patterns on the Mercury (little) fingertips will give these people a problem in their decisions. It will have a dual effect on their emotional life as well as their business decisions.

The Composite patterns on the thumb indicate difficulty over making up their minds. They often do things or say things they regret later. People with this pattern should not make quick decisions, but take time to think them out.

# Arches

The Arch patterned fingertips are thought to be our most primitive of all fingertip patterns. Anthropologists believe that horizontal arched skin patterns were probably developed by our ancestors to assist them in gripping things.

The Arch skin patterns on our fingertips indicate a practical, reliable and realistic type person. They are down-to-earth in their approach to life and people. They are trustworthy, capable, able to cope if things go wrong, and they have a natural inborn courage.

The Arch patterns on one Jupiter (index) fingertip, and a Loop or Whorl pattern on the Jupiter fingertip of the other hand will add reliability and practical sense.

Arches on both Jupiter fingertips can become a disability, especially if there are more than four on both hands combined. These people will have trouble expressing their thoughts or feelings. If these people have spatulate fingertips, they may be able to express themselves in writing or sketching when they have trouble putting their feelings into words.

Arches on the Saturn (middle) fingertips indicate a religious person who believes that religion will make them better and happier. They enjoy the study of the architectural and historical side of religion, rather than the elaborate ceremonies. In business they like to improve their properties and investments for better profits.

Arches on the Apollo (ring) fingers are very rare. If found, it indicates this person's artistic ability will be used in something useful.

Arches on the Mercury (little) fingertips are also very rare. When they do occur, they will be seen either on all of the fingertips of both hands, or with four or more on both hands. This is an indication that these people will be very domestic. Their home life and family devotion will be the most important thing in their life. Their interest in business will be only through others.

Arches are commonly seen on thumbprints; these people usually have a strong first phalanx of the thumb. These people do things with efficiency, and are practical in making any decisions.

Arches are a good sign on thumbs because it always adds a practical and constructive effect. They add stability and capability to any fingertip.

# Tented Arches

This Arch shaped Loop, straight up the middle of the fingertip is supported by a single tent-like pole or a stiff, narrow loop core. The Tented Arch is a very good symbol of the attitude of the mind this sign represents. The grace and flexibility of the loop has become stiffened and rigid. These people have a cautious personality. They often have very little to do with others, for it may reveal too much of themselves. Because of this they seem shy or even standoffish.

They have searching intellect, and can be creative and artistic depending on the shape of the fingertips. They are perfectionists and their main interest in life would be to educate themselves until they know as much as possible about any subject that interests them, and then continue on to other interests with the same intensity.

They are sincere, helpful people, though often misjudged by others because they only want to see the best in everyone.

They make good researchers and in any profession involving a need for creative analysis. These people want to achieve their highest goals and realize they will only do it through their own efforts. They tend to be attracted to others who are achievers.

Tented Arches are seen more frequently on the Jupiter (index) fingertips. These people have good concentrated mental powers and remarkable determination, enthusiasm and drive. Their goals in life are extremely important to them. If opposed, they can become very aggressive.

Tented Arch patterns on the Saturn (middle) fingertips indicate a strong personal ambition. These people have enthusiasm and drive with a great need to succeed in everything. They are always interested in self-improvement. They enjoy change and are interested in the latest ideas for themselves, as well as their careers, home and family to improve their lifestyle.

Tented Arch patterns on the Apollo (ring) fingertip indicates a gift for music and interest in the theater and art. These people are very self-expressive, socially active and are attracted to those they consider high achievers. One of the main reasons is in the hope that these people can help and support them in their own goals.

Tented Arch patterns on both the Mercury (little) fingertips indicates a desire for security and social status. Marriage is very important to them. They will invest time and energy to other close relationships, as a successful social life is very important.

Tented Arches on both thumbs add a very strong ambition to succeed in life, They are very active people, always interested in ideas and places. These people are always interested in the future and in seeing improvements that will help the world and its environment.

A Square-shaped hand with Tented Arch patterns adds character and technical skills. On a Conic-shaped hand, the Tented Arch patterns steadies the person and these people would rather specialize in one field than in many different types of work. On a Philosophic or Psychic shaped hand, it has a practical quality.

## The Whorl

The Whorl pattern on any fingertips is very important because it has a very strong influence on the personality of the person. It is sometimes referred to as the fixed sign. It is found more often on the Apollo (ring) fingertips, but can also be seen on the Jupiter (index) and thumb fingertips. There are two basic forms of the Whorl pattern, the Concentric Circle Whorl and the Shell pattern Whorl.

The Whorl patterns are easy to recognize. Equally easy to recognize are the people with the whorl-tipped fingers. These people have a strong definite personality, which makes them very individualistic. They always want to perform or organize everything themselves. They are usually brilliant and capable of conceiving and carrying out projects that others would not be capable of performing. They must have their freedom; they cannot tolerate supervision or restrictions and are better suited to work alone, especially in a high-pressured profession. They can be secretive and sensitive and are inclined to be tense. Because of this stress they may suffer form a nervous stomach or insomnia.

There is often a slowness about these people's reactions. You cannot hurry them into making decisions, although they can be extremely quick in an emergency because of their natural instincts and brilliant minds. They require time when deciding any change of view or programs which will affect them.

Whorls on all fingers and thumbs are extremely unusual. This person would be truly exceptional. They would have a tremendous amount of energy. This influence would be fixed and decided tastes, likes and dislikes

428

in everything. They would be strong-willed and would have the power to overcome any obstacles. They will want to continually prove their credibility and win the admiration of others. They are individualistic thinkers who can often see all sides of a problem.

If both Apollo fingertips have Whorls, these people have a flair for fashion and their homes will be intensely personal. They have their own ideas of beauty, even if it may be unorthodox. No matter how outrageous it may be to others, to them it will be a form of beauty. They know what they like and will not be influenced by their friends or family.

They are very creative and are usually talented in music, art, poetry and the theater. These creative people are always interesting to know. They are mentally alert and can see flaws in material objects, as well as flaws of their own. They can foresee problems and either will correct them themselves or assist others in correcting them.

However, these Whorls on the Apollo finger also indicate a born gambler and speculator; they are always ready to take a chance. To confirm whether they will be lucky or not, look for the Line of Success. If there is one and it ends under the Apollo finger, you can safely predict that good fortune will be theirs.

Whorls on the Mercury (little) fingers are often found when the first phalanx is long. This indicates a good power of self-expression, especially if they feel deeply about the subject. As a rule, though, they would rather be the power behind the throne.

Whorls on the Mercury fingertips usually indicate a person who is very sincere and will carefully complete anything they may undertake for others. They are idealistic and have very definite expectations of their close relationships.

If both Mercury fingertips have Whorls, it indicates these people are very appreciative of beauty, the arts and nature. They are creative and can produce original things that would be impossible for ordinary people. They are extremely passionate and expressive. They are intuitive and have the ability to grasp what other people are thinking.

The position of Whorl patterns on the thumbs is important. If the center or core of the Whorl pattern is low on the first phalanx, it indicates a person who will not be bothered about theories, but they want decisive answers to their questions. The opposite is true if the core or center of the Whorl pattern is high on the first phalanx. These people will not bother about where or how they live, but will be very decisive about their political or theoretical questions.

Whorls on both thumbs indicate a person with a strong will. Their will to live, to express themselves and to become achievers is very strong. They like to be in control of things, and prefer being the boss. Whorls are always a favorable sign of success.

The Whorl skin pattern is an extremely strong sign on any shaped hand.

## The Concentric Circle Whorl

The Concentric Circle Whorl is the most definite and easiest to recognize on the fingertips. It consists of a number of complete circles, one inside the other, like a bullseye. This Concentric Whorl is a sign of an almost complete non-conformist and individualist. They love a challenge, just tell them they cannot do something and they will break their neck getting it done. They always prefer to be their own boss, for they find it very hard to conform to authority. They prefer to live their lives in their own way.

The Concentric Whorl patterns are often found on the fingertips of criminals. This does not mean that all people with the Whorl pattern on their fingertips have a criminal personality. There are many other factors to take into consideration before any verifications can be made. There are many fine people with Concentric Circle Whorls.

## The Shell Whorl

The Shell Whorl patterns look as though an engraver started from the center of the fingertip and made a continuous shell-like open-ended circle. Depending which direction the circle started, it can have the open end to the left or the right of the fingertip.

The Shell pattern has all the usual influences as the Whorl, only to a less intense degree. This pattern is essentially the mark of an individualist.

The Whorl on the Jupiter (index) fingertip adds perception and signifies a person who can see the truth. They are hard to fool for they are a good judge of people and often see all sides of a problem.

These people can foresee so much, it is difficult at times for them to make up their minds. They show individuality when dealing with others. They are more concerned in learning about themselves and always try to analyze their own identity, rather than pursuing traditional roles. They have a strong ego and they are ambitious people with the energy to become successful. They are very interesting people and have individualistic life styles. They prefer to make their own decisions concerning their personal life.

When the Whorl is on both Jupiter fingertips, the pattern has its strongest effect. Their ambition in life will become their greatest concern. Their achievement must not only be their very own, they feel no one else could do it as well as they do.

If the Whorl is high on the fingertips, these people can become famous as writers.

If the Whorl is low on the fingertips, they will contribute to the community service, but with a flair.

The Whorl on the Saturn (middle) fingertip has its strongest influence. These people have fortitude, for they are always searching for wisdom. They are self-determined and excellent in the field of research.

If there are Whorl patterns on both Saturn fingertips, these people value their family, home and career above anything else. They will always do things out of the ordinary and their ideas of family life, home and career will always be unique. They have a gift or genius for organization and arranging things into categories. They are very capable of taking charge and know that what has to be done when things become confused or disoriented.

The Apollo fingertips will more often have whorled patterns, even when the other fingertips do not. It indicates the love of beauty and harmony.

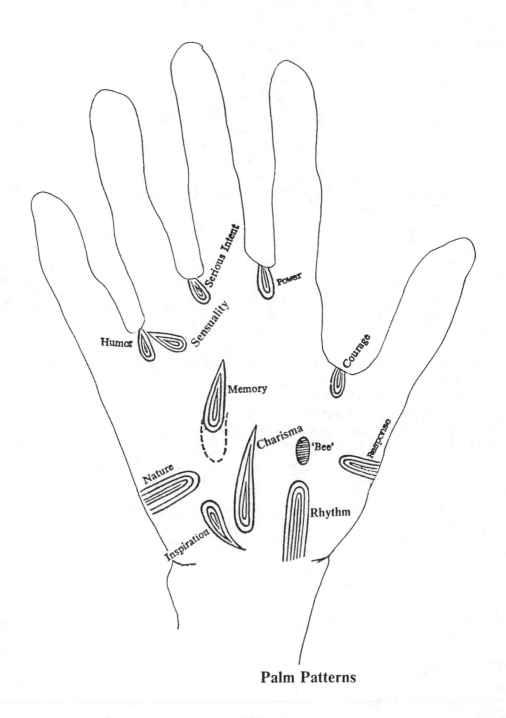

**Palm Patterns**

# Palm Patterns

Dermatoglyphics is the interpretation of the skin patterns made by the capillary ridges and furrows on the finger and the palm of the hand. As palmists we can only touch on its importance. Those who wish to become experts at Dermatoglyphics must do much more research, for it is a science of its own.

When reading skin patterns on the palm, as in reading the fingerprints, a strong magnifying glass is essential.

Skin patterns on the palm are usually Loop patterns, although Whorl patterns have been found on the palms of criminals.

## Loop of Power and Ambition

Loop patterns located on the palm between the Jupiter (index) finger and the Saturn (middle) finger are called the Power and Amibition Loops. This skin pattern is not a common sign and is said to be a sign of Royalty and dignity. These people are ambitious and are usually successful.

## Loop of Serious Intent

This Loop pattern located on the palm between the Saturn (middle) finger and the Apollo (ring) finger occurs frequently. This sign indicates sensitivity and good common sense. These people have a serious purpose in life, which gives the Loop pattern its name, Loop of Serious Intent. If on only one palm, these people will be content with just serious hobbies. When the Loop pattern is on both palms, they will want to do much more. The loops seem to unite the stability of the Saturn influence and the happiness of the Apollo influence so that they will choose hobbies, activities and work which they feel are a service and benefit to their communities, as well as their religious groups.

# Loop of Humor

Loop patterns located on the palm between the Apollo (ring) finger and Mercury (little) finger are called the Loop of Humor, and indicate a person who enjoys laughter and the humorous side of life. They enjoy the sense of the ridiculous, and laugh from the tummy. If they have these loops on both palms, they are often accused of artificial enthusiasm, but they don't care, for with their wonderful sense of humor, they can also laugh at themselves.

Sometimes the Loop of Humor goes astray and crosses in front of the Apollo finger on to the Mount of Apollo, which causes their sense of the ridiculous to become out of focus, and these people become warped by vanity. They cannot tolerate any laughter directed at them, only with them.

# Loop of Courage

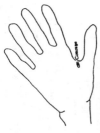

Loop patterns located on the palm between the thumb and the Jupiter (index) finger are psychologically attuned by the Mount of Mars beneath the Life Line from which this sign takes its influence of courage, and gets the name, the Loop of Courage.

The Loop of Courage sometimes enters the ball of the thumb from the Mount of Mars and this indicates physical courage. These people worship courage and have a longing to be braver than others.

This Loop adds forcefulness and determination to the personality, not just physical courage, and can be found on the palms of both men and women. These people are steady and unassuming, and have personality values such as stamina and fortitude.

## The Musical "Bee" Pattern

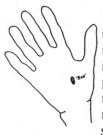

The Musical Bee pattern is an oval-shaped ring with a loop-type pattern inside the ring. This pattern indicates a person who has the ability to be a musical genius. If the patterns in the ring run straight across, the sign indicates a preference toward string instruments, and not only the ability to play, but to compose music as well. However, due to circumstances, they may never realize their unusual talents, but they will be tremendously moved by music. When this pattern is seen in the palm of a child, they should be encouraged to have a musical education.

# Loop of Response

The Loop of Response is located on the outside edge at the base of the thumb on the Mount of Venus. This pattern indicates a person with a deep response factor to their environment and surroundings, as well as music and rhythm. They love the sounds of brass instruments and their swinging rhythm.

These people respond strongly to the moods and emotions of those they associate with. They are affected very strongly by their surroundings; for example, if they are with a gloomy group, or if the weather is bad, they will become negative and moody. But if the weather is good and their surroundings pleasant, with the sounds of good music, they will be in a positive mood.

# The Memory Loop

The Memory Loop starts toward the Mount of Jupiter or below, near the Head Line and may flow onto the Mount of the Moon, about two-thirds of the way towards the wrist or higher up, about the middle of the palm. When analyzing this loop pattern, you must take into consideration where the apex of the loop is on the Mount of the Moon or the Upper Mars. These patterns are seen quite often. It indicates an unusual quality; these people can have an almost photographic memory or an extremely good one.

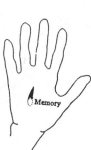

When the Memory Loop is found almost running straight across the palm, these people have no trouble remembering facts, figures, and they retain things they read.

When the looped pattern runs at an angle into the Mount of the Moon, these people have a good memory, but are strongly influenced by their emotions. They remember events of the past and how they felt at that time in their life.

The lower the loop pattern is found on the palm, the more their memory leans toward their feelings, rather than the actual facts.

This loop pattern also adds imagination and the lower the location of the loop the greater the imagination.

# The Nature Loop

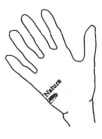

The Nature Loop is located on the lower outside or percussion edge of the hand on the Mount of the Moon. It can position itself anywhere from the Head Line down to the very base of the palm. This loop pattern is very significant and must be analyzed carefully.

This loop pattern is one of the marks seen on the palm of the mongoloid child. When it is found with the abnormal markings it is very significant.

On the hand of an adult or normal hand, it may only indicate a genetic or hereditary physical problem, such as asthma or diabetes.

On a good hand with good strength, this Nature Loop has positive and good qualities. People with the mark are often dowsers; they claim they can feel the water, oil, metal or even a person they seek. People with green thumbs of the gardner have this sensitivity.

They are people who do not like working indoors. They may have strong feelings towards animals and nature, and have a need to be near water. If the palm has the mark of the Medical Stigmata, the vertical little lines between the Apollo and the Mercury fingers, it can indicate a desire to be a veterinarian, as this would mean a positive and strong desire to work with animals and medicine.

Some people with this Loop can become claustrophobic when confined to closed areas; they must have fresh air and open spaces. The closer the Nature Loop is to the Head Line, the stronger the desire for freedom and outside activity. If the Loop is found very low in the palm, the aspects are not as strong.

# Loop of Inspiration

The Loop of Inspiration is located on the very center of the base of the palm on the Mount of Neptune. This loop begins almost from the wrist at the Bracelets looping upwards into the palm and down again toward the wrist. This marking adds a very special quality to those that have it, that of inspiration, for which the Loop is named. It represents deep inspiration, which can be very uplifting to an individual and at times can be given to those around them. This is a good marking, but a rare one.

With a long tip of the Mercury finger it adds the ability to inspire others.

This Loop is often found on the palms of radio and television personalities, self-made business people, teachers and leaders in all areas of life.

These people enjoy art, music, sunsets and nature itself.

## The Loop of Rhythm Response

The Loop of Rhythm Response is located opposite the Loop of Inspiration. It also runs upward from the base of the palm into the palm of the hand to the Mount of Pluto, toward the thumb side of the hand, and is a very unusual and rare formation.

This marking indicates a person who has a built-in automatic response to rhythm of any kind, whether it is musical or physical. They love any musical instrument which involves a definite rhythm. These people are good dancers and athletes. The secret of a good athlete is the rhythmic pattern of action and reaction. This marking indicates those that possess it have this rhythm response.

## The Loop of Sensuality

The Loop of Sensuality is located on the lower phalanx of the Mercury (little) finger, running crosswise on the phalanx. This marking is quite rare, but important when discovered. It indicates fulfilling our instinctive needs and sexual desires and the sexual and sensual nature of the person who has this marking. The loop also indicates the concentration of energy and response as well.

On a man's hand it emphasizes his masculinity. On a woman's hand it emphasizes her femininity.

## The Loop of Charisma

The Loop of Charisma is located on the lower phalanx of the Jupiter (index) finger and runs slantwise toward the inside edge of the palm, toward the thumb and looping back into the palm again.

This Looped formation indicates an unusual quality. The person with this marking has the ability to lead and sway others.

In an average person this marking will add the charisma to make them a leader among their peers. With a strong ambitious hand, it makes them irresistible. People will idolize them and become loyal and subservient followers.

People with loop patterns are capable of self service and dedication. They have the power that draws others to their cause and inspires them to complete devotion, whether they believe in their cause or not.

When they enter a room, their charisma draws others to them. A politician or a clergyman could be a very dangerous individual, depending on their honesty.

### The Winds of Fate

One ship drives East and one drives West
With the self-same winds that blow.
'Tis the set of the sails and not the gales
Which tells us the way to go

Like the winds of the sea are the ways of fate,
As we voyage along through life.
'Tis the set of the soul that decides its goal,
And not the calm or strife.

Ella Wheeler Wilcox

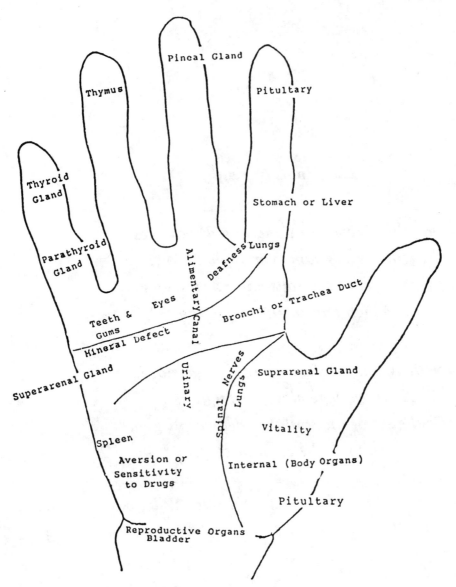

Thyroid
Gland

Parathyroid
Gland

Thymus

Pineal Gland

Pituitary

Stomach or Liver

Alimentary Canal

Deafness Lungs

Teeth & Eyes
Gums

Mineral Defect

Bronchi or Trachea Duct

Superarenal Gland

Urinary

Spinal Nerves
Lungs

Suprarenal Gland

Vitality

Spleen

Aversion or
Sensitivity
to Drugs

Internal (Body Organs)

Pituitary

Reproductive Organs
Bladder

## Areas of the Hand and Fingers that
## Correlate to the Body

# Health Areas of the Hand and Fingers
# Which Correlate to the Body

Two very valuable writers on the health aspect of
the hand were Noel Jaquin and Dr. Charlotte Wolff. As
long ago as 1823, Dr. Jan Evangelists Purkenji, who
was the originator of the scientific approach to skin
patterns, or Dermatoglyphics, wrote on the breakdown
of the skin patterns. Sir Francis Galton, the pioneer
of the basic studies on fingerprints, classified them
into Loops. Whorls and Arches, but it was not until
Noel Jaquin pioneered the work on the psychological
attitude of life indicated by fingerprint patterns of
the doctors working to interpret the skin patterns,
that they all agreed the physical make-up of troubles,
cancer, tuberculosis and forms of rheumatic fever is
indicated by the definite breaking up of the ridges
of the skin, long before any physical illness appears.
The skin patterns are believed to be formed by the
literally thousands of nerve endings and when the
skin pattern disintegrates, then the circuits of the
nerves seem to have been cut out so they can not no
longer function.

There is a lack of agreement on the exact location
of the various organs on the palm of the hand.

The following chapters are researched and condensed
from information gathered all over the world which
indicates the lines in our hands and the reflexology
locations.

# The Fingers

The Mercury (little) finger, the first phalanx, corresponds with the endocrine system; the secretion of a gland such as Thyroid and Pituitary. Prints of the Mercury fingertip showing little lines rising from the joint and eventually covering the whole area indicates problems with the Thyroid Gland. At this time it gives no indication whether it is under or overworking for both extremes are indicated by these little lines.

The middle phalanx of the Mercury finger indicates the Parathyroid can be detected by these little lines.

The Apollo finger correlates with the Thymus Gland. When the little lines are veiling the skin ridges, it indicates erratic blood pressure which may affect the heart.

The Saturn finger indicates one of the planes which is in sympathy with the Pineal Gland and responsible, with the spleen, for the intake and ingestion of the cosmic radiation which flows through all life. The Mount of Neptune also has a relationship to the Pineal Gland in that gland's physical manifestation and may gauge the cosmic radiation which boosts the life energy.

The Jupiter (index) finger is responsible for the Pituitary Gland which also is indicated at the lower angle of the thumb.

The Thumb rules all, and does not relate to any gland; however, the first phalanx of the thumb relates to vitality. When people are frustrated, unhappy, out of tune with themselves, the thumb becomes lined, usually with the cross frustration lines.

The Phalanx at the base of the Jupiter finger correlates to the liver and stomach, as well as the sense of taste, but to the height and size of the phalanxes rather than the skin patterns or markings.

# The Palm

From the base of the Saturn (middle) finger, for about two-thirds of the length of the palm of the hand towards the wrist, is the location which correlates with the alimentary tract which is the food canal between the mouth and anus, including the stomach and intestines. Any breakdown of the skin patterns in this area beneath the Saturn finger warns of digestive troubles.

From the base of the Apollo finger about two-thirds the length of the palm of the hand to the wrist, any breakdown of the skin ridges or veiling with little superficial lines indicates problems in the urinary system. These lines or skin ridges will sometimes rise from the Fate or Success Lines and proceeds upwards to the Head Line. They indicate acidity and digestive troubles and complaints of the kidneys, which can become dangerous.

The area where most people seem to have problems lies between the two horizontal lines on the percussion side of the palm (by the little finger). At first the skin patterns do not disintegrate dramatically, but the area becomes covered with many fine, upright lines. These become crossed and interwoven with lines which indicate that the Suprarenal Glands above the kidneys are not working properly, and warn of chronic rheumatic complaints. This condition indicates that some form of poisoning, which includes acidity, is the cause of the breakdown of the gland or the malfunction of the gland is allowing poison into the system. The skin ridges or lines can disappear in the course of only a few weeks when the cause is found and corrected.

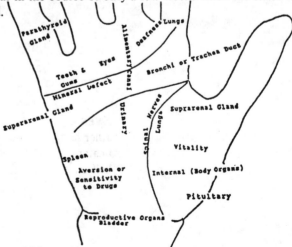

## The Spleen

The correlation of the Spleen with the Mount of the Moon indicates that when a Spleen is defective, the physical blood supply suffers and the whole body lacks energy.

## The Throat

When the Life Line is chained at its beginning under the Jupiter (index) finger, it indicates throat infection and bronchial trouble, especially in childhood. Deafness could be the cause from these childhood infections.

## Deafness

Difficulties in hearing can be caused from so many different problems. The traditional marking on the palm is a large Island on the Heart Line under the Saturn finger. The flexibility of the top joint of the Mercury finger is a guide to someone who has a quickness of hearing. A stiff first phalanx of the Mercury finger indicates problems with hearing even a telephone or doorbell.

## Eyes

Eye complaints can show as a rather large, definite Island on the Heart Line under the Apollo finger. Also cataracts make a small, clear circle on the thumb side of the Life Line, a half circle indicates only one eye.

## Teeth

Just above the Heart Line, between the Apollo and Mercury fingers is the area in correlation with the teeth and gums. Little fine lines that are very delicately etched are the usual markings, but the ridging can break into a skin pattern of missing nerve endings on each separate ridge instead of a smooth line. Should the condition become worse, and bacteria become stronger, the skin patterns will break up more and more.

## The Heart Line

The Heart Line, in correlation to the body, indicates the state of the blood supply as it passes through our organs.

## The Life Line

The Life Line, in addition to the relationship with the throat and respiratory organs, also correlates with the Spinal Column.

## The Head Line

The Head Line correlates with the mental part of our bodies and mental disorders. Cuts and Dots on the Head Line indicate the psychological aspects of the line. Islands indicate a period of anxiety or illness in which the head is involved, and a loss of energy. A chained Head Line is due to a deficiency.

# The Health Line

Perhaps the most important and certainly the most debated of all lines from the health aspect is the Health Line, which lies between the base of the palm of the hand and rises toward the Mount of Mercury. The older references named this line the Liver Line and assigned all alimentary troubles to its path. Its basic common denominator is that the Mercury Line represents our awareness of our autonomic nervous system. The longer this line runs, the greater the degree of awareness we have until the line crosses the Heart Line and ends on the Mount of Mercury. Then we respond all too quickly to our emotions. We feel literally sick when we are unhappy and recover from our ailments when we are happy or determined. People who do not have this line are unaware of all this nervous energy and go about their work and life without interference.

The Health Line may break and start again or have Islands which indicate loss of energy or ill health. When the line has little dashes, it indicates spasmodic conditions.

# Reproductive Organs

The true area of the Reproductive Organs is found at the base of the palm. A sharp rise of the first Bracelets into the palm is a warning of difficulty in conceiving or in childbirth or both. Also, a Tented Arch in the skin pattern, rising in the same place onto the Mount of Neptune has the same warning.

# Hand Reflexology

Hand Reflexology is the study and practice of working reflexes in the hands which correspond to parts of the body. With specific hand techniques, Reflexology causes responses or relaxation in corresponding parts of the body. Relaxation is the first step to normalization, the body's return to a state of balance: its equilibrium or homeastasis, the stability within and between the body parts where circulation can flow freely and supply nutrients and oxygen to the cells. With the restoration of the homeostasis, the body's organs which are actually an aggregation of the cells or the gathering together of its parts may return to a normal state and be able to function well.

Use the Reflexology Chart to locate the corresponding areas of each part of the body. The right hand represents the right half of the body and the left hand the left side of the body.

# Hand Reflexology Chart

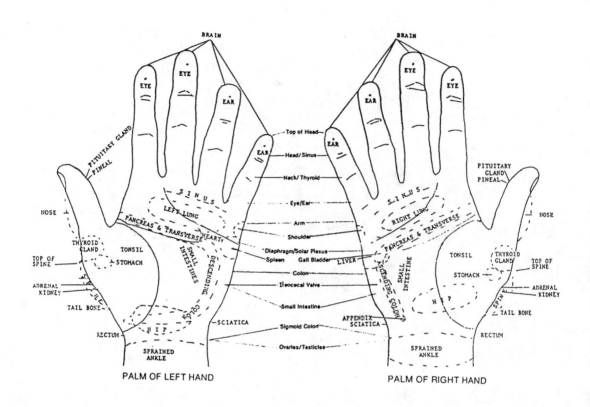

The reflex areas that correlate to the Mounts,
Fingers and Palms of the Hand

# Hand Reflexology Charts

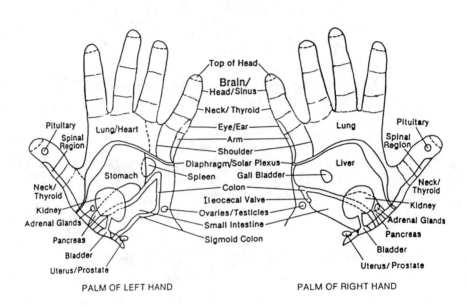

Top of Head

**Brain/**
Head/Sinus

Neck/Thyroid

Eye/Ear

Arm

Shoulder

Diaphragm/Solar Plexus

Spleen — Gall Bladder

Colon

Ileocecal Valve

Ovaries/Testicles

Small Intestine

Sigmoid Colon

Pituitary — Lung/Heart — Lung — Pituitary

Spinal Region — Spinal Region

Liver

Neck/Thyroid — Stomach — Neck/Thyroid

Kidney — Kidney

Adrenal Glands — Adrenal Glands

Pancreas — Pancreas

Bladder — Bladder

Uterus/Prostate — Uterus/Prostate

PALM OF LEFT HAND          PALM OF RIGHT HAND

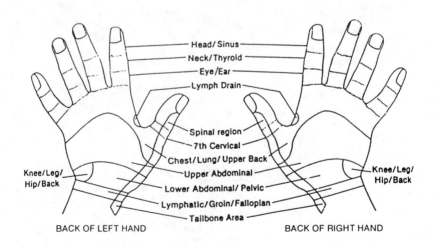

Head/Sinus

Neck/Thyroid

Eye/Ear

Lymph Drain

Spinal region

7th Cervical

Chest/Lung/Upper Back

Upper Abdominal

Lower Abdominal/Pelvic

Lymphatic/Groin/Fallopian

Tailbone Area

Knee/Leg/Hip/Back — Knee/Leg/Hip/Back

BACK OF LEFT HAND          BACK OF RIGHT HAND

## THERE IS NO ENDING

This book has no beginning or ending, you will want to
read and continue to refer to it over and over again.
Just ask a question of the hand and the answer will be
found in the book. Keep it on your coffee table so your
friends and family can study their hands. It makes a
wonderful conversational piece at your home or even at
place of work.

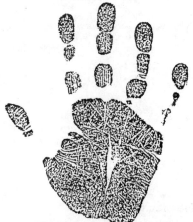